Blessed Are the Organized

*

Blessed Are the Organized

GRASSROOTS DEMOCRACY IN AMERICA

*

Jeffrey Stout

PRINCETON UNIVERSITY PRESS

PRINCETON AND OXFORD

Published by Princeton University Press, 41 William Street, Princeton, New Jersey 08540
In the United Kingdom: Princeton University Press, 6 Oxford Street,
Woodstock, Oxfordshire OX20 1TW
press.princeton.edu

Third printing, and first paperback printing, 2013
Paperback ISBN 978-0-691-15665-1

The Library of Congress has cataloged the cloth edition of this book as follows
Stout, Jeffrey.
Blessed are the organized : grassroots democracy in America / Jeffrey Stout.
p. cm.
Includes bibliographical references and index.
ISBN 978-0-691-13586-1 (hardcover : alk. paper)
1. Political participation—United States. 2. Democracy—United States. 3. Religion and politics—United States. 4. Social movements—United States. I. Title.
JK1764.S85 2010
322.4'40973—dc22
2010013800

British Library Cataloging-in-Publication Data is available

This book has been composed in Fairfield Light Std

Printed on acid-free paper. ∞

Printed in the United States of America

5 7 9 10 8 6

IN MEMORY OF

MARY DOUGLAS, HENRY LEVINSON,

AND RICHARD RORTY

*

ON RELATIONAL POWER:

Lupita tells me she has serious problems because she has no sewer service and the same with this one and that one and that one. This is the way we begin to have a relationship. And then, if you don't have water and I don't have water, let's have a meeting to fight for this.

—*Carmen Anaya*

ON ACCOUNTABILITY:

You said you were gonna, but you didn't. What's up with that?

—*Joanne Bland*

⁎ *Contents* ⁎

* *List of Maps* *

⁕ *Preface* ⁕

THIS BOOK TAKES A JOURNEY in search of democracy, through an America that Tocqueville and Whitman never knew.[1] It begins in New Orleans in the wake of Katrina and moves on to the Houston Astrodome, in the days when the hurricane survivors were there. It tours the borderlands of Texas, where hundreds of immigrant shantytowns somehow became habitable neighborhoods. It touches down briefly in Arizona, and then passes through some of the poorest communities in California, before ending in a well-to-do synagogue in Marin County.

In each of these places, we will meet people who want to explain, on the basis of their own experience, what they think citizenship means. Their stories will have much to teach us about the nature and prospects of grassroots democracy. Periodically, in the course of the journey, I will pause long enough to clarify some feature of life in a modern republic: citizenship, responsibility, authority, power, domination, freedom, anger, grief, leadership, ideals, values, ends, means, passions, interests, religion, secularity, and the concept of democracy itself.[2]

There is a lot of talk these days, most notably from the president, about grassroots democracy. Change, he says, needs to come from the bottom up. There is, however, a good deal of confusion over what this might mean, how this sort of change might work, and what it can achieve. To dispel the confusion, one needs to look away from the centers of elite power and ask ordinary citizens what they are actually doing in their own communities to get organized, exert power, and demand accountability.

How do they build an organization? How do they analyze power relations? How do they cultivate leaders? What role does religion play in the organizational process? What objectives are being sought? What concerns, passions, and ideals lie behind those objectives? What have concerned citizens actually achieved and how have they achieved it? What have their setbacks been? Who are their allies and their opponents? What obstacles stand in their way? By answering these questions, we can strengthen our grasp on what grassroots democracy is.

We will also need to consider the criticisms that have been raised against it. It is said to place too much faith in the myopic and apathetic masses, to undermine excellence and authority, to pursue unacceptable goals, to employ unfair tactics, and to mix religion and politics inappropriately. These are serious charges. The most important criticism, however, comes from people who think bottom-up change would be a good thing, but doubt that it, or anything else, can cure what currently ails our politics.

Grassroots democrats have had some success at holding members of local elites accountable: mayors, school superintendents, police chiefs, developers, and so on. But local political struggles disclose problems and structures that transcend the local level. This is one reason for undertaking a journey, instead of lingering for a longer time in one site. All of the stops along the way are nodes in a single network of cooperating organizations. If grassroots democracy is going to have effects above the local level, it will be because networks of this kind are strengthened, extended, and multiplied. I want to bring this possibility into focus.

Presidents, federal legislators, judges, bureaucrats, Wall Street bankers, insurance executives, media moguls, and generals are making decisions every day that have a massive impact on our lives. Together they wield unprecedented power. The sheer amount of power they exercise is worrisome, even if they aren't carrying out a grand conspiracy. Why think that ordinary citizens can end a war, deal adequately with global warming, achieve a just and wise resolution of the financial crisis, or bring multinational corporations under rational control if the most powerful people in the world dig in their heels? Why suppose that the establishment *can* be held accountable to the rest of us?

Candidate Obama's hopeful answer, born of his own experience as an organizer in Chicago, was that ordinary citizens can indeed "take the country back." His supporters chanted, "Yes we can!" as if trying to convince themselves of their power. He refers often to the need for "accountability."[3] Where, then, is the promised accountability going to come from? All indications suggest that accountability remains in short supply.

This thought forces us to confront a widespread doubt about democracy itself, the doubt against which "the audacity of hope" asserted itself, but which the election of Barack Obama seems to have put on hold only momentarily. If our most powerful elites are now essentially beyond the reach of accountability, as they increasingly seem to be, then why suppose that our polity qualifies as a *democratic republic* at all? It appears to function, rather, as a plutocracy, a system in which the fortunate few dominate the rest. And if that is true, then honesty requires that we stop referring to ourselves as *citizens*, and admit that we are really subjects. The question of democratic hope boils down to whether the basic concepts of our political heritage apply to the world in which we now live.

The stories I shall be recounting come from spirited, committed proponents of that heritage.[4] They think of themselves as citizens, as people entitled to demand a say in their society. Many of them are living under desperate circumstances. The law classifies some of them as illegal aliens. Yet, as Ernesto Cortés Jr., an organizer who will figure prominently in these pages, put it to me, "They do the work of a citizen." They have begun to lay their hands on the levers of power that a constitutional democracy puts at their disposal. They have entered into new relations of authority with one another, and acquired habits and skills they had formerly lacked. Their talents, virtues, and accomplishments are not ordinary at all.

There is no point in hiding the fact that my own democratic commitments incline me to identify with what these citizens are trying to do. In the eyes of some readers, this bias may threaten to spoil the whole project. The solution, I believe, is not to adopt a mask of value neutrality. Whether my sympathies have clarified or clouded my vision of citizenship is a good question, which is not for me to answer. Expressing my commitments clearly at least gives readers an opportunity to make allowances. Democratic social criticism, as I practice it, is not merely *about* democracy. It proceeds from a point of view shaped by commitments and friendships that are democratic in nature.

Listening closely while ordinary citizens describe their struggles, victories, and setbacks is itself a democratic act. One of its benefits is to bring the ideal of good citizenship down to earth. I want readers to experience something like what I experienced when talking, face to face, with citizens who believe that democracy's health depends on one-on-one conversations, small-group meetings, critical reflection, and organized action. I also want to explain clearly and precisely what these practices involve and set them in comparative and historical perspective. Contemporary grassroots democracy warrants the sort of respectful examination that is more often accorded to ruling elites and to the democratic heroes of the past.

To imagine the future of our politics in light of these stories is to allow the actual political practice of ordinary people to influence our vision of the politically possible. Saying this is not to prejudge the question of what one can reasonably hope for in politics. Perhaps there are insuperable obstacles preventing us from moving very far at all down the paths these people are treading. The only way to find this out, it seems to me, is to go down those paths and press against whatever obstacles one finds there. If the practices of organizing and accountability require modification or expansion in order to address the daunting problems now threatening democracy that is something to decide on the basis of experience. It is not the sort of thing one can deduce from a theory. This book is an expression of dissatisfaction with democratic theory in its current abstract form.

A degree of trust in the testimony of ordinary citizens is required to build up an empirically grounded sense of what citizenship is. I have been able to confirm some things that citizens have told me about their communities and campaigns, but news reports on local controversies tend these days to be rather sketchy. In any event, I am concerned here mainly with how citizens conduct their organizing when the media spotlight is not on them; what their motives, ends, values, and ideals are; to whom they attribute authority; and how they view their opponents. On all of these topics, my main evidence is what citizens have told me, and my main reason for trusting that evidence is my direct observation of what they are doing.

I do not think of myself as an ethnographer, let alone as an investigative reporter, but as an observer and critic of the political and religious dimensions of contemporary democratic culture.[5] My goal throughout has been to elicit from the testimony of active, hopeful citizens *a conception of what citizenship involves* and then to subject that conception to scrutiny in light of the most important criticisms that have been brought against grassroots democracy. These criticisms pertain to the ends and means of democratic action, the relationship of religion and politics, and the grounds for hoping that grassroots democracy can achieve major reform. My quarry is an informed, thoughtful view of what citizenship is, can be, and ought to be, not a detailed account of this or that campaign.

Readers are free to judge for themselves the credibility of the particular stories I have chosen to retell. Given that the testimony is coming from human beings engaged in conflict, one can safely assume that it is to some degree self-serving, self-deceived, biased, resentful, or based on wishful thinking. Yet it comes from people who are responding to demonstrably unjust circumstances, on the whole, with courage and restraint. These citizens do not present themselves as do-gooders. In fact, they speak with refreshing candor about the role self-interest plays in motivating them. But there appear to be other concerns in their hearts as well.

My impression, as someone who has observed them in action, is that they do spend as much time as they claim to spend conversing face to face, cultivating leaders, engaging in research, and reflecting critically. As a result of spending time in these ways, they have in fact acquired and exercised power, and won some significant victories. Whether the citizens who take hope from those victories always treat or characterize their opponents justly is impossible to determine on the basis of the evidence I have gathered. Another open question is whether the grander hopes for democracy harbored by some grassroots activists can be achieved. Hope, by nature, outruns the evidence that can be adduced for it and is inherently hard to distinguish from wishful thinking. Still, something will have to be said about its grounds.

At a minimum, the stories considered here can clarify what some citizens *take themselves* to be doing and the ideal of citizenship they *aspire* to embody in their conduct. It seems to me that the rest of us at least owe such stories a hearing and are ourselves to be judged by the quality of the hearing we give. Reading or listening to someone else's story, no less than telling one's own, belongs to the work of a citizen and brings with it an ethical demand, as well as a host of practical questions. The demand is to respond fittingly to one's fellows who seek partners in the formation of a just society. The questions include whether (and how far) to trust the people telling the stories, whether (and how far) to share their hopes and join their struggles. To answer such questions in one way or another, or even to refuse to answer them, is already to play a role in determining the kind of society we have.

Blessed are the organized. This is shorthand for the central claim of grassroots democracy. It needs elaboration and qualification. There are good and bad ways of organizing: effective and ineffective ways, democratic and nondemocratic ways. Only some of the ways now being tried have any likelihood of promoting the common good and thus any chance of making our communities happy and just places to live. I do not claim that the examples considered here give a full picture of contemporary democratic practice. Many groups of different kinds are needed to achieve a genuinely inclusive republic that is free from domination. Democracy would benefit from books on each kind. But I will try to show that the kind of group examined in this book, the broad-based citizens' organization, has an important contribution to make. I shall also try to show how the rest of the political landscape looks from the perspective of such organizations.

Will people who are now meek, weak, and isolated inherit at least some patch of the earth and establish there a society in which even the most powerful are held accountable in a system of just laws? I am not certain that they will. Neither, however, am I certain that they cannot. It is in the uncertain, broken middle that the hope for democratic accountability manifests itself in the deeds and words of ordinary women and men.

Blessed Are the Organized

*

✻ CHAPTER ONE ✻

The Responsibilities of a Citizen

Well and wisely trained citizens you will
hardly find anywhere.
—*Thomas More (1516)*

LATE IN THE SUMMER of 2005, somewhere in the Atlantic basin off the coast of Africa, an elongated trough of low pressure took shape and began moving west. Over the Bahamas, on August 23, it joined with the remains of Tropical Depression Ten to form the more powerful Tropical Depression Twelve. As it moved over the warm waters of the Atlantic, the system gathered energy from below. On August 24 meteorologists declared it a tropical storm and named it Katrina. By the time the storm reached Florida, it had become a hurricane. It weakened briefly while passing over land, but then rapidly gained strength from the Gulf of Mexico, before wreaking havoc on the Gulf coast on August 29. The damage done there had human as well as natural causes.

One evening, sixteen months after the storm, I was in Marrero, Louisiana, a city located on the West Bank in greater New Orleans. At St. Joseph the Worker Catholic Church, I met with several organizers and leaders of a citizens' organization called Jeremiah, which consists of churches, synagogues, parent-teacher associations, unions, and other nongovernmental groups. Each of these institutions pays dues to Jeremiah, with the money going mainly to the salaries of the organizers. By joining the organization, the institutions also commit themselves to a great deal of internal organizational activity. What that activity amounts to will become clearer in the next three chapters.

For now, it will suffice to say that the internal organizing going on in various New Orleans institutions is directed toward two initial objectives. The first is to get people within a given institution talking with each other about their concerns. In the case of a church this would mean hundreds of individual conversations and small gatherings—called "one-on-ones" and "house meetings," respectively—among church members. The second objective is to identify and cultivate leaders from within. These leaders represent their institutions in the citizens' organization and in the broader forum of public discussion. Drawing together institutional leaders in this way creates the sort of power base that the citizens' organization can then use to hold governmental and corporate officeholders accountable.

In the parlance of groups like Jeremiah, "organizers" are professionals tasked with helping ordinary citizens learn the practices of organizing and accountability. "Leaders" are citizen volunteers who have earned the right to represent an institution—such as a church or labor union—that has decided to join the organization. A "core team" is a set of leaders recognized as having the authority to formulate proposals and develop strategies on behalf of the organization.

Jeremiah is an affiliate of the Industrial Areas Foundation (IAF), a confederation of community organizations founded in 1940 by the legendary Saul Alinsky. Alinsky's mission was to be the kind of mentor to ordinary American citizens that Machiavelli had been to the princes of Renaissance city-states: realistic, pragmatic, and fiercely dedicated to the ideal of liberty. Alinsky is best known for his work in the Back of the Yards neighborhood of Chicago in the 1930s and in Rochester, New York, in the 1960s.

Two of Alinsky's books, *Reveille for Radicals* (1946) and *Rules for Radicals* (1971), vividly describe his experiences and tactics as an organizer.[6] He fashioned himself as an irreverent radical, but both books express reverence for a tradition whose heroes include Patrick Henry, Sam Adams, Tom Paine, Thomas Jefferson, John Brown, Thaddeus Stevens, Walt Whitman, Henry David Thoreau, Edward Bellamy, and Upton Sinclair (*Reveille*, 13–14; *Rules*, 7). The true democrat, Alinsky insisted, is "suspicious of, and antagonistic to, any idea of plans that work from the top down. Democracy to him is working from the bottom up" (*Reveille*, 17). The purpose of Alinsky's organizing, and of his writing, was to show ordinary people what bottom-up change involves.

Democracy, in his view, "is a way of life, not a formula to be 'preserved' like jelly" (*Reveille*, 47). Implicit in that way of life is a commitment to liberty and justice for all. These ideals become an ideological fog when they are abstracted from the activities of ordinary people. Liberty and justice are made actual in the lives of people who struggle for them. In the struggle to achieve liberty and justice for all, the "Have-Nots of the world" need to provide a counterweight to the "Haves" (*Rules*, 8, 18–23). Yet they can do this only by gathering in groups and exerting power.

> If we strip away all the chromium trimmings of high-sounding metaphor and idealism which conceal the motor and gears of a democratic society, one basic element is revealed—the people are the motor, the organizations of the people are the gears. The power of the people is transmitted through the gears of their own organizations, and democracy moves forward. (*Reveille*, 46)

Alinsky's books explain how such organizations are built and what they can do to seek democratic objectives by democratic means. By traveling to New Orleans and various other places where IAF groups have formed, I thought I might be able to see what Alinsky's heritage amounts to today.

Presiding over our meeting in Marrero was Jackie Jones, an African-American woman who used to be a teacher in New Orleans and now serves as Jeremiah's lead organizer. The leaders assembled at St. Joseph were all blacks, with the exception of one Latino,

Reverend Jaime Oviedo of Christ Temple Church. When we went around the table introducing ourselves, the leaders gave not only their own names but also the names of the institutions they represented, all of which happened to be churches.

Jackie invited Reverend Jesse Pate, of the Harvest Ripe Church of Christ's Holiness, to begin the meeting with a prayer. "Eternal Father," Reverend Pate said, "we do thank you again for allowing us to be here. We ask your guidance, for we do seek your mercy and your instructions. Give us the wisdom to follow your lead to heaven. You will be our guiding principle and our guiding light, for truly we are members of the same body. Together we have to know that all things are possible if we continually believe in trusting you. So, right now, guide us, strengthen us, and we thank you for the time you have allowed us to be here. In Jesus' name, Amen."

Reverend Pate describes Jeremiah as "a broad-based organization. We deal with a lot of issues. We do take on the IAF motto of not doing for others what they can do for themselves. But we also believe in being a voice for the people, and representing the people. We do research, actions, and things of that nature, we go into house meetings, we bring the public in, and we talk to them. We do community walks and things of that nature. So it's a lot of things that makes us what we are."

David Warren, a tall, elegantly dressed African American who wore shades throughout the evening, was representing the Living Witness Church of God in Christ. Jeremiah, he said, has its roots in faith: "We're a faith-based organization, and we believe in building relationships." David made clear that he wasn't disagreeing with Reverend Pate. Broad-based organizing encompasses, but is not limited to, faith-based organizing. Most member institutions in Jeremiah, as in many other IAF groups, are churches. The number of synagogues, mosques, schools, and labor unions involved in IAF is growing, and organizers hope to hasten this trend. Still, if one subtracted the churches from IAF and other similar organizing networks, then grassroots democracy in the United States would come to very little. In chapters 15–17, I will return to the significance of this fact for our understanding of pastoral responsibility, the training of pastors, and the proper relationship between church and state.

African Americans are heavily represented in the Jeremiah Group, and the leaders are quick to point out the role played by racial prejudice in the reconfiguration of New Orleans. But they have made a self-conscious decision to build a coalition that crosses racial lines, in the hope of accumulating sufficient power to address their concerns effectively. I found no reluctance among them to discuss the racial dimension of the situation. They present it, however, as one dimension among others; and they present it in this way, as far as I can tell, because they see it in this way, not merely because they are trying to draw whites, Asians, and Hispanics into the coalition. The major movers and shakers in the immediate wake of the storm were developers and bureaucrats, who took advantage of the racial prejudice in some sectors of the population to advance private interests at the expense of the common good. That is what happened, according to Jeremiah leaders, so that is the story that must be told.

Broad-based organizing aims to transcend racial boundaries.[7] It would be fruitless to fight racism in post-Katrina New Orleans by assembling a coalition consisting only of African-American churches and associations. What it will take to combat injustices caused in part by racism is a coalition in which the interests of many groups converge. If those groups are to be assembled, the identity of the coalition itself will have to be found in a conception of the city's common good. Racial *identification* cannot play the role in the process of coalition building that it plays in establishing solidarity within some of the groups participating in the coalition. Yet many of those groups will have less reason to join the coalition if racial prejudice is not named as one important source of domination in present-day New Orleans.

Jeremiah and the other broad-based citizens' groups discussed in this book all belong to a single network known as Southwest IAF, which stretches from Mississippi to Idaho to California. The ethnic, racial, and religious makeup of these groups vary considerably from place to place, yet they all employ the same political concepts and go about their organizing in a way that bears the stamp of Alinsky's influence. The network's supervisor is Ernesto Cortés Jr.

Around the time *Rules for Radicals* appeared, Cortés was a young organizer in Texas. His frustrations with his work led him to enroll in Alinsky's Training Institute in Chicago. By that time, however, Alinsky was spending most of his time on the road, giving speeches and raising funds. Within a few months of Cortés's arrival, Alinsky died of a heart attack, and Ed Chambers, Alinsky's successor, became the young organizer's mentor. After working on several projects in the Midwest with Chambers and a brief stint of organizing in California, Cortés returned to his home state of Texas in 1974, and began laying the groundwork for citizens' organizations in several major cities there. The first of these was COPS (Communities Organized for Public Service), an organization located in San Antonio that is known among organizers not only for building a power base for Latinos and for many concrete victories, but also for its longevity.

Ernie Cortés has since organized elsewhere in Texas and in California. In addition to coordinating Southwest IAF, he now serves as a director of IAF at the national and international levels.[8] Like his predecessors in that role, Alinsky and Chambers, Cortés teaches that democracy depends for its very survival, as well as for its health, on what citizens do. This claim is hardly new. Montesquieu inferred it from a theory of politics in *The Spirit of the Laws*, Tocqueville placed great weight on it in *Democracy in America*, and Whitman spun it into poetry in *Leaves of Grass*. Of course, these thinkers all had in mind a worry that goes back to Plato. The worry is that a democratic polity assigns to ordinary citizens a set of responsibilities for which they do not appear qualified.

If democracy depends for its survival on what citizens do, it could still be that citizens are not up to the task envisioned for them. Walt Whitman was as troubled as anyone by what he called the "question of character" haunting American democracy in the decades after the Civil War. In "Democratic Vistas," his long list of reasons for concern includes the "robbery and scoundrelism" practiced by economic elites. Justice, he wrote, "is always in jeopardy." Why, then, suppose that the people are capable of effective collective action on behalf of justice? His answer was grounded in "the experiences of the fight," including both successes and failures.[9] He witnessed thousands of acts of benevolence and courage during the war. He understood that the slaves would not have been emancipated unless countless ordinary people had campaigned for abolition. Whitman hoped that similar movements would eventually win the franchise for women and constrain scoundrels in high places from robbing ordinary folk.

Alinsky, Chambers, and Cortés all share Whitman's desire to prove democracy's detractors mistaken. Like him, they are committed to *grassroots democracy*.[10] That is, they hold that ordinary citizens can indeed act responsibly and effectively if they organize themselves properly and cultivate the virtues and skills of democratic citizenship. The belief that this condition can be met is grounded in the experience of particular examples of collective action—a social movement for Whitman, community organizing for Alinsky, and organizing on an increasingly broad scale for Chambers and Cortés. Abolitionism, the Back of the Yards organization in 1930s Chicago, and Southwest IAF represent three particular kinds of grassroots democracy.

In this book, I shall mainly be examining the third kind. Broad-based organizing differs from social movement organizing in that it does not restrict itself to a single issue and instead takes up different issues over time in response to concerns expressed by citizens. It differs from community organizing insofar as it sometimes succeeds in building lasting coalitions that involve multiple communities. Social movements are inherently limited in focus and duration.[11] Community organizations are inherently limited in geographical scope and have also often fizzled—or become corrupted by antidemocratic impulses—after a few local campaigns. Broad-based citizens' groups are meant to transcend these limitations. This is why the longevity of the COPS organization in San Antonio is significant for our understanding of grassroots democracy today. It is also why the network in which Jeremiah and COPS participate has importance for an appraisal of democracy's prospects at a time of worsening stratification. If grassroots democracy is going to address the most pressing issues now emerging at the national and international levels, and sustain itself over time, broad-based organizing will have to be expanded and strengthened.

On the many occasions when I have discussed this matter with Cortés, however, he has always underlined the importance of patience. In broad-based organizing that aspires ultimately to have a significant impact at the national and international levels, the standing temptation is, as he puts it, "to skip steps, to take short cuts." If the right sort of micro-organizational work is not being done, the macro-organizational work of connecting citizens' groups with one another in progressively wider networks will create only an illusion of democratic power. This can happen in two ways. In the first, the networks are too loosely connected with people on the ground to generate power. In the second, the connections linking network spokespersons with people on the ground are somewhat stronger, but function in a way that is not democratic. The first way creates an illusion of *power,* the second an illusion of *democratic* power.

If Cortés is right, it seems that high degrees of participation, vigilance, self-constraint, and patience on the part of organizers, leaders, and citizens will be required to scale up the organizational effort without sacrificing either effectiveness or internal accountability. In an era of economic crisis, globalization, terrorism, and melting ice caps, the task is as consequential as it is daunting. The trouble is that many citizens appear too alienated, deluded, ignorant, or fearful to advance even their private interests wisely. Still less do they seem capable of striving for the common good. Cortés would be the first to point out that elections are, for the most part, exercises in mass manipulation. Candidates declare their allegiance to democratic ideals, but behind the scenes something antidemocratic is going on. Citizens who sense that the puppeteers are pulling their strings are tempted to withdraw from the process in disgust.

An old adage has it that the cure for democracy's ills is more democracy. The adage assumes that there is a cure for those ills. It implies that the cure is to be found in democratic activity of some kind. But what sort of behavior, if any, could cure what ails democracy today? And why should one think that real-life citizens are capable of such a thing? Cortés argues that citizens who behave irresponsibly and ineffectively tend to be either disorganized or organized in a counterproductive way. The cure for the ills of democracy is therefore a more productive kind of organizing.

Skillful and virtuous citizens of any social class acquire their skills and virtues under specifiable conditions, as members of groups that gather people of good will, provide them with information, and cultivate their dispositions to behave well. The evidence that makes democracy seem like a foolish wager is best understood as evidence of how poorly organized, poorly trained people behave. The members of any social class, if poorly organized and poorly trained, are likely to behave irresponsibly and ineffectively. The issue, Cortés maintains, is not *which* social class to entrust with the responsibility of influencing and contesting governmental decision making but rather how to extend the benefits of good organizing and good training to the populace as a whole.

Citizens are individuals who have a share of responsibility for the arrangements and policies undertaken by a republic. A *republic* is a polity officially devoted to securing liberty and justice for its citizens. By separating executive, legislative, and judicial powers, and by granting citizens the rights of political participation, republics strive to make it more difficult than it would otherwise be for a single person or group to dominate others.[12] If a republic fails to secure liberty and justice, the citizens of the republic include all of the people who can legitimately be held responsible for permitting their polity to go wrong, whether it be by committing injustices or by neglecting available opportunities to influence and contest the decision making of officeholders.

An individual counts as a citizen in the formal sense only if he or she is recognized as such under law. The legal system confers the official status of a citizen on particular individuals. But when the legal category is applied in an arbitrarily narrow way, it can come into conflict with an informal process of mutual recognition among the people. In a broader sense, then, citizens are individuals who treat one another as bearers of the relevant kind of responsibility.

To be a citizen, in this sense, is to be recognized by others as such, or more strongly, to be worthy of being recognized. The trouble, of course, is that the informal process of recognition is a work in progress and has its own contradictions. The concept of a citizen, like other value-laden notions employed by citizens, is contestable. At any given moment, various people are applying it in somewhat different ways, and either recognizing, or refusing to recognize, certain others as legitimate bearers of responsibility in public life. These days the members of Jeremiah and certain other residents of New Orleans are applying the concept differently.

Citizens are supposed to be able to fulfill their public responsibility nonviolently: by casting ballots, speaking out freely, informing themselves, petitioning for the redress of their grievances, and assembling peaceably into groups. Beyond the affirmation of these rights, a republic is *democratic* insofar as it: (1) removes arbitrary restrictions on who counts as a citizen, (2) opens up sufficient opportunities for citizens to influence and contest official decisions and laws, and (3) is animated by a spirit of mutual recognition and accountability.[13]

The issue of immigration shows that the ability of the United States to satisfy the first criterion remains in question, despite adoption of the Thirteenth, Fifteenth, Nineteenth, Twenty-fourth, and Twenty-sixth amendments to the Constitution. Undocumented workers currently classified as illegal perform essential labor for legally recognized citizens, yet many are exploited in the workplace and live in fear of deportation. They are here because their alternatives are worse. Most Americans, if faced with the dilemma of undocumented workers, would do as they have done.

Some such workers contribute significantly to the civic life, as well as to the economy, of the United States. They bear civic responsibility while lacking the corresponding form of authority. This means that they are denied representation in the government, a denial that echoes the battle cry of the American War of Independence. Their defenders argue that the category of citizenship is being applied arbitrarily, at the whim of those already represented. The claim, in short, is that undocumented residents lack what our tradition calls liberty—security against domination. If so, then our treatment of them as noncitizens violates one of democracy's basic ideals.[14]

As for the second criterion, while there may be more opportunities than there used to be for legally recognized citizens to contest and influence official decisions, some of the most powerful people in our society are not in fact being held accountable for actions that have gravely negative effects on many of their fellow citizens. Economic power is accumulating in novel ways and is increasingly concentrated in the hands of a few. The multinational corporation and the modern banking system are plutocratic in tendency and have been extraordinarily successful in escaping and undercutting democratic attempts to rein them in. For several decades they have transcended all existing forms of accountability, and even the near collapse of international finance has not decisively changed the drastic imbalance of power in society. So long as economic power is exercised on a global basis, beyond the effective control of nation-states, and translates with ease into political power within nation-states, the existing means for influencing and contesting decisions made on high will seem feeble in comparison.

What, then, about the third criterion? Central to the *spirit* of democracy, as I understand it, is a people's disposition to care about liberty and justice for all and to act in ways that make this concern manifest. Caring involves taking an active interest in something, in contrast with being apathetic about it or unconcerned with it.[15] Caring about the goods of liberty and justice for all is manifested in striving for their realization in law and public policy; in joy, relief, or satisfaction when liberty is protected or justice is done; and in anger, grief, or disappointment when these goods are violated. But it also involves a disposition on the part of citizens to hold one another accountable for the condition of the republic and thus to treat one another *as citizens*.

The behavior of the American people has, however, hardly been consistent with concern for liberty and justice for all, and the habits of mutual recognition and accountability seem to have atrophied in most domains of public life. The hopes aroused by the emergence of Barack Obama as a political leader arguably show that many citizens yearn for bottom-up change. Cortés insists, however, that much more than electoral victories of this sort will be needed to revive the democratic spirit that once manifested itself in abolitionism, the struggle to win the franchise for women, the civil rights movement, and Alinsky's community organizing.

Grassroots democracy is an evolving collection of practices intended to perfect the exercise of political responsibility by citizens in a republic that officially aspires to be democratic. As such, grassroots democracy is essentially social, as well as essentially embodied in action. It takes shape in activities that link citizens together organizationally and relate them in various ways to governmental institutions and corporations, to officials and political parties, and to the general public. The activities are undertaken self-consciously, in light of value-laden conceptions of what democracy and democratic citizenship are. To the extent that the activities are successful, by the lights of the citizens participating in them, the activities *embody* an ideal of democratic citizenship and an ideal of democratic association.

Many people have construed the responsibilities of the average citizen in a more restricted way than grassroots democrats do. Beginning in the 1920s, Walter Lippmann argued that the main actors in a modern democratic republic are officeholders, political candidates, opinion makers, and other members of powerful elites. Ordinary citizens, he thought, have more limited obligations: to inform themselves about the issues and about the politicians vying for office, to conduct themselves with civility in public debate, to vote in a way that advances their own interests fairly, and to exercise their influence appropriately—for example, by contacting their elected representatives, signing petitions, or writing letters to the editor. Given that most citizens fail to fulfill even these limited civic responsibilities, Lippmann considered it foolish to expect them to do more.

John Dewey declared Lippmann's faith in elites undemocratic. Without a more extensively organized and active citizenry, Dewey thought, a nominally democratic republic would morph quickly into a form of oligarchy, or dominance of the lucky few over the unlucky many. The Lippmann-Dewey debate of the 1920s was not a merely verbal quarrel, and it remains timely. Lippmann's point was that grassroots organizing on a broad scale is unlikely to have the good effects democrats like Dewey envisioned for it. Dewey's point, which Alinsky wholeheartedly endorsed a decade later, was that grassroots organizing on a broad scale is *required* to keep elites from exercising their power *arbitrarily* over ordinary people.[16]

Broad-based organizing, as practiced by Cortés and others, is the latest version of a grassroots strategy designed to prevent a particular form of domination, oligarchy, from legitimizing itself through elections and the provision of certain constitutional liberties. When Cortés stresses the need for patient, indeed perpetual, micro-organizing as the basis required for genuinely democratic macro-organizing, he has in mind the delicate task of building sufficiently strong ties among citizens to generate power without creating, within the resulting networks of citizens' organizations, yet another version of oligarchy.

Cortés holds that the ideal of liberty and justice for all can in fact be achieved, provided that: the category of *citizen* is applied *nonarbitrarily*, ordinary people *cooperate* in the responsible and prudent exercise of their rights as citizens, and they embody *a spirit of mutual recognition and accountability* in their actions. He maintains that only by forming groups of the right kind and behaving wisely, as well as justly, are citizens able to fulfill their public responsibilities. Among their responsibilities is that of holding the most powerful members of society accountable. The accountability issue arises, however, within citizens' organizations and within networks of such organizations, as well as in relation to governmental and corporate elites.

But this realization obviously brings us back to the age-old worry about democracy: Where are the citizens who can do what grassroots democracy demands of them? The question is often asked in a dismissively rhetorical mode, but sometimes in a spirit of authentic inquiry. Either way, the reply will have to be specific if it is going to be effective. One needs to direct the skeptic's attention to particular people who are saying and doing particular things. If the skeptic responds by discounting as exceptional the examples being offered, one can always give more examples. There is a limit to how many examples can be discounted before the skeptic is exposed as impervious to evidence. In any event, such examples as there are require explanation. If there are citizens who are doing what grassroots democracy demands of them, how did that come to pass, and what, if anything, prevents the same process of socialization from being extended?

There are many books on the behavior of lazy or myopic or easily manipulated citizens, and many more books proposing abstract ideals by which the conduct and character of citizens should be judged and found wanting. There are also some books on what good citizenship used to look like in practice, as recently as the civil rights movement. But there are relatively few books on present-day citizens who are behaving as grassroots democracy says they must behave if democracy is to survive. Is that because such citizens are few and far between, or because the public hasn't paid much attention to them?

To see why the lacuna is worth filling, if it can be filled, consider a few analogies. In business schools future executives learn about something called "best practices." The phrase has become trite, but the wisdom behind it is that anyone who wants to run a business had better look closely at enterprises that are already being run well. A steady diet of bad examples would be dispiriting, as well as misleading. Some businesses succeed. Good examples promise to inspire and instruct. They show us what successful practice looks like, thereby giving us something to aim for.

Coaches, in any team sport, look to successful organizations for clues about how to win. If we want to start a sports team, we assemble it, and in doing so, we understand the value of a good coach. Ideally this turns out to be someone who has actually played the sport we want to play and has accumulated the relevant sort of practical wisdom along the way. Under his or her mentorship, we play the sport, and, with luck, get better at it as we keep playing. The game, our teammates, and the coach alike become our teachers.

This is not, however, how most of us approach politics. When the safety, well being, and freedom of a community are at stake, citizens who are not professional politicians rarely hire a coach, an "organizer," to help them. They do without mentors and good examples. They assemble haphazardly, if at all, giving little thought to building a powerful and skillful team. They spend little time reflecting critically on what they are doing. The likely results are defeat, disappointment, retreat, and eventually, resignation.

Not all citizens behave in this self-defeating way, however. In groups like Jeremiah and COPS, thousands of ordinary people gather regularly in living rooms, churches, synagogues, community centers, and schools. They swap stories, identify shared concerns, work through differences, investigate the relevant facts, and select leaders. Over time, with the help of professional organizers, they build powerful organizations. The organizations cultivate leaders, teaching them, among other things, the importance of reflecting critically on what they are doing. When the groups act, they often do so with a well-constructed plan and with considerable effect. Here are a few more examples.

In the southernmost region of Texas a Latino priest brings his parish into a citizens' organization known as Valley Interfaith. His motivation, he tells me, is fidelity to the church's teachings on social justice. Why does he think that something good can come of his efforts? It is because Valley Interfaith has already succeeded in transforming hundreds of impoverished shantytowns along the U.S.–Mexico border into habitable neighborhoods. An organizer is helping him figure out how to energize his parish. The heroes of the shantytown struggle enliven his imagination.

The section of Los Angeles formerly known as South Central is riddled with violence and ethnic tension. Yet in a public school there the principal, the teachers, and some of the parents, with the help of organizers, have constructed an island of civility where children can learn. The principal tells me that citizens of good will are in a life-and-death struggle with gangs over the allegiance of the young. He says that whoever does the best job of organizing, wins.

Near San Francisco, sixty delegates from citizens' organizations in northern California are meeting together for the first time. Among those represented are labor unions and religious institutions. In welcoming the delegates, a rabbi says that the work of a citizen pertains to the preciousness of human beings, to something one ought to hold sacred. The next speaker is a Latina, who represents farm workers in the Napa Valley. Later, a nurse asserts the need to build power. The chief organizer is a nun who tells me that it isn't enough to care about social change: "You have to know how to bring it about."

A priest, a principal, a rabbi, a farm worker, a nurse, and a nun: these leaders and many others like them will be heard from in chapters 2 through 17. Empowered citizens are eager to convey what they are doing. They take pride and encouragement from their successes. Their frustrations reveal what they are up against, what *anyone* who wants to hold elites accountable is up against. These ordinary people are practicing a kind of grassroots democracy and helping each other get the hang of it. Hearing them out is, I believe, a good way of learning what citizenship can be and an apt occasion for reflecting on the nature of power, authority, and domination in a society officially committed to liberty and justice for all.

Toward the end of the book, in an analysis that culminates in chapter 18, I shall consider the gap between grassroots democracy as it is currently practiced at the local level and the systemic imbalances of power at the national and international levels that have tilted politics in the direction of plutocracy and perpetual war.[17] The gap is large enough to make the future of democracy uncertain. For this reason, a lot hangs on whether existing networks like the one examined in this book can be broadened and linked together in a way that creates effective publics of accountability. It remains unclear whether grassroots democracy can be scaled up to address the realities of power in the age of global capitalism and American military dominance.

The scaling-up effort is certain to fail in the absence of democratic organizational structures conducive to both accountability and effective collective action. Most liberals, for all of their good intentions, are grouped too loosely to hold corporate bosses and public officials accountable. Stronger ties, however, would not *necessarily* be democratic. The challenge is to build organizations that can facilitate *both* the upward flow of influence *and* the exercise of collective power. Democratic change will happen on a large scale only if many organizations that are themselves democratically structured cooperate in bringing it about. Unfortunately, these organizational requirements are not widely understood by citizens who would be pleased to see stratification reduced and ruling elites held accountable to ordinary people.

Social critics have not provided much help on this matter. Many of them make careers of denouncing domination. A few are gifted at analyzing its systemic manifestations. But whether social critics earn a living as academics, as clerics, or as journalists, they nowadays give surprisingly little concrete guidance concerning the organizational means and institutional ends of change. The current crisis of democracy demands a precise, accessible, and detailed description of the organizational options open to people who seek large-scale change.

Loosely grouped liberals are doing some good. They express their qualms about the status quo mainly by casting votes, attending occasional rallies, signing petitions, and donating money to agencies like Oxfam and Amnesty International. Such acts have good effects. But they will never succeed in overturning plutocracy and militarism. The liberals' aversion for strong ties hampers them.

This does not mean, however, that radicals who specialize in debunking liberal democracy are doing any better. Anarchists offer a vision of a coming community without rulers but neglect to explain what would keep the strong from enslaving the weak if the vision were realized. Of course, the vision will not be realized. Academic Leninists suggest that we shall need to take orders from a revolutionary avant-garde if we want to bring about large-scale change. No explanation is forthcoming as to how this would differ from submitting to another mode of totalitarian oligarchy. Both the coming community and the future revolutionary avant-garde are, at this point, mere projections of the radical imagination. As such, they express a longing for a sublime break with the present, a desire for an identity apart from the complicities of an unjust order.

These feelings may be understandable, under the circumstances, but the resulting fantasies do not issue in informed or dependable guidance about how to move forward. The audience for these genres of radical theory tends to be short in either historical memory or moral scruple. We have been down these paths before. Somehow, people who wish to avoid domination need to fashion a clear, realistic, and ethically acceptable alternative to the unpromising options of lifestyle liberalism, anarchism, and academic Leninism.

Chapter 19 will show that the president who was once a community organizer has not done so. Whether wittingly or not, his rhetoric of grassroots democracy disguises the nature of his own partisan political apparatus. This option, too, needs to be understood for what it is. While much of what Barack Obama said when he first explained the need for grassroots democracy is true, anyone who thought that Obama's "grassroots" organization would be an apt instrument for holding him and his powerful allies accountable was bound to be disappointed. The extent of the disappointment his followers have experienced is proportionate to the extent of their confusion about what grassroots democracy is. Obama bears some responsibility for generating that confusion.

If bottom-up change is to be achieved, ordinary citizens will have to construct a network of organizations that are democratic in their internal structure, in the ends they seek, and in the means they employ. Citizens cannot rely on the political parties—or, for that matter, on radical social critics—to do the work of democracy for them. This book suggests that the effort is already underway. Our journey in search of grassroots democracy begins in New Orleans.

✻ CHAPTER TWO ✻

A Power Analysis

When the levees broke, Broderick Bagert Jr., a white native of New Orleans, was twenty-nine and for three years had been working as an apprentice organizer in Houston. At the time of my visit almost a year and a half after Katrina, he had been back in New Orleans, working for Jeremiah, for a month. The city was still in shambles, and there was much to be done. Ernie Cortés had urged Brod and his supervisor Jackie Jones to think big. Jeremiah could not serve its purpose well without encompassing the entire metropolitan area. The first step, with which Brod and Jackie had been occupied since his return, was to conduct a "power analysis" of the entire situation. Brod agreed to spend a day driving me around the city while explaining what Jeremiah had discovered.[18]

It is no accident that the group bears the name of a Hebrew prophet. The group's motto comes from Jeremiah 29:7: "Seek the welfare of the city, for in its peace you will find your own."[19] That passage "shows the link right there," said Brod, echoing David Warren. "There's no way you can be an active Christian without looking for the welfare of your own community." For many people in New Orleans, Jeremiah provides what Brod called a "bridge between Christianity and democracy."

Not everyone in New Orleans appears to have the same image of the city's welfare in mind. Brod remarked that the evacuation after Hurricane Katrina had led the city's economic and governmental elites to imagine that they "had a clean slate to work with"—an opportunity to remake New Orleans in the form of a wealthier, whiter place with fewer people. "All the things dreamed about in the deepest darkest secrets of their minds were now possible." Most of

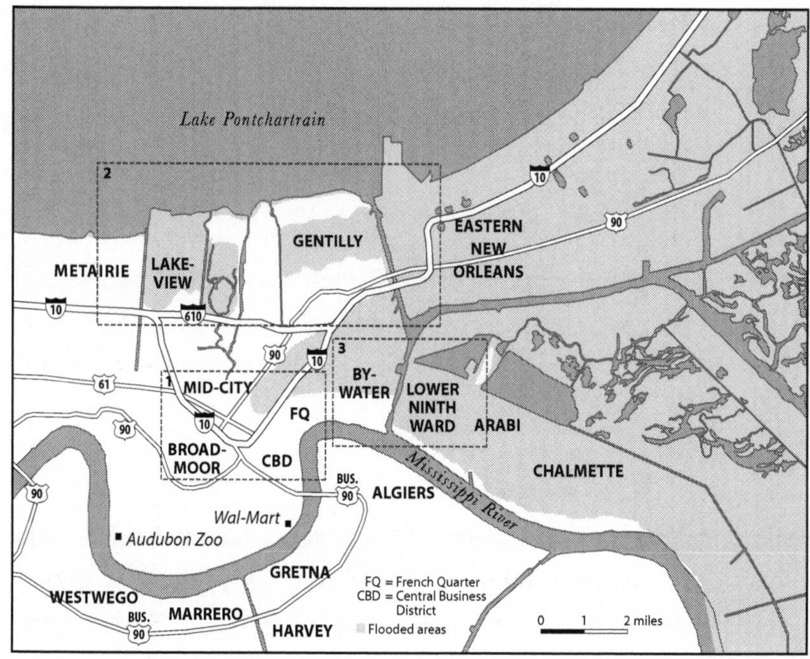

Map 2.1 Greater New Orleans

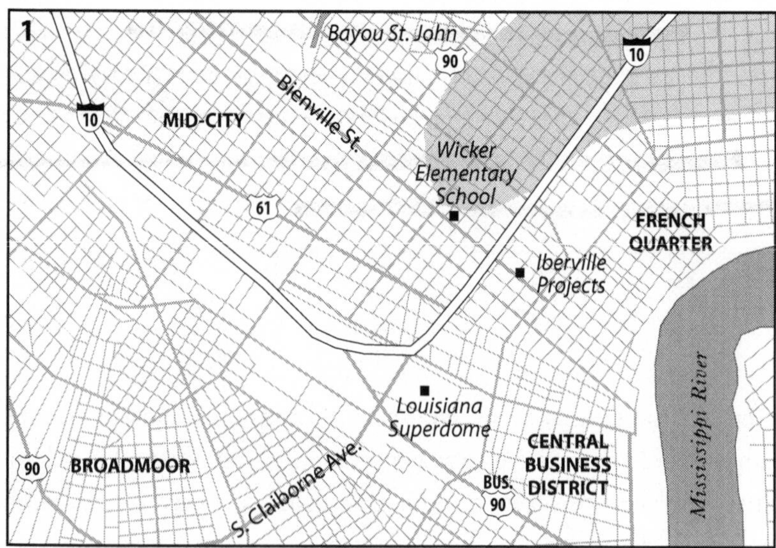

Map 2.2 Central New Orleans

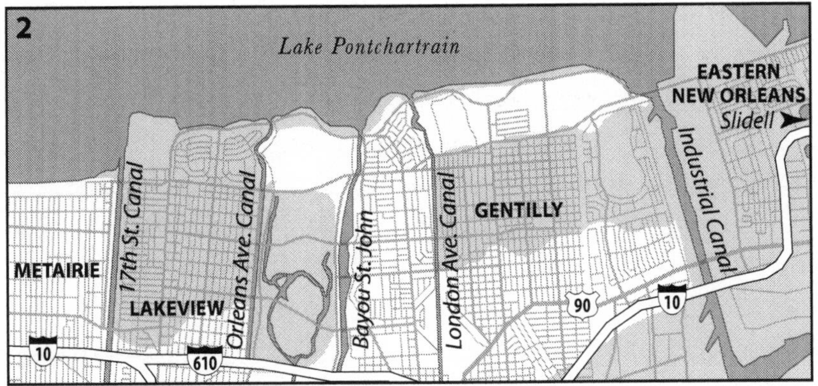

Map 2.3 Lakeside New Orleans

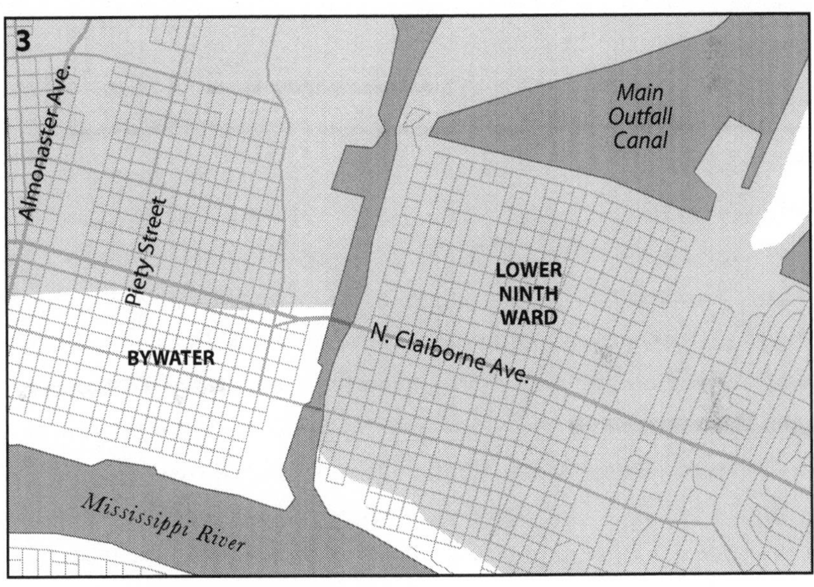

Map 2.4 Bywater and Lower Ninth Ward

the evacuees could now be ignored with impunity. Dysfunctional neighborhoods and institutions could simply be junked. With most of the population now dispersed in other states, it was time to reinvent New Orleans.

One of the first official actions taken was to fire "the entire workforce of teachers in Orleans Parish." The idea was that a broken school system could now be replaced by a brand new one. From Brod's point of view, it was the same kind of thinking that had led L. Paul Bremer to disband the army of Iraq. "Now they are really having a lot of trouble getting enough teachers. In some cases, nobody's doing the teaching, and there aren't schools open for children. . . . The stated goal of this was to hire one hundred percent certified teachers. The actual number is about sixty-seven percent, which isn't any better than it was before the storm. So, it's this kind of myth: slash, burn, and create things from anew." Brod grew up in a Catholic parish in the Gentilly section and attended Catholic schools. Most of those schools are still functioning, because the teachers were not fired.

As we passed through the warehouse district, Brod said that many residents of that area were angry even before the storm. A misconceived housing project there and controversies over how the arrival of Wal-Mart would affect residents and small businesses were the issues that had drawn Brod into public life in the first place. Unfortunately, the civic association that had picked fights over these issues possessed too little power to keep the developers and a major corporation from having their way. Anger by itself accomplished nothing, but it at least provided evidence that people didn't want to be pushed around.

In the period leading up to Katrina, the developer's stated objective, Brod said, was to "gentrify everything from the Central Business District to the Zoo," which would have an especially negative impact on long-time renters in the neighborhood. Residents wanted to fight the plan, but the organizational effort wasn't effective. "The worst enemy of organizing is bad organizing and there was no real organizing going on. . . . The [development] project got twenty-five million dollars in federal money, which was then topped up by some more federal money and state money and local money. And once they moved the residents out and started to demolish [the St.

Thomas public housing complex where nearly three thousand people lived], they brought in a different developer and canceled the choice of the original committee because . . . it had too many residents involved [in the decision-making process]. They accused the head [of the] housing authority of taking a proactive approach to resident participation.

"Next time," Brod continued, in the period after the storm "the housing authority freed itself from a proactive approach by having no residents [involved] whatsoever, picked the developer that had made that statement about gentrifying everything from the zoo to the Central Business District, and just made wholesale changes. It was going to be one hundred percent owned by the developer, a private company. The management company would be a subsidiary of the developer, and the housing started changing dramatically, to the point where very, very few of the former . . . residents were going to be able to afford [the new housing]. And it ended up being just a massive displacement program, subsidized to the tune of $100 million."

The Bring Back New Orleans Commission had held a press conference in this neighborhood a few months after the storm. The point was to say that this style of development would be the vision for the new New Orleans. Brod sees it as a "symbol of depopulation and displacement," and depopulation remains a major theme in the city as a whole. The population of Orleans Parish had "gone from four hundred and sixty thousand to somewhere around two hundred to two hundred and twenty thousand" since the storm.

We turned onto Claiborne Avenue, heading downtown. Historically this part of Claiborne was the center of black culture and commerce and religious life in the city. In the 1960s and 1970s, by building Interstate Highway 10 through the heart of the city, urban planners had eviscerated this area, which borders the central business district and the French Quarter. The interstate highway, which here looms above the city on two-story-high concrete pillars, had transformed this section of Claiborne, which had been a lovely boulevard lined with oak trees, businesses, churches, and homes, into an urban dead zone. The Louisiana Superdome, which was constructed in the Central Business District in 1967, has been a symbol of the city ever since, not least when twenty-five thousand New Orleans citizens, most of them poor and black, took refuge there immediately after the storm, before being evacuated to places like Houston and Baton Rouge.

An exit off of I-10 took us into the Bienville Corridor, where Wicker Elementary School became the focal point of the organizing that the Jeremiah Group carried out in the 1990s. The Bienville Corridor had been flooded during the storm, however, and still hadn't recovered. For every ten houses we saw, only three or four were in the process of being restored. This made it difficult, Brod said, to get organizing off the ground again, though some people were now asking what could be done for the school, which he took to be a sign that local democracy was beginning to come back to life.

"One of the most controversial issues right now is what's going to happen with these developments," Brod said, gesturing to a nearby housing project known as Iberville. "Some of them didn't flood, or only flooded on the first floor with a couple of feet, and could be used for housing [even] two weeks after the storm. The first thing that the city and the housing authority and the federal government did was to buy the steel doors that you see here, at a cost of several hundred dollars per door, and make sure that nobody could get back, not even to retrieve belongings." The idea, as the authorities saw it, was that "nature has taken care of this for us, that people aren't there." Keeping the former residents out would allow developers to build new housing to "attract a different kind of person."

"The official line," Brod granted, "is that the housing was substandard, there was crime, it was separated from the community, and we want to create better housing. The fight will be over what they replace it with. It's very attractive land, right off the Central Business District, and there will be intense pressure."

Closer to Lake Pontchartrain we found mile after mile of devastated neighborhoods, from the Seventeenth Street Canal all the way to Slidell. In these neighborhoods, Brod suggested, class differences go a long way toward explaining the rate and extent of recovery. Racially mixed working-class and middle-class neighborhoods like Gentilly were beginning to make a comeback, because homeowners from those areas felt they had little choice but to rebuild. They had to return if they were going to reclaim their investment, even though much of the city remained dysfunctional. Some of these homes were resting awkwardly on cinder-block stilts out of all proportion to their original design—little, one-story houses with daddy-long-legs, reminiscent of an Imperial Walker from Star Wars. It was an utterly surreal scene.

Another house we passed in Gentilly belongs to Catholic nuns, one of whom was Brod's principal at the school he once attended nearby. "They got lucky because a tree fell on their house," Brod said. Insurance companies classify damage from a fallen tree as caused by wind, rather than by rising water, which home-owner's policies in New Orleans don't cover. Middle-class luck in this place is to have a tree fall on your house. We passed Brod's old school and then his church, which he described as a "modernist monstrosity." From the building's spar, a cross, which had been broken off at the base, was still hanging. The water level had reached halfway up the surrounding houses.

Across Bayou St. John from Gentilly, moving west, is Lakeview. Being wealthier than their Gentilly neighbors, more of Lakeview's former residents were financially able to relocate elsewhere after the evacuation. They could afford to wait, at least until the city was fully up and running again, before returning, if they wanted to return at all. To the east of Gentilly is Eastern New Orleans, the home of the black middle class. And to the southeast is the Lower

Ninth Ward, another largely black area infamous after the storm as the most salient symbol of the city's devastation.

"The fight since right after storm was over whether there would be a smaller footprint," Brod said. "And what that meant was: Are the Lower Ninth Ward and New Orleans East coming back?" While we had seen many signs of recovery in white middle-class neighborhoods, we saw almost no such signs in New Orleans East. There were just rows and rows of solidly built wooden and brick homes, nearly all of them reduced to mere shells. The story of displacement in New Orleans isn't solely about poor people, as many outside observers assume. Most people who once lived in New Orleans East had had homes and jobs.

Brod recalled touring New Orleans East shortly after the storm waters receded. "At night it was like you dropped off the face of the Earth, or at least of civilization, because there were no lights, no electricity, nothing. During the daytime everything was dead." The only group that had made a visible comeback in New Orleans East was the Vietnamese community, which was able to take advantage of the strong network of institutions that it had built up over the decades leading up to the storm. The stronger the existing network of churches and other civic groups, the easier the process of recovery tends to be and the easier it is for an organizer to generate democratic activity. Brod was planning to meet with pastors from Vietnamese churches within the week.

Later that day we circled back to I-10, onto North Claiborne and entered the Lower Ninth, after passing streets in Bywater called Piety and Desire. "It's now almost green space," Brod said. "This was all as heavily populated as what we saw before. But the houses were just all over. There was no bulldozing, but they looked like that." In other neighborhoods there had been a great deal of damage, but the first time Brod was allowed into the Lower Ninth, he found it breathtaking, with the remains of houses in the middle of the streets, blocking the way. He pointed to an area where a gigantic barge had been pushed half a block into the neighborhood when a surge had broken the levee.

Brod mentioned a couple of groups that had been working in the Lower Ninth, in one case gutting houses, in another doing some organizing. The trouble with the organizing, he said, was that it was all cause oriented. The organizers thought they knew in advance what the issues were. Because the focus was on individuals, rather than on institutions and relationships, little power was likely to be generated. Everything depended on the charisma of the lead organizer. The Jeremiah Group follows standard IAF practice by treating institutions, rather than isolated individuals, as the basis for a citizens' organization. It is churches, synagogues, schools, and the like that commit themselves to organizing and contribute the money that provides for organizer salaries.

"When you're just organizing individuals," Brod said, "you end up hiring an army of low paid organizing staff, with whom turnover is extremely high. You just run through these folks. . . . There are dozens of these people running around making $6.50 an hour, knocking on doors. It ends up being organizer-driven, but without a culture of professionalism." Most of the work falls to young people who spend a couple of years after college accomplishing relatively little before burning out. The only way to generate bottom-up change, Brod insisted, is to develop a broad network of well paid "professional organizers" who are trained to be responsive to the citizens they are serving.

Which sectors of the city were relatively well organized? The developers are very well organized indeed. Executives associated with the city's most successful enterprises are well organized. As for the civic life of the city, there were some areas, including the Bienville Corridor and the West Bank, which had been quite well organized before the storm. But many of the leaders from Bienville who had returned after the storm were still living in trailers, trying to get their houses fixed. The Broadmoor District is a good example of an area being revitalized. The civic associations and neighborhood groups there have succeeded in getting "in touch with residents, identifying and bringing to the table some foundation resources." Not many civic associations accomplish much at all, because they are often handicapped by myopia and insufficient power. Most leaders in such groups, Brod thinks, just don't know what they're doing.[20]

Brod commended a leader of the Broadmoor Improvement Association and a priest at the Church of the Annunciation, on Claiborne Avenue, for being able to see beyond the immediate interests of the neighborhood. While there has been a lot of civic activity in some other areas, it has mainly been ad hoc. One of Brod's goals is to figure out how to build on those efforts. "The planning process is mostly meaningless because it's totally disconnected from power or any resources that are on the table. But there's a lot of talented people and a lot of interesting looking congregations and civic associations that have started to emerge. Part of what I'm trying to do is to create a picture with them of what it would look like to have a metrowide organization. Without organizing, those efforts are going to end in apathy, disillusion, and despair."

When Brod and I reached a white working-class neighborhood, he drew my attention to a sign bearing the name of a politician who had "led the effort to prevent evacuees from being able to vote" in the mayoral election of 2006. Brod found the campaign bizarre, given that the politician's constituents were all evacuees. Why would someone work to prevent his own people from voting? Because if eligible evacuees voted in large numbers, many of them would be from the Lower Ninth Ward and New Orleans East, and nearly all of those would be black. "There's a kind of objectification of the black community in some parts of the city, where it's just 'them,' and 'them' is associated with crime and danger and corruption."

"You wouldn't look around and say this is the seat of privilege, and by all standards it's not," said Brod as we entered Metairie, a white working-class municipality west of Lakeview, just outside the city limits, bordering on Lake Pontchartrain. "But it acted as though it is because it's constantly compared to 'them' in New Orleans." Brod is doing an analysis of institutions in Metairie and hopes to build a sponsoring committee. The Jeremiah Group hasn't organized there before.

We passed "a crummy, smelly drainage canal," which runs through the heart of residential Metairie. Brod finds it remarkable that citizens have tolerated this sort of thing. Metairie schools are ranked only slightly above New Orleans schools, which rank dead last in Louisiana. There is plenty for an organizer to work with in an area like this, which traditionally votes with the most conservative block in the entire state and more often than not against the interests of Orleans Parish. Brod is hoping to get Metairie residents talking with one another about their own fairly serious problems. But to build a public of accountability for the entire metropolitan area is likely to take between two and five years.

I asked Brod how he got into this line of work. "For reasons I don't understand," he said, "this kind of broad-based organizing is not on the radar of a lot of universities in the country." After his initial involvement in one of the pre-Katrina fights against developers in New Orleans, Brod did graduate work at the London School of Economics, culminating in a master's thesis on how that fight had failed. Before coming back to the city, he didn't know much at all about the IAF, but a friend of his had worked in a similar network of organizers called Gamaliel, the same network that Barack Obama had worked for in Chicago. "I started looking around in that kind of thing, despairing at the possibilities."

Brod was recruited, in the end, by Jackie Jones, before being sent off to Houston for seasoning. Prior to meeting Jackie he didn't know who she was, but he had been looking for someone with something like her approach and outlook: "I was hoping that there would be a serious group of professionals doing something in the right way. It seemed to me very strange that that wouldn't exist in some capacity. It didn't look exactly like I thought it might look, but [IAF] clearly included people who were serious and effective and who I could learn from. I have a fantastic job—very challenging and demanding and stimulating. I love it. I get energized by it."

Organizing can build to moments of high drama, and its victories can be deeply satisfying. But most of the work is an exercise in patient attention to detail, focused on building up relationships among potential leaders. Perseverance is as essential as patience, because there are many frustrations along the way. "You know, you'll just have gone through three separate and independent dead ends in one congregation. Sometimes you think you have found a leader, but it turns out to be someone who doesn't deliver anybody to the next meeting, and you realize that you were wrong. In some instances you find someone who can deliver a following, but their following are all followers. They'll always be just the same eight people. You think you're on to something. It just takes a while to realize that these eight people are going nowhere."

Renee Wizig-Barrios served as Brod's supervisor while he was getting his feet wet in Houston. "After I had been organizing for about a year, Renee got pregnant, and I was still learning my ass from my elbow, getting used to what I was doing and starting to put some things together. They made the decision that I would run the organization. As you can imagine, I learned more in those seven or eight months. Also I worked closely with Sister Christine [Stephens] on that part. That ends up being the most meaningful kind of training—mentoring. There's the five-day and ten-day training sessions, which can be real important for people to kind of step back from life and think about working on themselves, but what it took for me to grow up was applying that stuff and trial and error and seeing what people do in real circumstances, watching them make mistakes and helping them think about that.

"I think it's that culture of respectful, tough critique that I've never found anywhere else, where people can really just go at you." Brod recalled his first regionwide IAF seminar with other organizers in the Southwest. The topic was Charles Payne's book, *I've Got the Light of Freedom*, a history of grassroots organizing in the civil rights movement.[21] "I was very arrogant, intellectually self-confident, and was checking these folks out, you know."

"Meaning your colleagues."

"That's right. We did a reading group. Oh, by the end of the day I think four different organizers had come at me and really nailed me on something, taken me on, and said, 'I don't think you listened very well.' And I said to myself, 'JESUS CHRIST, WHO ARE THESE PEOPLE?' And, you know, that was the first of many lessons in humility and respect from this group of people.

"That's how I met my wife. We were going through the buffet line right after our reading group. She said, 'Can I give you a critique?' I said, 'Yeeaah.' And she said, 'Well, I don't think you listen very well to other people.' I said, 'Well, I don't think you know me, and I don't think you know what the fuck you're talking about.' [Laughter] And she said, 'Okay.' I found out a month later that she was moving to Houston to organize there, and I said, 'Aww shit! Now I've gotta call this woman and kind of depolarize.'"

"Apparently you succeeded."

"Well, yeah. I decided to take her to go hear this journalist talk. That's when we started a friendship, which eventually turned into a marriage."

"So you learned to listen to others? Or she learned to tolerate your inability to listen to others?"

"Probably a little of both."

✻ CHAPTER THREE ✻

Organizing for the Common Good

TOWARD THE END of my tour of New Orleans, I asked Brod how long it would take before one would know the fate of the new New Orleans. He originally expected to have an answer to that question fairly soon after the storm. He assumed that the $8 billion that had already been allocated by the U. S. Department of Housing and Urban Development would "start to go into people's pockets and knock around in the economy," which would immediately begin to pump up the recovery effort. "As it happens none of that eight billion dollars is in people's pockets. It was designed in a byzantine, complex way, a huge contract with an out-of-state contractor, and the upshot has been that only two hundred and fifty people have actually gotten money at this point [i.e., late January 2007]. So if it continues to go at this level we're in bad shape, and the long-term recovery is going to be as bad as the immediate relief effort."

"But if it goes that slowly, that already determines the fate of the city, doesn't it?" I asked.

"Yeah, that's right," Brod replied. "That's my point."

Developers and their allies had viewed the disaster of Katrina as an opportunity to wipe the slate clean and construct a smaller, richer, whiter population of its own choosing. They had made it difficult for evacuees to vote and had permitted the allocation of federal money to be delayed in a way that had effectively prevented countless black and lower-class evacuees from returning home. Social critics have coined a label for this way of seizing on the opportunities that catastrophes provide for the refashioning of the social order. They call it *disaster capitalism*.[22]

But Brod was not telling me that democracy had perished in

New Orleans. To the contrary, he was explaining why he considered democratic revival there both urgently necessary and a realistic hope. Some civic associations and churches had begun to see beyond the boundaries of their own neighborhoods and congregations. They were now considering joining forces with the Jeremiah Group, hoping to construct a metrowide citizens' organization that would have enough power to influence and contest decisions being made on high about the future of the city. There were a lot of institutions left to organize, to be sure, and a number of people who were organizing ineffectively or counterproductively. Nonetheless, it was clear what Jeremiah would have to do, and it had the accumulated experience of many citizens' groups in other places to draw on. No other organization in the IAF network had been through exactly what New Orleans had experienced as a result of Katrina, but they all had had to deal with the effects of a widening gap between rich and poor, racial and ethnic divisions among lower- and middle-class citizens, and a general weakening of institutions, such as churches and labor unions, that once mitigated the negative effects of a capitalist economy.

One effect of the widening economic gap is the ease with which elites are now able to translate advantages acquired in the economic sphere—such as money, wealth, organizational cohesion, organizational skills, communication technology, and ready access to information—into political power. The easier it is for elites to increase their political power by taking political advantage of their economic advantages, the more the political arena tilts in favor of the rich, which in turn diminishes the extent to which the rest of the population is able to exercise its countervailing power effectively. The greater the tilt, the weaker the system of political accountability becomes. The economically advantaged are then able to pursue their own private objectives with minimal resistance from others.

Katrina made a bad situation worse. Extreme stratification of wealth and power had already created many opportunities for the city's developers to do as they wished despite opposition from others. By scattering the population, the storm made it much harder for ordinary citizens to fight back. The basic rights to assemble peaceably, to speak out freely, to petition for the redress of grievances, and to vote suddenly became much more difficult to exercise. Indirectly, the New Orleans story shows how important the exercise of those rights is. A momentary weakening of citizens' counterpower left people in the top income brackets in a position to reconfigure the city's population, social structure, and culture. Power stratification, made worse by the storm, created an opportunity for domination. Developers in New Orleans were not disposed to let the opportunity escape their grasp.

Long-standing ethnic and racial divisions obviously come into play in many communities and are often exploited by elites that have their own reasons for favoring a particular kind of government-administered social engineering. If whites, regardless of class, would rather cooperate politically with the economic elite than with middle-class, working-class, and poor African Americans, or if African Americans become preoccupied with the points at which their own interests appear to diverge from those of Asian or Hispanic immigrants, it becomes more difficult to build the sort of political coalition that could counterbalance the economic elite's increasing political power. IAF's emphasis on the need for broad-based organizing of a sort that aims to bridge the divisions among identity groups responds directly to this widespread structural feature of American political culture. When Brod spoke of the need to create a "metrowide" coalition that would include the middle-class whites of Metairie, he was expressing Jeremiah's commitment to an approach that many IAF affiliates throughout the country have settled on as a way of addressing the fundamental problem of an increasingly tilted political playing field.

Saul Alinsky's organizing in Chicago's Back of the Yards neighborhood in the 1930s and 1940s was not broad based. Because his work focused on a single community of the poor and disenfranchised, located in the same geographical area and largely homogenous ethnically and religiously, it became known as *community* organizing. But as early as 1946, Alinsky noted the drawbacks of focusing exclusively on particular communities: "An organization founded on a limited program covering a limited community will live a limited life." The concerns of democratic organizing know "no boundaries, whether geographical, philosophical, or social. . . . Its philosophy, analysis of problems, and general objectives are at the very least national in character."[23] As time went on, Alinsky became increasingly worried by what happened to the Back of the Yards community after his organizing efforts there bore fruit. Poor whites, most of them Polish-Catholic immigrants, used the power generated by their community organization to improve their economic and political standing in the arena of Chicago politics. As they became middle-class and established their foothold in the Chicago political machine, they eventually used their power against other relatively disempowered communities.

Alinsky was forced to confront the question of what had gone wrong. How can an initially democratic organization prevent itself from turning into something that can be used to promote the exclusion of other groups? Contemporary organizers connect this question with Alinsky's hope for extending the effects of their work from the local to the state and national levels. A group like Jeremiah still devotes a lot of time to organizing in particular neighborhoods, but from the beginning an effort is made to build bridges across lines of geography, class, race, ethnicity, and religion. This explains why the term "community organizing" has largely passed out of favor.

The rationale for broad-based organizing, then, is twofold: first, to mitigate the tendency of groups organized around singular identities to use their power to advance only their own narrowly conceived interests; and second, to build up coalitions with enough power to address issues that cannot be resolved merely by applying leverage to local institutions. The first point is that the well-being of the city as a whole is actually in the interest of each individual and group in the city. There is no radical or permanent division between pursuit of one's own interests and promotion of the common good. The second point connects the convergence of interests in the common good with the need to amass power. If the well-being of the entire city can be secured only by a broad-based network that transcends neighborhood and ethnicity, then systematic efforts must be made to build up connections among groups with varying backgrounds in different communities.

The situation of the Have-Nots today, according to Cortés, is one in which many of the institutions that once buffered citizens from the market are themselves either falling apart or fighting for their lives. The main reason that IAF concentrates on building coalitions of institutions like churches, synagogues, mosques, parent-teacher associations, unions, and so on is that these entities are already to some extent organized and thus possess at least some money and power to serve as a starting point for defending the Have-Nots. Unfortunately, in many communities these institutions appear to have weakened.[24]

Cortés reports that in numerous settings where Southwest IAF has gained a foothold, there are fewer such institutions than there used to be for organizers to work with and that the institutions remaining are often attracting fewer members and generating relatively low levels of commitment, identification, and bonding among the members they have. More and more of the organizer's work must therefore, according to Cortés, be devoted to "reweaving the social fabric," which is largely a matter of strengthening the relational life of institutions that have chosen to join, or might be persuaded to join, a citizens' organization. "To rebuild our society," Cortés says, "we must rebuild our civic and political institutions. Under conditions of social fragmentation, it is a daunting challenge."[25]

Post-Katrina New Orleans is an extreme case of social fragmentation, where a process of disintegration that was already underway in some neighborhoods was exacerbated horribly, first by a catastrophe and then by decisions made on high that appear to have been intended to induce fragmentation and powerlessness within some groups. Yet, as Brod's comments on the Broadmoor District show, being confronted with catastrophic change can also be a stimulus to civic life. The need for cooperation is hard to deny when the tendencies of fragmentation are exaggerated in a moment of crisis. Catastrophes can clarify the mind.

A delicate balance needs to be struck if a multiracial coalition is to be constructed in post-Katrina New Orleans. Jeremiah leaders are taking four steps to achieve that balance. First, they are carefully distinguishing racial *identification* from being *concerned about* racism and its effects. Second, they are trying to explain in clear and accessible language how racial factors combined with economic factors to bring about the crisis they face. Third, Jeremiah is trying to show all groups, including corporate executives and the residents of Metairie, how their interests would be served by joining the coalition. And fourth, Jeremiah is trying to articulate a vision of a common good in which those interests converge.

The common good being sought consists in a way of relating to one another from which everyone who wishes to avoid domination would benefit.[26] But to provide a motivation for joining the coalition, a vision of the city's common good must be concrete. A concrete vision sounds like a mixed metaphor. What it means is simply a description of how the basic relationships among groups in the city *would* look if particular forms of domination were diminished or eliminated. It is visionary because it pertains to the impression one has of basic relationships. It involves an imaginative projection because it concerns how things would look if they were different in some respects. The projected vision is not utopian, however, in the sense of imagining how things would look if power and elites were eliminated from the community altogether—if, so to speak, the lion were to lie down with the lamb, or if there were no lions. A vision of a given community's common good is concrete if it projects an image of how the basic relationships among groups in the community would look if particular actions that *can* be undertaken by those groups *are* undertaken.

For a group of citizens to appreciate the attractiveness of such a vision, they will need first of all to perceive what the basic relationships among groups in the city already *are*. This is what the second of the four steps I have outlined amounts to. Perception of what the situation is usually precedes imaginative projection of an achievable alternative to it. But perception in this case isn't simply a matter of opening one's eyes and looking. Most people do not view their situation in terms of power relations. It is not in the perceived interest of the dominant to teach people how to conceive of and perceive power. Indeed, the dominant would often prefer that power remain invisible and unmentioned. If ordinary people view it as something inherently bad and therefore not the sort of thing one would like to acquire and exercise, so much the better, from the perspective of the dominant.

Jeremiah thus makes a point of teaching people how to use the word *power* and how to overcome their qualms about using it. The power analysis summarized in chapter 2 is designed to help them see what the existing power relationships of the city consist of, but also to project an image of an alternative set of relationships that they could achieve by collaborating with others in a certain way. The way of collaborating must be described as concretely as the current situation and the hoped-for outcome are. Jeremiah contrasts how things ought to be with how things are, but the *ought* being described is not a mere dream beyond the realm of possibility. The path leading toward it is also something to be made visible.

If the city's common good comprises a set of basic relationships in which everyone who wishes to avoid domination has an interest, this does not entail that everyone can already see their interests as converging in this manner. One purpose of a power analysis is to identify what is in the self-interest of key individuals and groups as those people already see it. For most of them, that means their self-interest narrowly conceived. *Self-interest* is, for this reason, another expression that organizers teach people to use, both in reference to others and to themselves.[27] Some people may already have an expansive conception of their own interest and understand that they would actually be happier living in a community freed from domination, but most people will not begin the process of transformation at that point. Some people serve their interests, consciously or unconsciously, by covering them in moralistic garb.

For all of these reasons, a citizens' organization needs to discover how narrow conceptions of self-interest currently operate in this or that segment of the community. The interest that everyone who wishes to avoid domination has in the common good is often as yet unknown to the individuals and groups themselves. It thus needs to be made explicit. Explicit recognition of one's interest in the common good is linked to explicit recognition of what the existing conceptions of self-interest are and how they currently operate to frustrate the achievement of relationships that everyone in fact has an interest in fostering and enjoying. The Jeremiah leadership holds, for example, that some of the key players in Metairie are wrong about what would actually be in the interest of the majority of Metairie's citizens. It remains the case, however, that the prudent way to reach out to those citizens is to treat their current conception of their interests as a starting point.

Some churches have the opposite problem. They are so enraptured by utopian visions of the lion lying down with the lamb that they are unwittingly assisting actual lions in the destruction of actual lambs. It might be that the meek and powerless will someday be blessed with happiness in God's coming kingdom, but Jeremiah leaders do not see this as a reason for encouraging people who are currently meek and powerless to remain so. Utopian visions have an uplifting role to play in some forms of religion but become dangerous when they interfere with legitimate attempts to constrain what lions are now doing to lambs. Caring about the vulnerable means little if one fails to name and prevent violence being done to the vulnerable.

Three institutions in the Bienville Corridor led the fight for revitalization there in the 1990s. Two were churches, but one was Wicker Elementary School, which became a focal point of Jeremiah's work. I asked Jackie Jones what happens when a school joins in. "To be a member of Jeremiah," she said, "you bring your talent and you bring an investment too." Public schools cannot pay dues to Jeremiah out of their own budgets, but parent organizations can raise money and make a donation. "We teach that organized people plus organized money equals power." The process doesn't amount to anything "if you don't invest in what you're doing. They sold ice cream in the afternoons."

The first step of Jackie's organizing in the Bienville Corridor was meeting with pastors, as many as eight one-on-one meetings a day. "Off of that we start bringing those people together through house meetings, through those institutions, then encouraging them to go out and talk to the community. It was urgent to do something about the prostitution and about the crime. So, you had those community walks. And I would say over a period of about three to six months, well over eight hundred individual meetings were done."

"House meetings" are small group discussions in which people exchange stories about their concerns. In these meetings people begin to discover that some their own concerns resemble the concerns that other people have. The organizers and leaders who sit in on the sessions are able to continue the process of identifying potential leaders, while also taking note of whatever concerns arise repeatedly in house meetings throughout the area.

Angela St. Hill, who represents St. Joseph the Worker Church, pointed out to me that the leaders of Jeremiah "don't decide what the issue is. In talking to the people in the community and doing walks in the community, and doing one-on-one meetings with people, they let us know what their concerns are and what their issues are." Once the issues of crime, housing, and schools were identified as central, Jeremiah "came up with a plan for the revitalization of that area." One victory came when the mayor agreed to fund after-school programs, which provide a safe and supervised learning environment for young people and which are proven to reduce truancy rates.[28] Parents from the neighborhood were hired to run the programs.

A related issue was what Reverend Pate described as the deplorable condition of the restrooms in the schools. Because toilets and partitions had been ripped from the walls, students were leaving the building to use facilities elsewhere. When they got back to the school, many were caught and suspended. By focusing on that issue, Jeremiah could win a fight, thus creating momentum for their organizing, while attracting public attention to the more general need to improve the schools. The city later allocated $1.5 million for restroom renovation. Every six months, local news reporters would bring television cameras into the schools for updates on the restrooms, and every time they did the members of Jeremiah were reminded that victory is possible.

Success breeds courage and hope. Many organizers say that it is prudent, early on, to pick fights that have high chances of short-term success: over issues like restrooms and traffic lights, rather than the minimum wage and job training. As an organization builds power and self-confidence, it can afford to take on riskier, longer-term struggles. A major objective at the outset is to endow the organization's members with self-trust, to persuade them that they really do have power in their hands. The particular issues matter less than the spiritual transformation of isolated individuals into citizens whose potential for agency is actualized.

Repeatedly engaging in face-to-face contact was necessary, Brod said, for "getting a sense of what the issues were, and looking for those interesting people who could be potential leaders in all of this, who can put passion and anger behind whatever is going on. And there was this continuous cycle of one-on-ones and house meetings in the Bienville area." One-on-one conversations, neighborhood walks, and house meetings are the basic practices of grassroots organizing. The view that they need to be conducted face to face was shared by all of the organizers and leaders I met with during my travels. As we will see in later chapters, when these basic practices atrophy, so do the organizations themselves.

✻ CHAPTER FOUR ✻

Rites of Solidarity, Commitment, and Mourning

WITH A MODEST, but encouraging victory behind them, the Jeremiah Group consulted with parents, teachers, and other members of the community about broader issues facing the school system. After the core team developed some proposals, the organization decided to hold an "accountability session" for local political candidates in the cafeteria at Wicker Elementary. About four hundred citizens attended, nearly a hundred of them standing.

At any IAF accountability session, officials and candidates are invited into the community itself. The session is held on the turf of the citizens' organization, not in a government building. The agenda is strictly controlled by organization leaders. Speakers from the community tell stories to illustrate what the issues are and dramatize their importance. Leaders lay out the organization's proposals concisely, and then ask the officials and candidates to say briefly where they stand. A politician who begins a stump speech quickly discovers that his or her microphone will simply be turned off.

The event is a rite of solidarity. By coming together in a public setting of their own choosing and enacting a script of their own devising, citizens make their collective power manifest. They articulate their shared values, sum up their experiences in representative stories, and celebrate their existence as a unified group capable of action. By assembling, they reinvigorate the group and charge up its members. They also make its life force and solidarity evident to others.[29]

The event is also a rite of commitment. For the rank and file attending the session, their cheers and applause express a willingness to act on the group's behalf in the future. The invited politicians are confronted with a series of dilemmas. Either they will accept the invitation to attend, or they won't. Either they will acknowledge the group's entitlement to perform a representative role in the community, or they won't. Either they will accept the group's formal proposals, or they won't. They are being asked to make a commitment. The pressure they feel comes from the implied threat of opposition.

At day's end, all parties know where they stand. The session personifies the role of leadership, as some speak publicly on behalf of others. The stories dramatize the community's concerns. The gathering makes visible the significance of membership in the social body. And the rite of political commitment draws the distinction between friends and others with unmistakable clarity. A public commitment from an official or candidate binds him or her to the group. Henceforth, the politician and the group can hold one another accountable for failing to live up to its side of an explicit bargain. Elections remain the primary means that citizens have for holding politicians accountable. An accountability session does not so much enact accountability as prepare the way for such enactment.

For its part, the citizens' group is promising to cooperate with candidates and officials who commit themselves to supporting the group's proposals. Nonprofit organizations like Jeremiah would lose their tax-exempt status if they endorsed candidates. So they simply publicize who agreed to appear, who did not, which proposals each official or candidate was prepared to endorse, and which he or she was not prepared to endorse. The political chips then fall as they may, but with predictable negative consequences for politicians who fail to make the commitments being demanded of them or fail to live up to those commitments down the road.

"In the process of building relationships, we are able to identify who our allies are," said Angela. "We never have permanent allies and we never have permanent enemies, because on some issues the mayor could be our ally and on some issues not. We meet with everybody we know that is connected to a particular issue that we're working on, and we identify our allies. So when we go forward we know in advance who is going to be with us and who is not."

One accountability session shortly before the storm focused on crime. Discussions with community members had established that a lot of local drug activity stemmed from one bar not far from St. Joseph the Worker in Marrero. "We had talked to a lot of different people, and brought them together," said Angela St. Hill during my meeting with Jeremiah leaders. "What we found we needed was a detox center right here on the West Bank for people who wanted to get off drugs, for people who wanted to go through rehab. Sheriff Harry Lee [of Jefferson Parish] came to that public action and said that he was going to donate X amount of money. One of the reporters there asked him, 'Is that all you're going to put up?' And by the next day, he had committed to about $150,000." Angela's point was that officials like Lee are responsive to citizens' groups that do their homework and learn how to exert power.

"Our concern was the sanctity of all life," Angela remarked. If "all life is valuable," that includes drug addicts, lawbreakers, and the victims of lawbreakers. "We had a very good conversation. We asked for a liaison from his office. We asked for some ongoing meetings with his officers and the community, and we were given those things. But one month later Katrina hit, everything went out the window. Since Katrina, we've found that crime has escalated both in Orleans Parish and Jefferson Parish, and in these neighborhoods where we have a lot of our leaders and our institutions: Marrero, Harvey, Gretna, and so on. So we met last Thursday with four of Sheriff Lee's chiefs, and reminded them of the meeting we had with Harry Lee himself prior to Katrina and let them know that we wanted this to continue, to reestablish the relationship, to come up with solutions that would help solve the crime problem."

The day before my visit, St. Joseph the Worker had buried a young man who had been shot, a case of mistaken identity. The church was packed for the funeral. "Eighteen years old," Angela said sadly, "but the grandmother's a member, the great-grandmother's a member, the aunties are members, the uncles are members, the cousins, you know. So, it touched home. Sometimes when things happen, especially like crime, people say, 'It's not happening to me. It's happening to somebody else over there.' So it's kind of coming home to us. When I first moved into Marrero twenty-five years ago, there was hardly anything happening here. But now Marrero seems like the capital of murders."

It used to be, Angela said, that "when there was a robbery, it was something, you know, something horrific. But now it's happening so often that you kind of get numbed to it." Angela described several other cases, ending with the story of a cab driver who had been killed right across the street. When she invites people to Jeremiah meetings in her neighborhood, they are reluctant to come. "It's getting in your backyard, it's getting in your front yard." The problems of post-Katrina New Orleans go well beyond the devastation I had seen from the passenger seat of Brod's car.

After Katrina, Reverend Jaime Oviedo said, there were many complications. Knowing that the schools are open and offering a decent education is essential to families considering moving back to New Orleans. "When schools were shut down and broken apart, it delayed the process of people coming home. You know, families can return home if there's a place to live and schools for their kids. I think more people would have been able to come home sooner had the school system been in place. But when everyone left after the storm, the school systems were just fragmented and broken apart by the state. There was really no reason for people to return home."

The group's pre-Katrina organizing had produced many leaders, some of whom had returned to the city after the storm and were ready to get things rolling again. But many others were now elsewhere, trying to reach out to their fellow evacuees. "As Jeremiah started to get back together," Brod said, "we started to get reconnected with the displaced folks in Louisiana. Central to all that was how people were affected, especially those folks who left the city. At the time, for those of us who were still here in the midst of this, something began to happen. A lot of the folks who were here were trying to make decisions for the city. They tried to take full advantage of the change in population and demographics at that moment and did their very best to keep people out while decisions were being made to reshape and reenvision what New Orleans would look like. . . . Democracy means participation by everyone regardless of race or social status or whatever. How do we make sure that no one gets missing when you talk about coming back home, where you've been for generations?"

Jeremiah held a conference of four hundred leaders from the New Orleans area in March 2006. Many were brought in on buses from Dallas, Houston, and other places where evacuees were living on a temporary basis. One-on-one conversations and "mini-house meetings" were used to identify shared concerns and collect information on how the storm had affected particular neighborhoods. Many people were concerned that they were being cut out of the decision making. With a clearer view of the situation, the group developed an action agenda. One issue that came into focus immediately was the need for affordable housing, which was related to the issue of home insurance. Other issues included job training, a living wage, the crisis in the public schools, and what came to be known in official circles as revitalization.

Karl Weber, another leader from St. Joseph the Worker, called attention to a map created by the Bring Back New Orleans Commission, which indicated the areas that had been slated, after the storm, for revitalization. If you know the census, Karl said, it's immediately apparent that the marked neighborhoods represent "the heavy concentrations of African Americans." In this context, *revitalization* means replacement of the neighborhoods that existed before Katrina with something whiter, wealthier, safer, and less heavily populated.

"The power play that was going on at the time was bald and naked," Brod said. "The first move with the Bring Back New Orleans Commission was a smaller footprint: 'We're going to turn these people's communities into a park or green space.' You had folks in the legislature who were trying to deny people the right to vote, because this was the big chance to take back the city from the undesirables and put it back in the hands of the responsible, the good and the great—you know, the people who ruled things until 1960."

With the mayoral election approaching in April 2006 and nearly thirty candidates still in the running, Jeremiah decided to hold an accountability session for the top eight. The candidates were asked whether they would work with the Jeremiah group on each of the main issues that had been identified. "We came up with a scorecard, and tracked how each of those candidates responded," Brod said. "We gave the results to all the leaders to see, to get a sense of who we'd be able to work with." Approximately five hundred people attended the session at Trinity Church in New Orleans. Hundreds more participated, by way of satellite broadcast, in Texas.

The runoff election pitted Mitch Landrieu against Ray Nagin. But in the confusion of post-Katrina New Orleans it was not clear who would be able to vote. Thousands of former residents were still scattered elsewhere. Many polling places had been destroyed, and many returnees were unsure where to vote. Jeremiah proposed that special polling sites be opened in cities outside of Louisiana where at least five thousand displaced citizens from New Orleans were now located. While that proposal was defeated, ten special polling sites were opened for evacuees outside of New Orleans in Louisiana. According to Jackie, one state legislator credited passage of the latter proposal to all of "those church people who were out there singing *Kumbaya*." Jeremiah was also able to work with IAF affiliates in other cities to deliver ten thousand absentee ballots. "It doesn't mean things are great," Brod said, "and there's a lot that's still screwed up. But the kind of drastic power play that I think a lot of people in power hoped for, they weren't able to pull it off, because of the organizing that Jeremiah did."

David pointed out that absentee ballots are always worth keeping in mind when you're organizing in prisons.[30] Prisoners "being held on charges still have the constitutional right to vote," David said. "So we went in and got those guys signed up for an absentee ballot. That was the first [effort of that kind] here in the state."

On the day of the runoff, Karl said, "We had a get-out-the-vote rally. We also brought in people that had been displaced from places like San Antonio, Houston, Austin, Dallas. We had a rally outside of City Hall. Just two weeks prior a lot of these folks had received notices from FEMA that their housing was in the process of being ended. So we were able to get commitments from the candidates saying that if elected they would go with us to Houston to make sure that that gets delayed, because these folks have no place to live. Nagin did win the election, he did go off with us to Houston, and we did get a stay on that decision." Displaced voters didn't just need a chance to vote, Karl argued. They needed information on what was happening back in New Orleans. Jeremiah therefore created "centers of information, or one-stops where people could find out what's going on in their neighborhoods."

"We went out into communities and knocked on doors," David said, "and found out the residents that were still there. Of course, the residents didn't know where the polling booths was at, but we had packets already designed showing where the polling booths had been moved to. Also we organized getting rides for them that day. Some of the city was still down. So we really wanted to know where most of the people were concentrated, where they had moved back to." David's approach in the more heavily populated areas, he said, was to get a band together and take it through the streets. Voting should be a celebration.

"Yeah, David," said Jackie. "Take credit, take credit! Go ahead!"

"So when they heard the music," David said, "they'd come outside and we had transportation ready to get them to the polls."

"I think they were playing 'Oh, When the Saints Go Marching In,'" Jackie laughed.

"It was a tremendous success in getting folks out and getting them engaged and getting them to the voting polls on that day," David said with evident pride. It was democracy, New Orleans style—black and blue, refusing defeat, improvising its way forward.

✳ CHAPTER FIVE ✳

Domination, Anger, and Grief

As I would not be a *slave*, so I would not be a *master*. This expresses my idea of democracy. Whatever differs from this, to the extent of the difference, is no democracy.
—*Abraham Lincoln*

New Orleans is a place where the social stratification currently threatening American democracy is impossible to ignore. Hurricane Katrina only made the divisions more obvious. The rain falls on the just and the unjust, but hurricanes mainly devastate the already destitute. In this city, the phrase "lower class" is not a metaphor. Many poor people lived on lower ground. No governmental agency, be it local, state, or national, managed to evacuate them in timely fashion. Accountability for this failure was minimal. Developers, with help from politicians representing the interests of big business and the white middle class, had used the disaster to reshape the city's population. The former residents of the Lower Ninth and New Orleans East were being denied a say in their own fate.[31]

It would be tempting to view New Orleans as exceptional. Before Katrina hit, at least nine American cities were economically worse off than New Orleans in statistically measurable terms, yet many Americans had trouble imagining that thousands of their fellow citizens anywhere were too poor even to get out of town. No one has to imagine this who has seen the pictures on television. President George W. Bush flew into town, toured the devastation, made his empty promises, and moved on. The American public, being too loosely organized to hold him accountable for his promises, allowed memories of poor people stranded on rooftops and the anarchy of the Superdome to recede from consciousness.

What those images of the New Orleans poor actually revealed was that a sizable fraction of the population lives in a continuing state of calamity and domination. Detroit looks a great deal like New Orleans. Miles and miles of devastation have replaced what used to be thriving neighborhoods. There are blocks in which a few houses stand, surrounded by vacant lots. But the damage has nothing to do with hurricanes. The poorest residents of New Orleans were already living in horrible conditions before Katrina compounded the hurt and drew our attention to it.

The picture of New Orleans that emerged from my tour of the city was even more disturbing than the images that I had seen on TV sixteen months earlier. Here was a city that had endured a catastrophe. The least well off, the residents of the Lower Ninth Ward, had taken the hardest hit. But how many Americans knew that the Lower Ninth, even a year and a half after the storm, would still be a wasteland? "Green space," Brod had called it.

How many realized, for that matter, what had happened subsequently to working-class and middle-class blacks in East New Orleans? We do not live in a postracial society after all. We live, paradoxically, in a society where blacks can become mayors and presidents, but also one in which even middle-class black neighborhoods can find themselves fighting for the right to return to their own homes. How many citizens outside the Gulf Coast, other than evacuees and their families, understand how concerted the effort was, on the part of the New Orleans establishment, to remake the city to its own specifications?

The standing possibility that our own communities will someday suddenly come to resemble post-Katrina New Orleans tells us something important about our social order. It tells us roughly the same thing that the subsequent global economic crisis tells us, namely, that governmental and economic elites are increasingly in a position to exercise their power arbitrarily over the rest of us. Among them, apparently, are people who are waiting for a chance to tilt the already-tilted playing field suddenly, drastically in their own favor. They already hold massive wealth and therefore massive power in their hands, and they are evidently using it to better their position in relation to the rest of us.

The question is whether the fortunate few are now in a position, or will soon be in a position, to have their way with us. I do not mean that their motives are wholly malevolent. No doubt, some of them sincerely think they know what would be best for all of us.[32] That, however, is beside the point. The case of New Orleans after the storm reveals a broader social structure nearing the tipping point between a society in which elites are held at least somewhat accountable to the people and a society in which elites can do as they please.

A power analysis like Jeremiah's aims to determine how power is currently distributed in the broader community. *Power*, in the sense at issue here, is the capacity that an individual, group, or institution has to produce effects that people would have reason to care about.[33] It is because individuals in isolation have little power that a power analysis focuses mainly on institutions and on the people who play consequential roles in them.

In an economy based on the market system, corporate bosses always have the advantages of institutional power at their disposal. By using the inducements of wages, salaries, and other benefits to secure the cooperation of others, they are able to achieve things that would be impossible without the collaboration of many people.[34] The bosses of large corporations, in particular, tend to have enormous power in their hands. So a power analysis of any community that resembles New Orleans does well to begin by looking closely at the corporate sector.

Bosses share an interest in using whatever organizationally aggregated power they have to acquire other advantages for themselves, including the knowledge that is required to establish and maintain political dominance over other groups. The top bosses know a lot about how to build organizations and amass power. They know this because they study such matters in school and get a lot of practice while on the job. Bosses specialize in organization building. That is what they do for a living. The top bosses are very good at what they do. That is how they got to the top.

Jeremiah's power analysis also took account of the governmental sector. Here too we have a set of institutions and a set of people holding office in them. In a country like the United States, these institutions are, at all levels of government, supposed to serve a common good, above all by establishing a framework of laws that make it difficult for some people to treat others horribly, for example, by murdering, raping, kidnapping, or exploiting them. Any legal framework of this sort is necessarily coercive, because protecting people from horrors requires the threat and, at times, the use of force against those who would otherwise stand to benefit by using their power arbitrarily over others.

To achieve its beneficial purposes, the framework must include governmental institutions of some sort, and there must be officeholders exercising power within those institutions. The institutional design of a modern republic, with its separation of legislative, executive, and judicial powers, expresses a widely shared concern to prevent some groups from dominating others. If domination were not widely counted as intolerable by the dominated, there would be no republics. The idea is that an arrangement which separates governmental powers, with each providing checks on the others, makes it harder than it would otherwise be for any single person or group to use governmental power simply as they wish, arbitrarily, without giving due consideration to the concerns of all citizens.

In a republic the rights of a citizen—to vote legislators and governmental executives in and out of office, to assemble peaceably, to petition for the redress of grievances, and to speak out freely about matters of public concern—create counterweight to governmental power as an additional protection against domination. A democratic republic modifies the basic conception of a republic most importantly by adopting an inclusive, nonarbitrary criterion of citizenship. As we have seen, however, social dislocation can render an inclusive conception of citizenship null and void.

The classical ideal of a republic, in which no one dominates others and in which rulers give each person affected by governmental action his or her due, has been transformed over the last two centuries into the modern democratic ideal of a nation dedicated to liberty and justice *for all*. The latter ideal is a core commitment in all of the citizens' organizations examined in this book. It matters in the context of a power analysis, however, mainly because it informs institutional design in modern democracies, not because it is fulfilled in practice, which is hardly the case.

Thus a power analysis of New Orleans must take into account the structure of all relevant governmental institutions, the legal framework as it currently stands, and all individuals and groups that are well-positioned to achieve their own ends or cause worrisome side effects with the help of legally sanctioned coercion. On the one hand, Jeremiah leaders were struck by how easy it is, under the current arrangements, for major corporations and their executives to turn governmental institutions to their own purposes—how easy it is, in other words, to translate economic into political power that can be exercised *over someone else*.[35] On the other hand, Jeremiah leaders believe that the powers of citizenship are currently being used with less than maximal effect to hold economic and governmental elites accountable.

These thoughts, taken together, highlight the issue of domination in post-Katrina New Orleans. Wherever economic power translates easily into political power and ordinary citizens exercise their rights haphazardly or ineffectively, the economic elite tends to be in a position to dominate. It has the capacity to exercise its considerable power arbitrarily. The dominant position of economic elites is enhanced under circumstances where a natural disaster frustrates the efforts of ordinary people to get organized and make themselves heard.

It is therefore crucial, when conducting a power analysis, to determine what institutional resources ordinary citizens already have at *their* disposal when exercising their rights to assemble, speak out, and petition. To what extent are ordinary citizens already gathered in institutions of their own making? What institutions are present in the community apart from the economic and governmental sectors?

So long as ordinary people remain unorganized, they will lack the power to prevent bosses, developers, and bankers from achieving economic dominance and translating it into political dominance. A citizens' organization aims to enhance the power of ordinary people to achieve basic social relationships that are not marred by domination. Exercising this power involves taking advantage of the institutions they have already created. Organizers need to find out what those institutions are and then begin the process of contacting the people associated with them. This is what Brod and Jackie were doing at the time of my visit.

One major obstacle that tends to impede this process is a particular kind of ignorance. The relatively disadvantaged, insofar as they are politically isolated from one another, tend to be unaware of the benefits that organized political power could bring to them. Detailed knowledge of those benefits—and of how elites turn modern economic and political systems to their own ends—can be hard to come by. It belongs mainly to the members of organized communities that are dedicated to acquiring and disseminating it. Such knowledge is itself *one of the benefits* that organizations of certain kinds confer on those participating in them. Because isolated citizens tend not to know what they are missing by virtue of being isolated, they often lack the motivation to overcome their isolated condition.

Building citizens' organizations takes a lot of time and energy, which one will be disinclined to spend unless one has a clear view of the potential advantages of aggregated strength. Even when those advantages become clear, however, they do not necessarily provide the sort of stable and strong incentive to cooperative activity that bosses provide to their managers and workers by paying them. For this reason, citizens' organizations consisting mainly of volunteers and operating without large infusions of capital from the wealthy are at an organizational disadvantage relative to corporations. They need to rely for the most part on incentives of other kinds.

The organizer is a paid employee of the citizens' organization, but other people involved in the organization, the "leaders," are not paid. The most important incentives motivating the leaders of Jeremiah in the wake of Katrina appear to be hatred of domination, anger at having been dominated, and a longing to be treated justly. The political traditions of democratic republics are replete with talk about justice and liberty. Because a just society gives everyone his or her due, the circle of moral concern must be expanded to include everyone affected by society's arrangements and policies. This means that every citizen's voice must not only be heard, but given due consideration. To be denied such consideration is an affront to liberty, as well as to justice. Liberty can be defined as security from domination. Love of liberty and hatred of domination are two sides of the same coin.

Abraham Lincoln articulated the primacy of liberty with marvelous concision in the definition of democracy I have used as the epigraph of this chapter. The relation of master to slave is a paradigm of domination because it is so lopsided that one party is *obviously* in a position to exercise power arbitrarily over another, with no recourse for the party being dominated. The master forces the slave to work for him. The slave labors under the constant threat or use of physical coercion. Everyone knows what could happen if the slave refuses to cooperate. It is easy to recognize the slave as a vulnerable party and equally easy to see that the master is in a position to exercise power arbitrarily over the slave. That power takes the form of chains, whips, and branding irons.

In a modern state that has outlawed slavery and prohibited child labor within its own borders, the coercive forces at work in a capitalist economy can, however, be much less visible. The military force used to secure access to foreign labor and markets and to dominate potential rivals is often unjust, but it is deployed outside the democratic republics themselves and therefore tends to go unnoticed in a power analysis that is local in scope. Equally important, much of the power exercised in the domestic economy is located in an impersonalized market rather than in the hands of a particular person. The function of the police is in part to preserve the conditions in which the market can function smoothly, not to compel workers to enter into specific contracts with particular employers. The worker-employer relationship appears to be one entered into freely by both parties. Within the boundaries of the wealthy democracies, at least, it is nowadays rarely forced on the worker by the employer's threat or use of violence. Indeed modern capitalism can plausibly be characterized as an economic system that has largely escaped the need for "extra-economic coercion" in providing incentives for workers in developed countries to submit themselves to the demands of employers.[36]

This does not mean that power plays no role. Nor does it mean that the power being exercised within contractual relationships between employers and workers is free from arbitrariness and injustice. The business elite derives *profits* from the workers' labor. This implies the production of a surplus of value for which the worker is not being compensated. Even if we reject the Marxist notion that any surplus value automatically renders the exchange of work for wages unjust, we can still conclude that when the surplus becomes disproportionate in the form of extremely high profits for the elite, then the contractual relationship between employer and worker rapidly degenerates into one of domination and exploitation. This is especially true under circumstances in which the elite uses its disproportionate political power to cut taxes and weaken governmental programs designed to protect ordinary citizens from the consequences of unemployment, poverty, and illness.

In a society where surplus value in the form of profits is taxed in order to benefit the entire populace, including bosses and investors, it should be possible in principle to compensate workers adequately for the imbalances implicit in the basic contractual arrangements of a profit-driven economy. In the absence of a political system that can deliver adequate compensation and protection, however, capitalist economies often create situations in which workers are compelled, by fear of homelessness, to work for wages that still leave them in misery. Executives in a company employing such workers often make millions of dollars a year, and then use a portion of their profits to influence the political system to deregulate corporations and to drastically cut the taxes paid by the wealthy. The resulting imbalance of power typically leaves executives relatively unconstrained in their treatment of actual and potential workers. Meanwhile, workers suffer under forms of constraint sufficiently extreme to eliminate all hope of mutual accountability in setting the terms of the basic economic relationship they participate in. It seems likely that the imbalance of power will tilt even more drastically in favor of corporate executives in the wake of the Supreme Court's 2010 decision, in *Citizens United v. Federal Election Commission* (No. 08-205), to overrule two precedents intended to restrict corporate spending on electoral campaigns. A bad situation now threatens to worsen.

The relationship between executives and workers can qualify as a relationship of domination, then, even when the compulsion to work is not the result of physical coercion applied or ordered by the dominant party. The relevant criterion is whether the advantaged party is in a position to exercise power arbitrarily over the disadvantaged party, outside the bounds of mutual accountability. The attempt to downsize the population of New Orleans after Katrina is a blatant example of domination in contemporary American life, but it is hardly the only one.

In a capitalist economy the worker's wages are set by the employer in response to market considerations. When workers are compelled to take work on the terms offered to them in order to keep their families alive, there is no whip being brandished; nor is the employer readily identifiable as someone personally responsible for compulsion. Because the compulsion operates through the market, the responsibility for it is diffused so broadly as to be virtually invisible. If an employer profits excessively from the relationship, the extent of the profit derived from any one worker is typically small, as a percentage of the executive's overall wealth, and difficult to estimate, let alone specify. Unjust employers typically acquire the advantages of domination by exploiting many workers in less than fully blatant ways, and then using the political system to manipulate the coercive effects of the market and the law on worker conduct.[37]

All these considerations are relevant in the case of New Orleans. What makes this case instructive, as a starting point for our examination of grassroots democracy, is that in post-Katrina New Orleans forms of domination that many people fail to notice suddenly became visible. What had seemed like strictly impersonal forces now had a human face. In other communities, similar forces are in play. To feel like a pawn being moved about by forces outside one's influence, as many ordinary people do, is to be at least vaguely aware of those forces. Relatively hidden forms of arbitrary power need to be described in suitably revealing terms, however, to be resisted self-consciously. The market and the state are not gods. They are institutions given shape and substance by the actions of human beings. The people who benefit most from them are often in a position to set the rules governing them, and in doing so they sometimes determine the fates of millions.

Power minus accountability equals domination. The remedy for arbitrarily exercised power that the Jeremiah Group proposes for New Orleans is therefore public accountability. A culture of accountability would be one in which the Haves and Have-Nots share the responsibility of shaping and reshaping the city's basic arrangements: its institutions, policies, and laws. It would be a culture in which citizens of many different kinds are able to hold one another accountable for those arrangements and disposed to recognize one another as entitled to do so. The members and organizers of Jeremiah do not suppose that a culture of mutual recognition is a gift awarded charitably by the Haves to the Have-Nots. It is rather something that the Have-Nots must win on behalf of all, and something they can win only by learning to name power and by learning how to acquire and exercise it responsibly.

The power imbalances between business enterprises and citizens' organizations—with respect to both the acquisition of knowledge and the provision of incentives for cooperative activity—help illustrate why the danger of domination by economic elites is great in our time and why the task that the Jeremiah leaders are undertaking is an uphill battle. Here we have an initial glimpse of the broader systemic issues that can make democratic organizing seem both needful and hopeless.

The people who run business enterprises and profit most heavily from them are constantly accumulating economic power and using it to acquire political power and influence. When one business enterprise fails, others immediately arise to take its place. New business elites are always in the process of emerging, fueled by the knowledge and incentives generated by the market system, and they are well positioned to affect political decisions at the local, county, state, national, and international levels, regardless of the constitutional separation of powers instituted at the founding of the American republic. The democratic expansions of citizenship that were instituted when former slaves and women won the vote have not altered this basic imbalance of power between the well heeled and the rest.

Citizens' organizations have trouble achieving even the basic levels of solidarity and knowledge required to have an impact on a local scale. With this thought in mind, I want to return for a moment to the question of what motivates people to participate in Jeremiah. Brod had twice underlined the importance of anger, and during my travels elsewhere in the Southwest IAF network I heard many other organizers do the same. Anger is one of the most important traits they look for in potential leaders. Someone who professes love of justice, but is not angered by its violation, is unlikely to stay with the struggle for justice through thick and thin, to display the passion that will motivate others to join in, or to have enough courage to stand up to the powers that be.

The ideal future leader is not someone possessed by blind rage, but rather someone capable, at least in the long run, of focusing anger on injustices and of achieving the emotional balance required to think clearly about what is actually going on, how wrongs can be righted, and how broken and distorted relationships might be repaired. It can take stern guidance from mentors to bring a potential leader's emotional life into order.[38] The ideally organized citizens' group has leaders whose motivations are both spirited and well organized. But a person who doesn't initially feel angry—say, about attempts to exclude Katrina survivors from the political process—is unlikely ever to lead others in a successful fight against an establishment that is intent on dominating.

IAF's emphasis on the importance of cultivating anger differs from the celebration of rage one sometimes finds in separatist groups organized along racial lines. While rage typically begins as a response to real injustices, and therefore can legitimately claim to have just cause, it shows little or no concern for focusing its emotional energies and actions in accord with justice. Rage is what anger becomes when justice, courage, temperance, and hope do not shape it into a perfected response to a situation that merits anger.

Mere rage tends to be unfocused, rather than discriminating in the way that justice demands. An enraged person can easily become deluded about the people, acts, or situation to which his anger responds and about the prospects for achieving redress of grievances and setting the situation straight. When rage is mixed with fear, it can slide into passive dejection and thus into despair over the prospects for achieving a just outcome. When it does not slide into dejection, it tends to vent itself in rituals of scapegoating that achieve little more than symbolic consolation for those who have been wronged and repeat the original injustices by returning them indiscriminately.

The sort of anger that IAF organizers hope to cultivate stands midway between despairing rage and liberal squeamishness about the vehement passions. A politics of just anger aims to restore the *spirit* of democracy to democratic culture, a spirit disposed to become angry at the right things in the right way and use this passion to motivate the level of political involvement essential to striving for significant social change. A politics completely emptied of the vehement passions, of spiritedness, tends in practice to be antidemocratic. It cedes the authority of decision making to elites—experts and social engineers—who characteristically present themselves as disinterested and rational agents, intent only on maximizing fairness and efficiency. The actual victims of injustice are thus assigned to passive roles, as objects of pity and as potential beneficiaries of properly rationalized decision making. Expressions of anger on the part of the underclass violate the elite code of decorum. IAF sets out to oppose that code. It searches out leaders who are capable of disrupting it.

In public life, no less than in private life, the experience of anger usually tells us that we take ourselves to have been wronged, not just by anyone, but by someone who is related to us in a way that matters to us.[39] One often responds to a stranger's flagrant insult with cool disdain or even indifference, but if our spouse, sibling, or friend slights us, our response is often vehement.[40] The vehemence can express the importance we attribute to the underlying relationship. What the slight means is that the terms of the relationship, as we understand them, have been violated. What makes the action a slight is that it can reasonably be taken as such a violation. One's thought is something like: "Am I not, in your eyes, still your lover (brother, buddy)? Are you now thinking of me as your servant (an enemy, a stranger)?"

Anger, when experienced in the context of a purportedly democratic society, goes hand in hand with the thought that a particular act or set of arrangements is not only in fact unjust, but also, implicitly or explicitly, a sign of disrespect, a slight, a diminishment or humiliation: "Are we not *citizens*? Am I not a *human being*? Do you seek to *dominate* us? Do you intend to be our *masters*?"

The experience of anger can reveal to us that we do indeed care about being treated as citizens. If we did not think of ourselves as bound together to some extent by mutual respect, then we would not be angered by the behavior and negligence of elites. To feel anger is to have the importance of the relationship and its demands drawn to our attention. Accordingly, the individual who rarely experiences anger in response to injustices that express disrespect, or who represses anger under a veneer of niceness, is ill-equipped to lead others in a struggle for equal consideration. Apart from the pseudo-virtue of niceness, the marks of a person like this are often slavishness and apathy. A central task of a leader, in IAF groups, is to help others transform themselves from slavish or apathetic victims into people who behave and feel as citizens do.

The public *expression* of anger is of paramount importance in political life, not least in an IAF accountability session. The more intimate relationships of spouses, siblings, and friends can again help us see why. If Fred repeatedly leaves the dishes for his wife, brother, or roommate to clean, there might well come a day when doing so can reasonably be taken to imply that Fred is redefining the underlying relationship as something other than one of a bond between equals. If his significant other surveys the pile of dirty dishes with this thought in mind, the result might well be not only an experience of anger but an expression of it, perhaps a quite vehement one. What expressed anger does, within the context of an important relationship, is to put the other party on notice that the terms of the relationship will have to be respected, or perhaps redrawn, if the relationship is going to continue. Expressed anger performs the same function in political communities. A community that does not have expressed anger in its symbolic repertoire is one that lacks one of the central communicative means of restoring significant relationships to equilibrium and, when necessary, redefining the roles and expectations that constitute them.

The political significance of anger takes on another dimension in communities that have been devastated by catastrophe, as New Orleans was by Katrina. When disaster strikes, the first of the passions to make an appearance are typically sorrow and grief—for lost lives, but also for the loss of a way of life as it was before disaster struck. Grief, like anger, shows us what we care about, including what relationships we care about.[41] But because it enters the picture in the wake of loss, it tends to adopt a retrospective stance, whose most natural modes of expression are symbolic and commemorative. The mourner stricken by grief at the funeral service described by Angela St. Hill is someone who cannot do what he or she would most like to do if only the world, or God, would permit it, and the process of grieving is largely a matter of coming to terms with an unwelcome impossibility. The work of mourning consists for the most part in disentangling one's life, strand by strand, from the way things were before one's loss. That disentangling is hardly a merely passive endeavor, but it is necessitated by a crucial respect in which action has been permanently limited. There is no going back to life as it was before the catastrophic loss occurred.

When grief begins to give way to anger, however, the self is able to move into another, more prospective, mode of action. The question is what form that action will take. The *merely grieving* Katrina survivor isn't yet ready to lead others in a fight of any sort. The *enraged* Katrina survivor, however, is apt to engage in acts of revenge against those thought to be responsible for the broken levees, the mismanaged relief efforts, and the attempt to exclude evacuees from a fitting role in determining the city's future. There are many possible scapegoats to choose from, if that's the way one wants to go, and many of them have already been slain, at least symbolically, in post-Katrina New Orleans. But what lasting satisfaction is the formerly grief-stricken, increasingly enraged heart likely to find in rites of sacrifice or exclusion?

The anger that marks the leaders of the Jeremiah group offers a different sort of therapy for grief. It overcomes mourning not with a spirit of vengeance, but with a courageous determination to reconstitute the basic social relationships of New Orleans on even terms. Vehemently, sternly, and without cowering before the city's establishment, Jeremiah's leaders declare unacceptable an order in which some people are dominant and others are dominated.[42] If there is going to be a new New Orleans, it will be on terms that all who should be counted as citizens have a role in setting. The *spirit* of Jeremiah, as a group prone to oppose domination angrily, implies something about the group's *ends*. Put in positive terms, this is a group striving for a city marked by mutual recognition and democratic accountability. It takes offense at violations of the common good it strives to achieve. And its *means* —including one-on-one conversations, house meetings, neighborhood walks, accountability sessions, and get-out-the-vote bands—for the most part enact the very sort of relationships that define the common good for which Jeremiah strives. To act as Jeremiah acts is already to instantiate that good to some large extent. Means, ends, relationships, and spirit are in this case largely of one piece.

✻ CHAPTER SIX ✻

Public Address

VOTING IS ONLY ONE WAY of holding elites accountable. It gives citizens a nonviolent means for deposing despots, and is therefore to be prized as one of the powers essential to democratic action. But when used in isolation from the exercise of other political rights, voting often provides too little accountability, too late. The electoral process, when not invigorated by a culture of accountability, often becomes a vehicle for domination, rather than a corrective for it.

The right to assemble peaceably, the right to petition for the redress of grievances, and the right to speak freely are as essential to modern democracies as the right to vote. Even where all of these rights are constitutionally guaranteed, however, if they are not exercised courageously, skillfully, prudently, and justly by enough people enough of the time, democracy gives way to domination. Assembling, petitioning, speaking out, and voting are all crucial components of democratic culture. Of these activities, assembling is the least well understood by the public as a whole. It is by assembling as groups capable of concerted action that citizens are able to generate the power required to prevent elites from dominating.

In the previous two chapters, we have begun to see how organizations like Jeremiah go about assembling, and we have learned something about the importance of face-to-face communication. Let us now look at the process from the perspective of the dislocated evacuees. What did it take for them to get organized and address their concerns to the officials exercising power over them? It took a *call to assembly*, a particularly important sort of speech act.

But the call was itself dependent on prior acts of organizing. And what the call led to was more assembling, more organizing, as well as many other acts involving the full range of political freedoms.

When thousands of Katrina survivors arrived in Houston shortly after the storm, they were taken to the Reliant Complex and placed in three shelters: the Astrodome, the Reliant Arena, and Reliant Stadium. Mayor Bill White immediately began putting together a team of people who could help him deal with the situation. One of the people he called on was Renee Wizig-Barrios, the senior organizer of the Metropolitan Organization (TMO), Jeremiah's sister organization in Houston. Renee, a Jew and a member of Congregation Beth Israel in Houston, served as a Peace Corps volunteer in Nicaragua before becoming an organizer. Her first organizing jobs were in Austin and El Paso. Brod Bagert was working under her supervision in Houston at the time the Katrina survivors arrived.

"I met with our leadership," Renee told me, "and asked them what roles they thought we should play in this situation. We decided we had to play the role that we always play, which was to organize. In the first meeting with the mayor's team, he basically gave us carte blanche to go into the shelters and do whatever we wanted to do."

When Renee and Brod went into the Astrodome for the first time, the scene was surreal. Oprah Winfrey, the talk show host, and Bishop T. D. Jakes, the leading African-American televangelist, were taking turns consoling the vast crowd. The situation was a circus, as far as Renee was concerned, and she grew impatient while the two celebrities dominated the public address system. Jakes's message was in keeping with the gospel of abundance that has attracted thirty thousand members to his megachurch in Dallas: the good news is that God rewards the faithful, not only spiritually in the afterlife but also materially in this life. Given that the survivors had just been stripped of whatever material abundance they once had, Renee found his message "very patronizing." The disaster that had befallen the Gulf Coast, Jakes implied, was a providential judgment on the faithless, as well as a test of faith for the faithful. "Just trust in God," Renee remembers him telling the survivors. "Everything is going to be fine."

Renee had already gathered a few pastors, who understood what needed to be done. She urged one of them to get his hands on the public address microphone. When he managed to do so, Renee recalled, his message to the crowd took issue with Jakes's theology: "I'm a believer, but I believe God expects us to do our part of the work too. So if you've been a leader in New Orleans, and you were a leader in your church or your school or your neighborhood organization, whether you were a teacher or a deacon, we're asking those of you who were leaders in New Orleans to come forward and have a conversation with the Metropolitan Organization about what's happening, and about doing something."

As yet, there was no room to meet in, but slowly a group of about a hundred leaders assembled on a set of bleachers. "The pastors prayed," Renee said, "and then we did house meetings." These were house meetings for the homeless. Many of the people assembling had been Jeremiah leaders in New Orleans. "We began to hear people's stories of what they had gone through to get there. And they were horrific. Once people began to be able to process that pain, we asked them: What did they want to see different? What needed to happen?"

Many of the survivors had had their cell phone service cut off, because there was no way under these circumstances to keep up with their payments. Without their phones, they were cut off from families and friends. "Families were separated, children were missing, grandchildren were missing, and the elderly were mixed in with everybody else." The children had no place to play. The house meetings portrayed the situation in the Astrodome as mass chaos. "We made a deal with the leaders, which was that we would go back and represent those interests to the mayor and the county judge if they would begin organizing and starting a petition drive and begin to find other people that they knew. Then we'd come back and meet with them. And they accepted that offer. We went back to the mayor and the county judge, and said: 'You know, people don't even have a way to communicate.'" Renee negotiated an agreement to authorize an automatic extension of cell phone service for evacuees and the provision of playground equipment for children in the Astrodome.

The Red Cross had set up a relief program in the Astrodome, but its work was hampered by a failure to find a computer system that could be used to register evacuees. Renee talked the mayor into outsourcing the operation, which meant that the process could go forward much more quickly. When the Red Cross decided to distribute debit cards with two-thousand-dollar accounts to evacuees, another parody of bureaucratic inefficiency unfolded. "So it's about one hundred and two degrees," Renee said, "and there are about twelve thousand people in line in the scorching sun waiting to get these cards, and you've got elderly people and children, and people are sweating. Several people have already fainted. They've all been asking the police why they can't go inside. Because here's this air conditioned facility, taxpayer supported, and the police are all in the air conditioning, and outside is the line of ten thousand people, and we're supposed to have our meeting in there.

"We got the line inside, which to the leaders was a really important victory, because they had felt that they had constantly been treated as though they were not citizens, as though they were not human. That set the stage for the rest of the aid distribution, which was done differently." As the organizing efforts continued, TMO was able to involve evacuees in decisions being made about plans for housing them in Houston.

The Red Cross is a nongovernmental institution intended to deliver relief assistance in emergency situations. The mayor was in charge of a set of governmental institutions intended to serve the well-being of the Houston community. None of these institutions can do their work without a bureaucratic administrative structure of considerable size. Bureaucracies have value to us, not least of all because they are structured to operate according to publicly transparent, fairly applied rules. Decision making within a bureaucracy is supposed to provide an alternative to nepotism and other forms of favoritism that would otherwise govern the distribution of essential goods and services to people in need. But it also tends to be slow and inefficient. Bureaucratic procedures tend to become disconnected from the values they are meant to serve. When Katrina survivors complained that they had not been treated as human beings, let alone as citizens, they were voicing a concern distinct from the worries about domination examined in the previous chapters. Here the immediate concern had to do with the tendency of bureaucrats to lose sight of the people their institutions are meant to serve.

Democratic activity in the contemporary world necessarily seeks to influence and contest decisions made by the bosses of corporate enterprises, on the one hand, and by the officials of nongovernmental and governmental agencies, on the other. It is significant that all three of these types of institutions not only wield massive power of a sort that tends, when left unchecked, to insulate itself from accountability, but also that their internal structure is often bureaucratic and hierarchical. In dealing with corporate bosses, citizens' organizations like Jeremiah and TMO need to find ways to constrain the translation of economic power into political power. This means organizing ordinary citizens to exert their power within the political sphere to pass laws that protect basic political relationships from domination. Because the administration of such laws requires governmental bureaucratic structures as well as threats of punishment, the alternative to being dominated by the economically advantaged is inherently risky.

It takes power to limit power, and the power structures required to keep economic power from becoming both arbitrary and pervasive include legal and bureaucratic modes of organization. Similarly, it takes power for a nongovernmental agency like the Red Cross to deliver goods and services to thousands of people in desperate need. If the principle of distribution is to be nonarbitrary, the organizational mode will have to be bureaucratic and is thus bound to have the drawbacks, as well as the benefits, of the bureaucratic mode. In all of these cases, power tends toward arbitrariness unless citizens organize themselves in a way that permits them to generate power of their own—enough power to influence and contest decisions of great importance being made at the upper levels of corporate, nongovernmental, and governmental bureaucracies. That the internal structure of a citizens' organization like TMO is itself hierarchical to some degree is something we will need to examine in later chapters. But it is crucial for a citizens' group to avoid congealing into an entrenched bureaucratic structure of its own. Its practices are designed to inject accountability into its own operations, while also holding accountable institutions like the development companies in New Orleans, the Red Cross, and the municipal government of Houston.

In the Astrodome it was a nongovernmental agency that behaved with maximal inefficiency and minimal regard for the particular individuals being served. It was the head of the local governmental bureaucracy, the mayor, who had the wisdom to permit TMO organizers to help evacuees have a voice in decisions being made on their behalf. This key decision was itself the product of years of relationship-building on the part of TMO before the storm. It is chilling to imagine what the Astrodome would have been like had the trust created by years of prior work not been in place.

The decision to require cell phone companies to extend service to their customers in the disaster zone is a clear instance of reasonable governmental constraint on corporate behavior with an eye toward the common good. The constraint was necessary to protect the social fabric itself. By using governmental power to open the basic means of communication for people whose families and friends had been dispersed, the Federal Communications Commission made a crucial contribution to civil society. But this decision also depended on the mayor's prior decision to include both federal officials and a TMO organizer on his crisis management team.

It is a commonplace in social criticism that modernity is typically experienced by ordinary people as a war between two great forces: the market and the state. We become resigned to being pawns moved about by economic forces and bureaucracies over which we have no control. The market and the state are the secular gods we fear and serve. We quarrel over which of them can save us from the other, and propitiate each in turn, but view ourselves for the most part as essentially powerless. The Katrina survivors in the Astrodome came close to having an extreme version of this experience. Another force, nature, had destroyed their homes and forced them into exile. Many of them had been through hell in the Superdome. Now they were in another stadium in another state. Cell phone contracts and structures of political representation alike had lapsed. For a moment, market and state appeared to be jointly omnipotent, while nongovernmental agencies seemed utterly incapable of providing a humane alternative to the powers that be.

But this mythic picture does not capture the whole truth of what happened in the Astrodome, let alone the whole truth of our society. The morals of the Astrodome experience are rather different: no governmental bureaucracy, no capacity to constrain corporate power from dominating. No autonomous citizens' organization, no effective power for citizens. No effective power for citizens, no accountability for corporate, governmental, or nongovernmental power. No accountability, no way for power to be anything but arbitrary in its exercise and dehumanizing in its effects. It is not generally the case that nongovernmental agencies behave more efficiently or more humanely than governmental agencies do. Neither is it the case that unconstrained markets necessarily serve the interests of the ordinary people affected by them. Corporations, governments, and nongovernmental agencies will not soon pass from the scene. Massive power will continue to appear in these guises. Yet our politics should not be about which of them is our true god. Our struggle, like that of the Katrina survivors, is to hold all of the relevant elites accountable insofar as we can.

By the time Hurricane Rita hit Texas and Louisiana on September 24, about eight hundred evacuees remained in the shelter in the Reliant Arena. The mayor, in consultation with federal agencies, decided that those evacuees would be sent to Arkansas. Again, the evacuees insisted on being heard. "People were just disgusted with this decision," Renee said. "They didn't want to go to Arkansas." TMO brought a group of evacuee leaders to meet with the political officials, arguing that with five hundred apartments still available in Houston, it was unnecessary to send people to Arkansas. Renee recalled that the assistant fire chief running the operation was enraged when survivor leaders refused to cooperate with the order for deportation to Arkansas. "He was very, very angry, and said, 'People are going to Arkansas. We have policemen here with guns, and people are going whether they want to or not.'" Luckily, the mayor agreed to intervene on the survivors' behalf, and citizens were not moved against their will. Renee was a bit embarrassed, though, by a statement attributed to her the next day in the *New York Times*. I asked her what she had said. "It was, you know, that these people are American citizens, and they shouldn't have to go to Arkansas."

Why were survivors of Katrina able to win victories in the Astrodome? Renee underlined two factors already touched on. The first was how much it helped, in the context of a disaster, to be able to identify evacuees who had already acquired leadership experience and training before the disaster struck. A group of a hundred was able to create an agenda that authentically represented the concerns of survivors in Houston and to mobilize roughly six thousand people to sign a petition in support of that agenda. They knew how to earn the right to represent others and how to use the power that this status gave them to influence and contest decisions that were being made about their fate. The second factor was that TMO was able to rely on established relationships of mutual respect with the mayor and the county judge. Without the trust that TMO had earned over time, Houston officials would have had trouble recognizing the displaced New Orleans leaders as legitimate spokespersons for the survivors.

"I have never had so much fun in my life," Renee said. "It was enormously exciting and exhilarating. It was also the most anxiety-increasing period as well, because we really did have enormous power and there were enormous things at stake. But we were able to accomplish something because we knew an enormous amount of people to begin with."

It is instructive to note that the right of the evacuees to vote became the focal point for organizers only after what might be called the Astrodome phase of the crisis. The transformation of the evacuees from victims into agents, their reconstitution as citizens, relied in the first instance on their exercise of the rights to free speech and to peaceable assembly. Some skeletal structure of representative authority among the evacuees was necessary if they were to have a voice. Potential leaders had to assemble. For that to happen, they needed to receive a message, a call, through a public medium of communication, which in this case amounted to nothing more than an amplified microphone. Once they had gathered, they could begin the process of face-to-face interaction in which they could earn the license to speak *for* those to whom they had listened, to *represent* them when petitioning officials for a redress of grievances. Had none of this transpired, there would have been no effective way for evacuees to influence or contest what the public officials were deciding. In short, there would have been no accountability.

If we take a step back from this crisis situation, what we see is a motley collection of displaced citizens reconstructing the rudiments of a democratic culture on the fly. This case makes clear how freedoms guaranteed by First Amendment clear space for democratic culture. It was by exercising the right to speak, to assemble, and to petition for the redress of grievances that the evacuees were able to create a public of accountability. And it was by treating the Astrodome's public address system as a *public* address system, as something they had a right to use, in the manner of a free press, that they were able to initiate the process.

Renee's story about organizing in the Astrodome calls to mind a story that other organizers told me about their work elsewhere in the Southwest IAF network. Jorge Montiel described Arizona, where he works, as an example of extreme inequality, but also as one of several states in which immigration policies are a major source of strife. In 2004 Arizona passed Proposition 200, which requires individuals to prove their citizenship before they can register to vote or receive state benefits. "There wasn't any organized opposition to this proposition," Jorge said, until IAF groups in Arizona began to focus on the issue. At one point, forty-five bills directed against undocumented immigrants had been filed in the legislature.

"The right-wingers were in control of the legislature," said Jorge's colleague Joe Rubio, "and they basically had everybody running scared. Without any opposition, this is the way it would work. They'd bring forth five or six bills at a time, and they would allow Russell Pearce, the leader of the anti-immigration effort, to get up and talk ad nauseam on each of these bills." Opponents of the bills weren't being recognized. "This happened repeatedly over the course of two weeks. So we decided we were gonna go back into this hearing. Representative Chuck Gray was the chair, and he was one of the right-wingers running this."

Forty-five minutes before the hearing, a hundred leaders from the Arizona Interfaith Network—a mixture of young and old, Anglo and Latino—occupied all of the seats in the hearing room. Joe recalls a rumbling outside the room, as lobbyists gathered in the doorway, wondering where they would get to sit. The Speaker of the House came in and surveyed the scene. The meeting started fifteen minutes late, and the published agenda had been abandoned. Bills pertaining to the treatment of immigrants were not going to be discussed. The new topic of the session was going to be automobiles.

"They do this for half an hour," Joe said, "and they even let some of the high-priced lobbyists, who hadn't signed in, come up to speak. Finally, Tom Donovan, one of our team leaders, who has been in the organization forever, a big Teddy bear of a guy, gets up to speak, goes up to podium, and says 'I signed up to speak on a bill and I'd like to be recognized.' Chuck Gray says, 'Mr. Donovan you're out of order. Please sit down.'" While telling this part of the story, Joe pounded on the table, imitating the sound of the gavel, while the other organizers who were with us, listening to the story, laughed hard.

"Now all our leaders stand up, all hundred of them. Another one of our leaders standing right up behind Tom, he's about six feet three, puts his arm up like this. This is the signal, and then all our leaders in unison say, 'Let our people speak! Let our people speak! Let our people speak!' Everyone stayed up, standing, while Gray kept saying, 'You are out of order, people. This is a mob scene. I'll get the . . .' 'Let our people speak! Let our people speak!'"

"Then Tom says, 'I have a letter to read to you and to deliver to the Speaker.' And the leaders say, 'Let the people speak! Let the people speak!' Gray says, 'I'm going to have you people thrown out.

Bring in security!' All of a sudden you see these big potbellied guards. They're coming up each side of the aisle. And so Tom says that we're going into the hall to hold a press conference.

"The immediate reaction to this action is very negative: how rude these people were, they broke the rules, this is not the way citizens should behave in the legislature. But slowly, as some more informed TV reporters and others began to look into this, as we began to talk to them, they began to understand that not only did this happen to us on immigration issues, it had happened in the state chamber on budget issues, AARP, a lot of other groups. They would have been treated the same way. We broke it open. Finally, the newspaper comes out a week later with the headline, saying the legislature should stop muzzling the public, they're behaving like tyrants."

That headline, Joe claims, was a turning point in Arizona politics. With the press now focusing a spotlight on the conduct of legislative hearings, the atmosphere changed. The anti-immigrant bills were still under consideration, however, and Arizona Interfaith decided to assemble a group of religious officials in the capital to assess the situation. When Arizona Interfaith leaders described the forty-five bills, the religious officials were taken aback. "They were aghast," Joe said. "They had no idea it was this bad. 'What can we do?' they said. 'We need to talk to the governor. We've got to get her behind this to veto.'" Arizona Interfaith arranged a meeting attended by the governor, Christian, Jewish, and Muslim leaders, and executives of companies relying on immigrant labor. "The governor comes in the room in a bright yellow suit," Joe said. The religious leaders explained the importance of vetoing any of the bills that managed to be approved by the legislature. The governor's reply was simple: "Make me do it!"

"We put together an interfaith prayer service on the capitol grounds a couple weeks after that," Joe said. "This is about the time the immigrant marches are appearing. You know, you have all these brown faces, marching, hundreds of thousands of them. Our group looked different. It was a thousand folks, mostly Anglo, folks from across the state, bishops and leaders. We were basically saying, 'Let's deal with the real business of the people, and [get] real solutions to real problems. Let's work together.' A lot of the legislators came out to see it. It was the right-wingers who stayed. When they saw those religious leaders on the stage, they didn't leave. Particularly one state senator from Paradise Valley, Barry Goldwater's turf. She had a bill to make it a first-offense felony [for undocumented immigrants] to be in the state. She saw her rabbi on the stage, got up close to him, and when he was done, she basically was on him for half an hour, explaining that she wasn't a bad person, but that her relatives came legally, and everybody else needed to. The next day she amended her bill. Now it said: first offense, misdemeanor. All these bad bills got rolled up into one. The governor vetoed it, found a very clever way to do it. Our action gave her the political courage to take those steps."

Joe remarked that the religious officials had played a crucial role, not only by appearing at the public event, but also by issuing statements that gave room for others to organize within congregations. The level of involvement "depended on the level of courage in the particular individual," but all of them had managed to come forward in some way. Here we see another First Amendment freedom coming into play. Could it be that freedom of religion has a political function that its defenders and critics have not yet fully fathomed? I will address this question and related issues in later chapters. For now, I want to reflect for a moment on free speech and a free press.

The right-wing legislators who were trying to push through the forty-five bills pertaining to undocumented immigrants hoped to get their way by controlling the agenda and access to the microphone in the hearing chamber. A reader might ask whether this is any different from the control that IAF groups exercise over accountability sessions. The difference, it seems to me, has to do with the purposes being served. It is legitimate for legislators, no less than for citizens' organizations, to run their public meetings in accordance with agendas and rules of order that are in keeping with democratic ideals. The goals of accountability sessions are to enhance the ability of ordinary citizens to present proposals, to offer reasons for those proposals, to elicit commitments from candidates and officials, and thus to set the stage for future attempts to hold candidates and officials accountable. A citizens' organization aims to enhance the ability of citizens to influence and contest the decisions of elites, a central democratic value. It is therefore appropriate for a citizens' group to set an agenda and adopt rules of order for its own meetings with this value in mind.

The right-wing legislators, in contrast, used a similar form of control over a legislative hearing to inhibit public expression of opposition to their proposals. The agenda and rules of order were used in order to diminish the opportunity of Arizona citizens to influence and contest the legislature's decisions. In this respect, the legislators were behaving with antidemocratic intent, as they seemed to have done on other similar occasions in the preceding months. Under these circumstances, what it took for democracy to be defended was a refusal, on the part of Arizona Interfaith leaders, to be shut out of the public discussion. This meant rejecting the authority of an unjust attempt to exclude their speech from the hearing. When the presiding officer declared them out of order, they persisted, even in the face of threatened punishment.

In reporting and commenting on the episode, the press played a crucial role by interpreting what the legislators were doing as antidemocratic. Reporters had a democratic responsibility, as well as a right, to act independently of state officials. The function of the press in a democratic republic is in part to inform citizens of all abuses of power that diminish the opportunities citizens have to influence and contest governmental decisions. In this case, the responsibility went beyond merely reporting the spin that the legislators and the Arizona Interfaith leaders sought to put on the event when discussing it with reporters. The press needed to make some judgment about what the threats to democratic values actually were. To avoid committing itself to such judgments, case by case, would leave the press unable to distinguish political news fit to print from events that are lacking in political interest. Among the stories that are printed, distinctions must be made between those that are highly important and those that are not. A press hiding behind a claim of evenhandedness cannot perform the role that justifies its constitutionally protected freedom. A press that pretended to be neutral on the difference between domination and accountability would be a press that had already sided implicitly with domination.

✻ CHAPTER SEVEN ✻

Ain't It Awful?

IN 1976 SISTER CHRISTINE STEPHENS was part of a planning group that lured Ernie Cortés to Houston, to get grassroots organizing going in Texas. Two years later she joined him as a fulltime IAF organizer. She has served as the lead organizer in Houston, Dallas, San Antonio, and the Rio Grande Valley. Some of the Texas initiatives, she says, have been in place longer than any others currently affiliated with IAF. Christine now supervises IAF projects throughout Texas and in Louisiana and Mississippi. She is one of the four officers who alternate as director of the IAF at the national and international level.

She speaks of Ernie with admiration. "At the time when we were fighting for our lives here in Houston [back in the 1970s], Ernie was saying to me, 'Someday we're gonna have these projects and we're gonna be across the Southwest.' I would say, 'My God, Ernie, we're *dying* and you are telling me how we're building.' Ernie's style would be to find us, find the organizers, and put us together, and then he moved on and started another project. He just kept expanding the network to what it is now." Ernie's way of going about his business remains a work in progress. "It was something we invented as we went along." Christine utters that "we" with pride. She feels she "was present at the creation." Most of her adult life has been poured into this work.

One afternoon in Houston, Christine, Ernie, and three of their associates, Sister Pearl Ceasar, Sister Consuelo Tovar, and Elizabeth Valdez, told me about the fights in the Rio Grande Valley of South Texas in the 1980s that led to the transformation of the disease-riddled shantytowns just north of the U.S.–Mexico border

Map 7.1 Rio Grande Valley

into communities with access to safe water, sewer systems, and paved roads. "Those of us who worked out there," Christine said haltingly, "this is not our story." She paused, steadying her emotions. "But it is partly our story because we worked with them on the politics."

The Valley is one hundred miles by fifty miles and includes the cities of Brownsville, Harlingen, Mercedes, Weslaco, Edinburg, and McAllen, as well as Willacy County. The shantytowns where the poorest of the poor lived at the time Ernie began organizing in the area are known as *colonias.* Most colonia residents are farmworkers or their families. The attraction of living there was an opportunity to own a bit of land, but most homes barely qualified as buildings. As Christine put it, they consisted of "whatever could be put together." Grove owners would sell off land they couldn't use, much of it on floodplains, but without giving a thought to the provision of water, sewer services, or drainage, apart from the occasional ditch.

A 1995 study by the Texas Water Development Board put the number of colonias at nearly 1,500, with a total population of more than 300,000. The latter figure might be low, given the difficulties of taking an accurate census among impoverished immigrants, especially along the border. The largest of the colonias was Cameron Park. A 1994 survey by the Texas Department of Housing found that nearly 90 percent of the families contacted in Cameron Park had annual incomes below ten thousand dollars, with about 60 percent bringing in half that much or less. About 65 percent of colonia residents were U.S. citizens at that time. Like the other colonias, Cameron Park was an unincorporated subdivision, lying outside of existing municipalities in a kind of legal limbo. It was located just beyond the city limits of Brownsville, and comprised approximately five hundred lots. Brownsville had not extended the city limits to include Cameron Park because doing so would have significantly increased the city's obligations to provide services.

Migrant workers would purchase a small lot under an arrangement known as *contract for deed*, which leaves ownership of a property in the hands of the seller until payment is complete. Consuelo estimated the average deal as one hundred dollars down, ten dollars a month. It was difficult to keep up on payments because of their seasonal employment in the north. As a result, Christine said, colonia residents rarely built up any equity. They would hold a contract for a while, struggle with payments, and then lose their investment. They would clear the land one year and come back the next to lay a slab. Gradually, a makeshift house would appear, only to be sold again to someone else. What the migrant workers sought to do was own their own land, but actual ownership mainly eluded their grasp.

The combination of unpaved roads and the floodplain location meant that most colonias became ponds of mud after rainstorms. "Consequently," Consuelo said, "if children would walk to school they would be full of mud and would be embarrassed. They would not want to go to school because of the mud. Buses would not be able to get into the colonias to pick them up." Worse, the absence of effective sewerage meant that the flooding would bring fecal matter to the surface and distribute it everywhere. The resulting health conditions were "horrific." Incidence rates for hepatitis, salmonellosis, and tuberculosis in the colonias far exceeded rates elsewhere in Texas. Christine recalled a case of leprosy. It was, she said, "a Third World" situation. "If you had a septic tank you were doing pretty good," said Elizabeth Valdez. Outhouses were especially vulnerable to flooding. Given the high water table, even after light rains children would end up playing in water "that was not water." When the ground eventually dried out, the smell of fecal matter remained. "Everyone knew in the public schools who the colonia kids were because they were dirty and they smelled," Christine said.

Things were somewhat different in El Paso, where Pearl had been organizing. Rainfall was minimal, on average about seven inches per year. Colonia residents, knowing that the water table was high, would dig wells, but the water they tapped into was dangerously high in salt content. Hence, in addition to "Third World diseases like hepatitis C, they'd also have skin rashes." When water trucks came to the colonias, residents would purchase water and store it in oil barrels, which led to other health problems. The city initially refused to extend its water lines into the colonias. "As we developed the issue there," Pearl said, "there was a whole mentality that these are poor people who are not capable of living with dignity."

Ernie reported that a "fairly liberal" state senator had told him that the colonia residents should just be deported. Ernie's response, as he remembers it, was that deportation would be difficult, given that most of the colonia residents are U.S. citizens and hold a deed for the land they are living on. However, Lieutenant Governor Bill Hobby agreed to tour the schools of the Rio Grande Valley. Hobby had a major project of his own, for which he was soliciting political support in the Valley. Valley Interfaith was looking for a deal. Hobby and his allies would have to give something to get something.

When Hobby and other state officials arrived, a bus picked them up at the airport and took them to Cameron Park colonia. "It was probably the first time any state official had seen something like that," Christine said. "Consuela and the priest had organized every resident. They were just out there in force, and a priest was standing there with a bullhorn." According to Christine, one state official, being uncertain about the mood of the assembled colonia residents, was reluctant to get off the bus. "Finally one of the men said, 'Get off there, and tell them why they don't have water.' They got off the bus, but they were scared, so we did some presentations for them." One of the presenters asked the state to map all of the colonias and get a clear picture of what the basic needs were for water, sewer systems, health care, and education in the entire area. The next step would be to negotiate plans for meeting those needs.

"Slowly," Christine said, "we began to talk about bonds that could be floated but that would get repaid over thirty to fifty years. And together we [eventually] fashioned a very complicated piece of legislation that had the Texas Water Development Board issue these bonds." Because the legislation required passage of amendments to the state constitution, Valley Interfaith needed to rely on IAF organizations throughout the state to muster support for the various initiatives. Christine credited preachers in Austin, Dallas, Houston, and Fort Worth, among others, for their help in these fights. "Preachers went to their pulpits and said, 'Everyone deserves water. Everyone deserves a decent place to live.'"

Pearl described a visit to the Valley by Republican U.S. senator Kay Bailey Hutchison: "As God would have it, the day she came it rained. I mean it was just cats and dogs, so the colonia streets were muddy and slippery. We had her in a van. And she gets ready to get out of her van for her photo op walking through the streets. She says to her aide, 'Can you please get me my other shoes?' She changes her shoes, so she can walk through the mud. Elida Bocanegra, a Valley Interfaith leader, was with her. The senator hugged Mrs. Bocanegra, they had their photo op, and they come back and get in the van. Kay Bailey changes her shoes again. Mrs. Bocanegra says, 'Senator Hutchison, you're very fortunate. You can come in, and take a picture and change shoes when you leave. We have to live like this every day.'"

Kay Bailey Hutchison and Bill Bradley were the two U.S. senators to play central roles in securing massive federal support for the transformation of the colonias. Press coverage of conditions in the colonias helped Valley Interfaith increase the pressure, Christine said, because it "shamed all the people in Texas in the legislature." A story in the *Washington Post* had been embarrassing to Texas politicians in Washington—not least of all, according to Christine, House Speaker Jim Wright. A similar story in the *New York Times* had sent ripples of shame through the business community.

"One of the major bankers, Hal Dougherty, was at a bankers' meeting that weekend," Pearl said, "and when he came back to El Paso he was furious because he described the scene at this bankers meeting. He says, 'I walked into this meeting on a Sunday morning and here are all these easterners reading their bible, the *New York Times*, and they said to me, Hal, how can you let people live like this?' And he says, 'Do you know how embarrassing that is? Do you know what kinda slap that is in our face?' And he goes on and on and on. Long story short, they extended water after that, because the business leaders didn't want that kind of publicity for El Paso. They didn't want people thinking they were that heartless. It was a case of people doing the right thing for the wrong reasons."

When producers for one of the network morning television shows came to the Valley, they wanted to film colonia residents. Pearl recommended a handful of families for one of the producers to contact, but the producer wasn't happy with the recommendation. "That's not the kind of family I want to interview," the producer said. Pearl asked why not. "She said, 'Well, they have hope.' Could I make up this story? 'They have hope.'" Pearl explained that these families included prominent leaders in Valley Interfaith. "They do have hope. They have a strategy. They know how they want this to be done." The producer said, "No, you don't understand. I want dirt. I want to see them dirty."

Pearl told her that if she wanted dirt, she'd have to find somebody else to talk to: "If you want strategy and power and people who have organized to do something about their situation, then we're willing to talk to you. There are two stories here. One is: Ain't it awful? See them grovel, or see how dirty they are! And the other story is: see what people can do when they organize! Now, that's our story. If you want the other story, go to someone else." The producer decided to pursue her story elsewhere. She contacted the county health department, who then took her to a house in a colonia at eight in the morning. The plan was to film a woman, still in her housecoat, washing clothes in her backyard.

"I just want to emphasize," Christine said, "that people like Carmen Anaya and Alida Bocanegra were leaders in the colonias, but also leaders in their congregations. *They* did the organizing." Christine, Elizabeth, and Pearl had to cover a vast region. The professional mentors had to concentrate on finding leaders to organize their own communities. The leaders of the colonia fights were not posing for a Walker Evans portrait. It was their right, as they saw it, to hold political officials and corporate executives accountable. It was their responsibility to do so. And it was in their power to do so. To my mind, the fight over the colonias represents one of the most impressive victories for grassroots democracy in the United States since passage of the Civil Rights Act of 1964.

The *Washington Post* and *New York Times* reports that caused embarrassment to Texas businessmen and political officials were straightforward depictions of misery in the colonias. They were meant to raise the question, "Ain't it awful?" in the mind of the average reader. That is why they were capable of shaming people who had ignored or tolerated the dreadful conditions being portrayed.

Such depictions have a place in media coverage of political issues, just as they do in social criticism more generally. There are times when human misery must be shown or described if shame is going to be triggered in the hearts of those who bear responsibility for injustice and if sympathy is to be evoked in the hearts of people of good will.

On the other hand, as Sister Pearl pointed out, depictions of this kind also render invisible the political agency, indeed the dignity, of the very people whose suffering is being portrayed. The nearly complete failure of social critics, as well as the mass media, to depict the democratic *practices* that have occasionally produced victories like the transformation of the colonias is a major source of desperation in our politics. One senses that something has gone terribly wrong. Pictures of the suffering poor confirm our fears and call forth our sympathy. And in that moment, we are imagining ourselves as either the saviors of these people or, more likely, as unable to do anything meaningful to alleviate their condition. Either way, we are taking the wretched of the earth to be the essentially passive recipients of our sympathy or beneficence. We do them an injustice even in our way of bemoaning their plight.

✻ CHAPTER EIGHT ✻

The Authority to Lead

There were those . . .
who led the people by their counsels . . .
and their inheritance [remains] with their children's children.
—*Sirach 44:3–4*

The understanding of what constitutes a genuine
native, indigenous leader is rarely found among
conventional social do-gooders.
—*Saul Alinsky*

DEMOCRATIC CONSTITUTIONS place power in the people's hands. That power might rein in powerful elites if enough citizens made good use of it. But few citizens make much use of it at all, and many of those who do use it stumble so badly that they give up. Their potential power is never actualized.

What kind of practice is it, then, to cultivate one's power as a democratic citizen and use it well? It is a *political* practice because it attends to shared human arrangements in light of concerns and judgments that are not always in harmony. It is a *social* practice because the ends it pursues and the means it employs involve building up human relationships of certain kinds. It is an *egalitarian* practice in the sense that it is open to anybody who wishes to master it and in the sense that it aspires to create a society in which no one is in a position to dominate others.

A practice can be egalitarian in this sense without eradicating all forms of authority and hierarchy. In a culture of democratic accountability some people hold high office and exercise the powers thus accorded to them, and some people serve as mentors or leaders to others without holding office. Elites will always be with us. They rise and fall, but are unlikely to disappear. The question is how to tame and civilize them, not how to eliminate them. Grassroots democratic organizations need leaders and work hard at identifying and cultivating them. The internal structure of such organizations is not anarchic. As a social formation democracy has more to do with structures of *earned and accountable authority* than it does with leveling.

Democratic action aims to create a society in which even bosses, generals, and presidents are held accountable to the rest. Holders of high office will always have power at their disposal, but in a healthy democracy that power can be held in check. What holds it in check is itself a kind of power. Ordinary citizens, by relating wisely to one another and to elites, are able to influence and contest decisions made on high. No society can free itself of domination unless citizens make good use of the power at *their* disposal. And citizens are likely to do that only if some of them acquire the moral authority to lead, represent, and advise their associates and only if those associates are prepared to acknowledge whatever moral and intellectual authority their leaders, representatives, and advisors have earned.

In this chapter I will examine what the resulting relationships are like, how they are built up, and what their effects are. The memory of one leader in particular personifies democratic authority as it is now understood throughout much of the Rio Grande Valley, but we would hardly do justice to the topic—or to her—if we merely called her *charismatic*, a term that more often mystifies than instructs. To have charisma in the original biblical sense is to possess a divine gift and exhibit its spiritual fruits in one's conduct. Modern sociological theories of charismatic authority apply the concept to persons capable of winning followers purely on the basis of their own gifts, but how authority of this kind is bestowed and exercised remains mysterious.[43]

I have no doubt that the strongest leaders of grassroots democratic groups are gifted in ways that contribute to their authority, but their gifts can be described. So too can the discipline of cultivating those gifts and matching the people who have them with the responsibilities of leadership. I want to take seriously the thought that the authority of a grassroots leader needs to be earned, that the sort of authority that such leaders ideally, or even typically, possess is not merely a matter of natural talents. And I want to warn against the temptation to wait passively for a great charismatic leader, like Sojourner Truth or Martin Luther King Jr., to follow.[44]

"Carmen Anaya never learned English," Christine remarked. "But she would be the major speaker when we would have Mark White, who was then governor, come down. And she had this habit, she would put her hand on her hip and she would kinda shake her finger. She would be speaking Spanish to Mark White and he wouldn't know a word, but he was afraid to look away. So he would be looking intently at her, and she would be going like this [wagging her finger]." On one such occasion White is reported to have said, "I don't know what you're saying but I know I'd better say yes."

Valley Interfaith interviewed Carmen Anaya in 1998 and translated some of her recollections for a report to the Ford Foundation. In those remarks, she took pride in the material and spiritual transformation of the colonias. The colonia streets are now paved. The water is safe. Everyone has access to an adequate sewer system. More important, the people of the colonias now carry themselves with dignity. Valley Interfaith has brought about that transformation, she said, by serving as a "university" for the people. There is much to be learned in a university of this kind. It is no accident that the leaders of Valley Interfaith speak knowledgeably about the basic processes of the political system, many aspects of the law, the economics of the minimum wage, scripture, and the social teachings of the churches. But the central lesson being taught in Valley Interfaith's public university, Carmen Anaya said, is

> how to deal face-to-face with a politician and not humiliate ourselves or beg. We have the right to negotiate and tell him, "You are not our patron—you are our servant." This is very important. This is the most important point because through this organization we have brought accountability to these politicians. And I believe we have made them more responsible.[45]

Carmen Anaya had died before I joined a handful of organizers on a several-day tour of IAF activities in the borderlands of Texas, but I heard many people in Brownsville, McAllen, and Las Milpas speak of her. I also heard her spirit echoed in the voices of many others. Her willingness to stand up to mayors and governors in public settings had served as an example to people throughout the Valley. The current population of the area is 1.2 million, with 40 percent falling below the poverty line. The gap between rich and poor remains massive, but many of the poor no longer carry themselves in a posture of submission. They do not take themselves to be begging the rich for a handout. "What we regard as ours by right," according to moral philosopher Annette Baier, "is what we are unwilling to beg for and willing only within limits to say 'thank you' for."[46] It is appropriate, according to Carmen Anaya, to bow down and beg God for forgiveness, but not to bow down and beg CEOs and politicians for decent working and living conditions.

Donna Rodriguez is a teacher in Brownsville who once lived in a colonia known as Sebastian. The only employer in the vicinity at the time was a cotton gin that emitted pollutants. It became clear early on that a solution to the problem would be found, if at all, only at the state level. Donna was warned that she wouldn't be listened to in Austin. "We were terrified," she told me. This was why she was reluctant to get involved in the first place. Donna and other leaders were determined to get to Austin, but they had trouble finding money for the trip. State officials agreed to hold a hearing in the Valley. The gin brought lawyers from Indiana, Michigan, and San Antonio.

"We had us," Donna said proudly. When it was time to negotiate, "we were able to tell them, 'This is our table. You go over there.'" Here one sees a recurring IAF theme: the importance of meeting with governmental and corporate officials, at least on some occasions, in a space over which ordinary citizens exercise control. To be in charge of the meeting place and to be able to set the agenda of discussion are significant sources of empowerment. "They had maps," she continued. "They had data. I had no idea about this kind of stuff. But I was able to negotiate, because Valley Interfaith helped me get a voice." Donna was able to explain what the problem was, because it was part of her experience. "After that meeting we had so much fun learning. I'm still learning. Now, at my home, I have a sewer. We have paved streets. We have a park for our children. It's because we believed that we could get together and learn." When she is in the classroom, Donna teaches her students that they, too, have a voice, that they shouldn't be afraid of the wrong things or overwhelmed by fear, as she once was. One of the marks of leadership is courage.

Lupita Torres, another Brownsville leader, spoke to me in Spanish, with Elizabeth Valdez, the lead IAF organizer in the Valley, translating. For a long time, when others asked her to attend meetings, Lupita held out. "I am a very spiritual person. I didn't believe in politics. I didn't want to get involved." Finally, she gave in and attended a meeting, which was part of a parish development project that Elizabeth helped run. "I began to hear scripture stories that opened my eyes to think, 'This is what I need to be doing.' Before, I knew that there were a lot of needs in my neighborhood. We needed drainage. We needed lighting. We needed everything. But for me that was not the work that I was supposed to be doing. In the end, understanding scripture helped me understand my role."

Lupita recalled the day when Valley Interfaith took all of the politicians on a bus tour of the city. She asked the officials why the community was being charged for irrigation, since there was no farming going on. One official said that the charges had to do with taking care of drainage ditches. "I told him that the ditches aren't taken care of at all. They are full of weeds, people dump garbage in them, and sometimes, even bodies are found there. How are you cleaning the ditches, and we're paying all of this money?" She told the mayor that she wanted him to come to the neighborhood on foot, so he could see it and smell it. By the time the visit ended, officials had promised to pave the streets before the end of the month. "And so by the end of April, they were fixing the streets and putting streetlights in the neighborhood."

Another woman who admitted an initial reluctance to get involved pointed to Judy Vera as her role model, saying that the example of Judy's involvement had grown on her. How, then, did Judy get involved? "I was born in Brownsville," she told me, "and didn't know the Cameron Park colonia was located just outside the city limits next to a golf course. I was really shocked to see what the conditions were there, especially no water. How can people live without water? I asked a lady, 'Where do you take a bath?' And she told me, 'Well, when it gets dark you put up a tarp and get behind there and get a bucket and take a bath.' I thought I'd never do that. I'd be scared, you know, of animals. We worked real hard for water and sewer. If you saw the colonia then and you saw it now, it's different. You wouldn't recognize what it was when we started working on things there." It was the visual experience of conditions in the colonia, combined with the words of colonia residents, that motivated Judy to get involved. For some of those in her sphere of influence, however, it was Judy's exemplary conduct that moved them. Judy is *their* Carmen.

When Judy first got involved, the issues were unpaved streets, sewer systems, and lack of running water. When I visited Brownsville, however, the leaders were mainly talking about education, wages, job training, and health care. In each of these areas, Valley Interfaith had identified the community's concerns in the same way, by building up from one-on-one conversations to house meetings and research committees and eventually to programmatic proposals and accountability sessions. Stories about the original fights for decent conditions in the colonias continue to reinforce the sense that ordinary citizens have of their own agency. To hear the stories retold, even as a newly involved participant, is to be symbolically integrated into a group that has the capacity to achieve significant change and the moral authority to demand a hearing. It is also to affirm the desirability of overcoming the attitudes and habits of bowing and scraping in the presence of one's alleged superiors.[47] As our meeting in Brownsville drew to a close, Christine spoke of the stories of past victories as "construction with dead stones that you put in the ground" and build on. But the current leaders, she said, are "the living stones. Really our best achievement, I think, is the leaders."

Elizabeth later commented that one of the leaders who had spoken at the meeting in Brownsville, "the one with the rosary," was still undocumented. "None of her kids have papers either. She's almost at a 4.0 average. She did an internship at the capital, and the supervisor there said that when she graduated she wanted her to go work for her. [The supervisor] kept pushing her and pushing her, and she finally had to admit that she didn't have papers. And [the supervisor] said 'Well, we'll figure something out.' You don't have to be born in the U.S. to do the work of a citizen. You still have the responsibility. Father Jerry says she's involved in all sorts of organizations in the church. He says, 'You have been released from all your obligations in the church. All I want you to do is Valley Interfaith.' At the end she was the one leading the charge."

In a situation where many undocumented immigrants have become heavily integrated into the life of a community, as they have in Brownsville, Father Jerry's concept of a citizen applies to anyone who has a share of responsibility for social and institutional conditions, regardless of whether the state grants that person the right to vote. The moral concept of a citizen can outstrip the corresponding legal category. Anyone who enters so deeply into a community's life that he or she is reasonably taken by others to be partly responsible for that community's arrangements is a citizen in the moral sense. Father Jerry was not being unreasonable in treating his parishioner in this way. Neither was she being unreasonable in taking it to be her duty to do the work of a citizen. It belongs to the work of other citizens, who already have the legally recognized right to vote, to bring application of the legal category into line with realities of social life in the borderlands.

Her supervisor, her pastor, and many members of her community treat the woman with the rosary as someone with a share of responsibility for communal arrangements. They recognize her as someone with the authority to make claims on others and as someone with the moral authority to lead.[48] When she speaks about her experiences, expresses her concerns, or offers reasons for a proposal, she is *entitled* to gain a hearing from others. Hers is one of the voices to be taken into account. In some cases, hers is a voice to which other members of the community *ought to defer*. This is what it means for her to have the authority of a leader, which in a citizens' organization must be earned by demonstrating the reliability of what one says. The authority of a leader is earned entitlement to deference. A citizens' organization without relations of authority cannot perform its representative functions. If the relations of authority within a citizens' organization are not earned in practices of democratic accountability, the organization lacks the very sort of authority it claims for itself in public settings.

When an organizer like Elizabeth goes into a community in search of leaders, the existing patterns of deference speak volumes. Which people in the community are already treated by others as reliable and wise, as well as courageous, just, and spirited? Alinsky pointed out that authority relations within any given community tend to be patchy. Within a particular circle of associates, one person will have earned respect on some topics, but not on others. It is rare that one "stumbles across what might be defined as a complete leader—a person who has a following of forty or fifty people in every sphere of activity." There are not many Carmen Anayas. At the beginning of the organizing process, one typically finds "a large number of partial leaders or leaders of small groups and particularized aspects of their life." Most of these partial leaders "occupy the most humble roles in the community."[49] Their authority as leaders does not derive from an office or a title that they hold.

The organizer's work of leadership development therefore involves a number of distinct tasks. The first is to identify those who already possess an earned entitlement to deference on some topics. A second task is to widen the range of topics on which these "natural" leaders can speak with genuine authority. Another is to expand the scope of the groups that recognize that authority, thus expanding the influence of someone like the woman with the rosary beyond the circle of her immediate friends and family. Yet another task is to place leaders repeatedly in situations where what they say and do can be held accountable by other leaders and by rank-and-file members of the institutions they represent. This last task is essential, because it increases the likelihood that power being exercised on behalf the organization, in its external as well as its internal dealings, is grounded in *earned* attributions of authority. Ideally, those who come to hold office in the citizens' organization or who speak on behalf of the organization in a public setting have the moral authority to exercise the collective power that in those moments rests in their hands.

The case of Carmen Anaya shows that authority relations within a community are not exhausted by patterns of deference to living persons. All communities are shaped by traditions of some sort, which Alinsky defined as the "collective habits, experiences, customs, controls, and values of the whole group." In democratic politics, Alinsky wrote, "*the tradition is the terrain*." It is a fatal error in organizing, he thought, to "indulge in the sterile, wishful thinking of liberals who prefer to start where they would like to begin rather than with actual conditions as they exist."[50] Most of the beliefs, values, and dispositions shared by any group, and taken for granted by default as the starting point of its reasoning on political questions, are acquired through acculturation.

By undergoing novel experiences, considering new evidence, or engaging in reasoning, we can call some of our cultural inheritance into question, reject received commitments, and adopt new ones. But the process of critical reflection would not be aided by confining ourselves to premises already certified by critical reasoning as sound. How, in that case, could one begin? Critical reasoning is itself dependent on a cultural inheritance. Imagining ourselves to be operating with a blank slate, on which we are free to inscribe the deliverances of pure reason, would be self-deceptive. Each of us gains access to a cultural inheritance in the first place by deferring to our elders on a range of matters that is too wide and too deep to be fully acknowledged. To be able to think critically is itself initially to be acculturated into practices of accountability of a particular kind, practices that permit us to call some things into question, but only while taking others, for the moment, as the default starting point of our questioning. So it is with the woman holding the rosary beads, with Carmen Anaya, and with thousands of others in the Rio Grande Valley. And so it is with the rest of us.

Most people currently associated with Valley Interfaith are Roman Catholics. They were raised to treat a particular ecclesial tradition as authoritative on matters of faith and morals. This tradition not only identifies scripture as a source of normative authority but also specifies what books belong to scripture and whose interpretive authority must be taken into account when reading it. The woman with the rosary beads began her moral and political journey with these commitments in mind. Thinking back to the parish development program, Elizabeth Valdez remembered a session that had focused on Saint Paul's Letters to the Corinthians. The assignment was to write one's own letter, to play the role of Paul with respect to the contemporary church. "What would you tell Brownsville? And they posted their letters on the church. They did that, and they did the Beatitudes, to teach the qualities of leaders. They did the Road to Emmaus as a way to teach individual meetings. Everything was scripture oriented." This process of reading, discussing, and writing was a crucial turning point for the woman with the rosary, Elizabeth said. "In the end, she was like, 'We must do this. We don't have a choice. Why haven't you told us about this before?'"

One morning Elizabeth took me to meet with leaders from the McAllen area at Saint Joseph the Worker Catholic Church. After Father Alfonso Guevara welcomed us, Father Carlos Zuniga began the meeting with a reading from Psalm 44. "We commend ourselves to the Lord as we continue to live this day in the light of God's presence," said Father Alfonso. "We pray in God's name, Amen."

Ninfa Guerra described Valley Interfaith as "the conscience of the business community, in making sure that they don't forget the persons that are going to be affected by the policies they set." For a long time, Ninfa said, the Valley "has been known as a source of cheap labor. The chamber of commerce advertized our low wages and hard work as selling points. We decided we really had to change that culture if we wanted to make enough money to live on."

"Professor Stout," she told me, "you need to know that I'm very selfish. I do it because of what I'm learning. I like that I'm contributing to community, but most of us in here do it because it's developing us, as well, as individuals. I'm from McAllen. I was born here, raised here, and I want to die here. I love McAllen. But I didn't always like the politics. The story of McAllen is really interesting. For twenty years we had a mayor who ruled with an iron hand. He hated organizers. He told us right up front. He also hated unions, the reason being that he made his money off the backs of the poor. And to tell you the type of person he was, he was placed in a committee that oversaw the use of pesticides in agriculture, and his response to why everyone was making such a big deal about pesticides was, 'Well, they're going to die anyway. So, what's the big deal, right?'"

Ninfa met with a similar response when dealing with other sorts of programs. Students enrolled in a training program to become dental and medical assistants came out making only six dollars an hour. When Valley Interfaith challenged that figure as inadequate, the medical establishment's response was that the market sets wages.[51] As Ninfa now sees it, wage levels are the product of the decisions made by everyone who participates in the market. Inaction on the part of workers and self-interested behavior on the part of CEOs were jointly responsible for low wages in the Valley. Organizing the working poor to challenge the CEOs is a way of participating in the market with open eyes.

At the beginning of the learning process, workers are inclined to defer to CEOs as authorities on all matters pertaining to the market. CEOs do tend to know more about the operations of markets than others do. The CEO's informational advantage derives both from prior education, the organizational resources of the corporation, and the ability to hire academic experts, including economists, to produce information of a certain kind. To level the informational playing field, the citizens' organization provides educational opportunities to those who participate in it and procures help from experts of its own. Paul Osterman, the author of one of the best books on IAF and a professor of management at MIT, has been especially valuable in contributing his expertise to Valley Interfaith. Ernesto Cortés deepened his own grasp of economics by spending the 1997–98 academic year as a visiting professor at MIT in the Department of Urban Studies and Planning. The seminars that Cortés runs for organizers and leaders in the Southwest region are intended in part to provide ordinary citizens with access to information and expertise that has not been filtered through the biases of big business. Equal access to information and direct access to experts tend to democratize the distribution of intellectual authority.

The need for this sort of redistribution is underlined by the work in the economics of information for which Joseph Stiglitz, currently a professor of economics at Columbia University, won the Nobel Prize in 2001. Stiglitz and one of his associates demonstrated in a paper published in 1986 that an unequal distribution of information, such as that which typically puts workers at a disadvantage in relation to their actual or prospective employers, skews the ways in which markets operate, not least of all in the setting of wages.[52] Orthodox economic models that abstract from asymmetries of information suggest that the way to achieve higher levels of employment is to lower wages. The work of Stiglitz and others implied that abstraction of this sort has tended to produce policy advice that advanced the interests of those already benefiting from a high degree of access to information. IAF organizers have attempted to redress asymmetries of economic information directly through education, but also by giving considerable weight to the findings of economists who focus empirically on existing economies that are imperfect in various ways.[53]

IAF's practice of consulting experts of its own choosing when crafting its policy proposals is part of a worldwide shift in the distribution of information that has been underway for some time now. As anthropologist Arjun Appadurai has argued,

> A series of social forms has emerged . . . to create forms of knowledge transfer and social mobilization that proceed independently of the actions of corporate capital and the nation-state system (and its international affiliates and guarantors). These social forms rely on strategies, visions, and horizons for globaliza-

tion on behalf of the poor that can be characterized as "grassroots globalization" or, put in a slightly different way, as "globalization from below."[54]

The network of organizers and citizens' groups Ernie Cortés supervises is itself part of IAF's national and international networks, which are themselves exchanging information with other similar networks around the world. Globalization from below represents a significant challenge to the authority-claims of many experts holding appointments at prestigious universities.

Appadurai has referred to globalization from below as "cellular democratization at work" and as an "exercise in capacity building." The term *cellular*, as Appadurai employs it, contrasts with *vertebrate*. Cellular democratization involves the creation of relationships among citizens' groups that permit them to be connected to one another and to exchange information without relying on a vertical, top-down, unidirectional model of authority. It is characteristic of cellular democratization that the groups involved in it do not feel bound to think of themselves, or to present themselves to others, as representatives of a national or international "movement" or as incarnations of a single idea or principle. In contrast with the "great progressive movements of the past few centuries," cellular democratic networks tend to build "solidarity from smaller convergences of interest," in "a more ad hoc, inductive, and context-sensitive manner."[55] I am suggesting that Alinsky's decision to found a *network* of citizens' organizations can be viewed as a harbinger of this contemporary global development and that latter-day IAF groups can now be seen as part of a much bigger democratic transformation that affects authority relations of many kinds, including those that pertain to expertise and political legitimacy.[56]

It should not be surprising, then, that in tackling the issues currently on Valley Interfaith's agenda, the organization has repeatedly drawn on the experience of other citizens' groups elsewhere. IAF has developed an approach to education known as "Alliance Schools," which applies the basic democratic practices of face-to-face interaction, coalition building, and accountability within a school district. The "alliance" being constructed as a basis for successful education is meant to bring together parents, teachers, local businesses, and other constituencies into a collaborative and continuing exercise in problem solving and mutual accountability. The approach was first hammered out by COPS in San Antonio and later spread to many other communities that are part of the IAF network. Similarly, the job training program promoted by Valley Interfaith, which is known as the Valley Initiative for Development and Advancement (VIDA), is also modeled on a COPS program called Project Quest. The "living wage" campaign in McAllen took inspiration from an initiative in Baltimore by an IAF affiliate known as Baltimoreans United in Leadership Development (BUILD).

Consuelo Maheshwari has been principal of Sam Houston Elementary School in McAllen since it became an Alliance school about fifteen years ago. "That's when everything happened," Connie told me. "We really became different people, as far as how we saw our role as teachers. Once we started with house meetings, we got to know the real issues of the community, the real issues the children were facing. We had students coming in our offices, saying that if they sell a package of cocaine, they can afford to buy a TV. We had children in very dire, horrible situations. When we started talking to the parents, they said, 'We're scared.' Safety was one of the major issues they were concerned about. It was education and the safety of the children.

"We didn't have a playground, and behind the school was where a lot of the drug dealings were going down. So then we brought community leaders into play: the city leaders, the chief of police, the commissioners, and the mayor. We started to have one-on-ones with them. And we started to have the teachers and the parents meeting with these individuals, talking about what the issues were impacting the students. At that point, we also partnered with St. Joseph the Worker. So now we were a much larger force.

"I remember the first accountability session. After we had done the research, we all teamed together and we invited these key leaders—the mayor, the chief of police, the superintendent, the board members, and commissioners—to come in and talk. And the school was packed, to the point where I started to get calls from people, saying, 'You know, Connie, I know your board members, and they don't like it. They don't like Valley Interfaith.' That was a very good sign that they were starting to respect us and they were starting to be afraid. And sure enough, from that meeting, we got four more police officers assigned. The City of McAllen and the district partnered and made new streets all around the school."

IAF organizers teach that it is crucial for a citizens' organization to win recognition from the political establishment as a source of power and moral authority. Both the power and the authority are rooted in the organization's ability to demonstrate that it is recognized by those it claims to represent as entitled to speak *for them* in public debate and at the negotiating table. Some degree of recognition of the organization's representative status in the eyes of those being represented comes first. It emerges initially in one-on-one conversations, house meetings, and neighborhood walks, and is raised to consciousness when individual citizens who have engaged in these practices see each other coming together in public assemblies and accountability sessions, where what leaders say on behalf of those being represented can be tested against a shared experience of the interactions that informed the content of the group's demands and publicly stated reasoning.

But public assemblies and accountability sessions must make the organization's representative authority visible even to people who have not participated directly in the organization's internal practices of consultation and decision making. The need to achieve this second sort of recognition dictates the initially strident tone of many IAF public events. The organization must not only get the attention of public officials but must also give evidence that its constituent institutions and many of the people associated with them are prepared to resist those officials in publicly visible ways—in particular, in ways that might well cost those officials something, whether it be a policy they favor, the image of themselves they wish to project to the public, or the office they hold. In other words, the organization must make clear to public officials that it is a source of power capable of frustrating their own intentions. To achieve a relationship of mutual recognition with public officials and other elites in the broader political community, a citizens' organization has to put officials in a position of needing to negotiate with it.

"What we gained was a seat at the negotiating table," said Connie. "The other thing that happened was a change in us as teachers. We realized that the parents were the true teachers, because we learned so much from them as we walked the streets, as we partnered with them. We would meet with the commissioners, and it was our parents, like Rosa Gutierrez, who were the ones making the demands and understood the history of their area and the issues."

The organization's internal process of consultation also required potential spokespersons to earn their entitlement to speak for others in a particular way. This mainly entailed listening to and demonstrating an empathetic understanding of those they sought to represent. The internal participatory process permitted someone like Rosa Gutierrez, a parent, to be recognized as an authoritative spokesperson by others within the organization.

The transformations I have just analyzed are democratic in tendency. They involve earning recognition of one's representative authority from others on the basis of one's responsiveness to their experiences, concerns, proposals, and reasons. When the citizens' organization wins recognition from public officials, it constitutes itself as a legitimate counterpower over against those officials, not only as an agent capable of frustrating an official's hopes and plans, but also as a group of citizens to whom the official owes an account of his or her decisions. The result is the formation of a public of accountability.

By constituting enduring publics of accountability, citizens' organizations can make the activity of holding officials responsible a perpetual, rather than merely episodic, affair. The same interactive process also increases the chances that citizens will vote and will inform themselves and one another about matters of public concern. Officials who are interacting with the leaders of an organization like Valley Interfaith quickly acquire the sense of being held accountable to citizens on a day-to-day basis.

It also becomes clear to all concerned, however, that those speaking for the citizens' organization can themselves be held accountable, both by the officials whose decisions they seek to influence or contest and by those for whom they claim to speak. A public of accountability opens up a zone of interaction within which officials and the spokespersons of citizens' groups hold each other accountable, while simultaneously being held accountable in various ways by the ordinary citizens being represented. The spokesperson who, acting on behalf of others, holds officials accountable in meetings of various kinds expects to be held accountable in turn by the ordinary citizens on whose behalf she speaks, as well as by the officials she addresses. Democracy resides in these relations of accountability.

"Basically," Connie said, "I'm from Las Milpas. It is one of the colonias. It's south of Pharr. I was born and raised there, and go back every chance I get. My father still lives there. My mother lived there. My mother organized there. I learned a lot from her."

"Who is your mother?"

"Carmen Anaya. My mother and the church are what got me involved. Until a few years ago, when she passed away, she was just there every single day. Her presence was very much a part of Valley Interfaith, the church, and the community."

Ernie Cortés is fond of quoting Jaroslav Pelikan's distinction between tradition, as "the living faith of the dead," and traditionalism, as "the dead faith of the living."[57] Stories about Carmen Anaya are retold in part to reaffirm the shared values of Valley Interfaith, but they also serve as an example for a generation in search of guidance concerning how leadership is to be earned and exercised. The life presented in the stories is an example *of* democratic moral authority and an example *for* those who wish to acquire it.

A woman who acquires even a fraction of the moral authority Carmen Anaya had in the eyes of the wider community can meet with opposition and constraint at home. Some husbands put their foot down, and when they do, their wives have hard decisions to make. Elizabeth mentioned a man from San Juan parish. "His wife went to national IAF training, and he went berserk. He was going nuts without her and he asked her to come back." She decided to keep the peace and accede to his wishes.

"That was one of the worst national training experiences I've ever had," Ernie said. "I got so mad at her. 'You know,' I told her, 'you let the men in your life hold you back: your father, your husband, your children.'" She remained somewhat involved after that but "never realized her potential."

Renee Wizig-Barrios suggested that "the women seem to have been the strength of the leadership" in the Valley. Elizabeth agreed. Renee asked Elizabeth whether there has generally been "a *machista* reaction to that?"

"Rosa had to take Father Bart with her to go talk to her husband to be able to let her go even to Austin," Elizabeth said. "She had a baby when she started getting involved, and her husband would hold her back." Christine mentioned a woman who was the secretary at a church in San Antonio. "She could have been COPS president. She was attractive, she was smart enough, but she just didn't make the commitment. Her husband didn't want her to do it, and she didn't challenge him."

These cases were memorable in part because they are less common than one might expect. It was Renee's experience, when she was organizing in El Paso, "that not only would the women change, but their marriages would change because of them becoming leaders. It would create real tension, but in the end it would create a transformation in that relationship."

On the last day of my tour through the Valley, Elizabeth, Christine, and Ernie introduced me to a number of the local leaders from Las Milpas. Elizabeth had posted some photographs on a bulletin board in a meeting room in a church there. Christine, fighting back tears at first and then shifting to laughter, identified a picture of Senator Hutchison on a walking tour of Elida Bocanegra's colonia, with the senator's pants rolled up comically above the ankles. Another picture showed the colonia roads at their muddiest. Next, an attorney was supposed to make a PowerPoint presentation on the colonias, but he had been held up in court, so Elizabeth took us through it. One of the slides depicted Carmen Anaya, standing near an outhouse, "speaking with her hands," as Elizabeth put it. In another, Mrs. Anaya and all of the other Valley leaders are standing behind the governor, witnessing his signature on a bill. "Carmen was pushing his hand, saying, 'Sign!'"

I heard a good deal from various leaders over the course of the next hour. One story illustrated a division between north and south McAllen. People on the poorer south side wanted tax money to go to El Milagro Clinic. Many people on the wealthier north side were saying, "Let the south side take care of themselves." One leader recalled a story from one of the house meetings that helped bridge the gap: "One lady had a maid from Mexico. She would go there on Sunday night, pick her up, and take her back on Friday afternoon. She paid her, what, fifty dollars, sixty dollars for the whole week?

Well, this maid had TB and the family never knew. She was taking care of the newborn baby in this family. The baby developed TB in the spinal cord and died. So we are all connected." The story was vintage IAF. The moral was that the enlightened self-interest of relatively wealthy people in the United States overlaps with the interests of Mexicans. Intertwining lives disclose a common good.

Near the end of the meeting, the attorney who was supposed to have made the PowerPoint presentation arrived, apologizing for being late. Ernie asked him to identify himself. "I'm Eddie," he said.

"And who was your mother?" Ernie asked, prompting him to answer for my benefit.

"Carmen Anaya," Eddie said.

✻ CHAPTER NINE ✻

On the Treatment of Opponents

And why not say (as some people slander us by saying that we say), "Let us do evil that good may come"?
—*Romans 3:8*

As for those who persist in sin, rebuke them in the presence of all.
—*1 Timothy 6:20*

OPPOSITION TO IAF is hardly limited to the private misgivings of husbands of female leaders. Every IAF group in Texas has had the moral authority of its leadership challenged vehemently in public. "We got labeled communist and every name in the book," Elizabeth said. Leaders were often unprepared to hear such accusations being flung at them. Christine thought back to her early experiences organizing in Houston. Some opponents "sent letters to every parishioner in St. Jerome's, attacking us." To avoid early attacks of this sort, she would try to keep her organizing efforts relatively quiet until she had established enough credibility to survive the attacks.

"We would really fly underground for a long time," Christine said. "But in one community, when the religion reporter for the *Houston Chronicle* found out what we were doing, he was furious. He was like, 'How dare you?' because at that point, we were strong enough that they couldn't kill us. 'How dare you organize here and not tell me about it?' So he wrote all of these stories about us." The reporter was close to a former mayor, who had become the head of the Chamber of Commerce. His attacks on churches committed to the IAF coalition in Houston became daily fare. He told Christine:

"Churches shouldn't do anything but run soccer." The newspaper stories kept coming. At one point, Christine said, Ernie took a vacation, and left her in charge of the Houston organizing. She had been an organizer for about three months, so she wasn't fully prepared for the negative reactions. Every morning she would wake up and read another story attacking her efforts as either evil or useless. "It was the most nerve-wracking thing."

Christine called Ernie, and told him what the former mayor was saying through the press. She remembers Ernie telling her to call the Houston leaders together. They should call a press conference, and when the reporters arrive, the leaders should tell them, "This guy has syphilis of the brain." Most of the leaders at that point were Protestants, one of them a "very proper Presbyterian minister." When Christine called them together, explained the need for a press conference, and told the leaders what Ernie wanted them to say, the minister said, "I don't think I can say that." They didn't end up saying anything that harsh, Christine admitted, but they did get the point that the attacks had to be answered in a forceful way.

Ernie then told us about an experience he had had in El Paso, where he met opposition from a man who had previously been chairman of the Water Board in San Antonio. "We had gone up against him in San Antonio," Ernie said. "He was also a developer, but the developers had taken over the city council and got the city council to appoint their candidates to the Water Board. They changed the Water Board to basically subsidize development outside of the city limits. In San Antonio every new capital project was outside the city limits—way out, thirty or forty miles. Basically it became a bank for developers, with no-interest loans and that kind of thing. That's where we got the idea for some of our programs, because if you can do this for rich people, you ought to be able to do it for poor people. We took this guy on and ridiculed him for doing these things. So, he had gone through this experience with us in San Antonio.

"Anyway, a reporter from El Paso calls me up, quotes this guy ripping us apart, and says, 'What do you say to that?' I said, 'Are you going to print that?' 'Well,' he said, 'yeah, I'm going to print it.' 'Well, then, you print this: The reason he said that is because he's got syphilis of the brain.' And the reporter says, 'I can't print that.' 'Why not? I said it.' 'Well, I can't do it.' So I said, 'Okay, then don't print what he said either.'"

Another opponent of organizing projects in Texas, according to Ernie, had charged that IAF treats public officials as if they were prisoners in North Korean POW camps. Members of the business establishment began reading Alinsky. "You know that line from *Patton*," Christine said, "where Patton says, 'Rommel, you magnificent bastard, I read your book!' Well, that's what it was like. When I was first in San Antonio, one guy kind of leans back at his desk, opens his drawer, and pulls out Alinsky's *Rules for Radicals*. They called it the Little Red Book. He throws it down, and says, 'I read your book!'"

In 1988, when Othal Brand was mayor of McAllen, he was quoted in the *New York Times*, saying of IAF: "There's not much question their basic philosophy is basically a communistic philosophy."[58] Aside from being mayor, Brand was a major landowner in Central America as well as in Texas and a significant figure in the Republican Party at the state and national levels. His complaint was about IAF's ends, but I found no evidence, either during my travels through the Southwest or in my other research, that the charge is true. IAF groups are not striving for the elimination of governmental and corporate elites, but rather for a level of democratic participation, on the part of ordinary citizens, that can permit elites to be held accountable.

A kind of equality is being asserted here, but it isn't the perfect economic equality of communist utopias, and it certainly doesn't involve promoting an all-powerful state. IAF groups tend to view state bureaucrats and corporate bosses as more or less equally disposed to insulate themselves from accountability. It is no solution to this problem to place one or the other in complete control. The kind of political equality that IAF groups affirm is centered in the notion that every law-abiding adult resident in a society bears responsibility for the condition of that society's arrangements and ought therefore to be recognized by others—and under law—as entitled to fulfill that responsibility. This is what it means to embrace an inclusive conception of citizenship.

IAF also affirms the priority of the political over the economic. Economic arrangements are among those for which all citizens are jointly responsible, and such arrangements tend to get seriously out of whack when representatives of the corporate sector have unchecked power in determining what those arrangements will be. This, surely, is what Brand and others have had in mind when referring to IAF's philosophy as communistic, but the charge simply conflates a desire for nondomination with a desire for the elimination of private ownership of the means of production.

On the ethics of *means*, it must be admitted that Alinsky's position was neither coherent nor entirely in keeping with the positions of most religious groups that have joined IAF coalitions over the years. The chapter entitled "Of Means and Ends" in *Rules for Radicals* begins by heaping scorn on "means-and-ends moralists" for implicitly providing ideological assistance to the Haves.[59] No doubt, there are cases in which this is true, but there also appear to be cases in which it is not. Alinsky was simply wrong to claim that *"one's concern with the ethics of means and ends varies inversely with one's personal interest in the issue"* (*Rules*, 26, italics in original). Gandhi and King were obviously concerned with the ethics of means, while maintaining a high level of interest in the issues at stake in their respective political struggles, and the same holds of countless others who understand that one cannot consistently object to the unjust means of oppressors without applying the standard of justice to one's own actions.

Unjust means are unjust, regardless of who sets them in motion. Willingness to use unjust means corrupts the characters of those involved. It also opens a citizens' organization to charges of hypocrisy, thus yielding the high moral ground to its opponents. People genuinely committed to justice will not want to be complicit in an organization that exempts itself from the standards it applies to others.

Alinsky once wrote that in the struggle "against social evil there are no rules of fair play" (*Reveille*, 133). In some passages, he debunked moral reasoning as mere "rationalization," a covering worn by "self-interest" (*Rules*, 43). On the other hand, there are many other passages in which he extolled the importance of respecting the dignity of human beings, of valuing the preciousness of each human life, and of freeing ourselves from slavery in all of its forms (e.g., *Reveille*, xiv, 9, 56, 92, 100, 103, 190; *Rules*, 12, 20, 46, 60, 93, 123, 124). Yet these are the very sorts of concerns that motivate many people to place moral constraints on means.

In the context of social conflict, the ethics of means mainly has to do with the question of how one's opponents should be treated. Citizens' organizations strive for a society in which no one will be in a position to dominate others. Domination is not merely bad, but horrendous. The horrendous, etymologically, is that to which we appropriately respond by shuddering.[60] It violates something held especially dear or sacred. By speaking of the dignity of human beings and the preciousness or sanctity of human life, the friends of democracy try to name what it is that domination violates. A society of liberty and justice for all is meant to provide security against such horrors.[61] But the fellow citizens who occasionally oppose the democratic struggle are human beings. So presumably there are things that shouldn't be done to them. In particular, *whatever violates their dignity, or does them a grave injustice, or arbitrarily exercises power over them should not be done*.

When political and corporate officials complain about IAF tactics, they repeatedly mention the moment in accountability sessions when an official's microphone is switched off if he or she starts giving a speech in response to a yes-no question. "It never seemed right to me that I or other elected officials should have to get up in front of our constituents and follow a script written out by Valley Interfaith," Brand once said. "Those accountability sessions never give anybody a chance to explain why they have a position. It's just set up to put a lot of pressure on you to agree with whatever Valley Interfaith wants."[62] Brand's frustration is understandable. Officials like him have powerful institutions at their disposal. They use that power when they determine where meetings of various kinds will be held, what will be discussed, who will be allowed to speak, and for how long. It can be frustrating for officials to find themselves in a public meeting that they cannot control.

Brand's complaint glosses over the need for ordinary citizens to compensate for what happens on the numerous occasions when officials like him are in charge. The sort of compensation that is ethically relevant here is not a matter of tit for tat. The point of restricting officials from giving speeches at accountability sessions is not—or should not be—that they deserve a taste of their own medicine, as if the point were retribution. No doubt, a desire to dominate officials who are accustomed to dominating does sometimes taint the motives of the citizens running a given accountability session, or even the spirit of a given campaign. When this happens, undemocratic motives threaten to corrupt a citizens' group, to drive people of good will away from it, and to make eventual reconciliation more difficult.

A better reason for running accountability sessions as IAF groups do involves a desire for a different sort of compensation—namely, that of leveling the playing field. If a few powerful people are in charge of all meetings where issues are discussed publicly, the playing field will tilt, perhaps decisively, in their favor. If it tilts enough in their favor, they will be dominant in the sense of being in a position to exercise power arbitrarily over others. One way to compensate for this, as we saw in the Arizona case, is to resist arbitrary attempts on the part of public officials to change the agenda of a given meeting in ways intended to deprive citizens of their voice. Another way is to create additional meetings, such as accountability sessions, that are controlled by people who are neither public officials nor leaders of a political party. The right to convene meetings and to set agendas and rules for running them is, in practice, much of what the freedom to assemble amounts to. Multiple meetings, run in different ways by different people, tend to counteract the dominance of elites.

What matters most in this context is the overall relationship between elites and other groups, not who controls the agenda and administers the rules in a particular meeting. In a genuinely democratic polity, people take turns calling meetings and determining how to run them. Officials are free to decline an invitation to an accountability session. They are also free to schedule their own meetings and to run them according to whatever rules they deem suitable for the occasion, provided that the rules do not establish or reinforce a pattern of domination. If officials or candidates for public office wish to explain their positions at great length, they can always create a forum for doing so.

In accountability sessions citizens' organizations give public articulation to the concerns and issues that have emerged in one-on-one conversations, house meetings, and community walks. Public officials who do attend are expected, first of all, to listen. When the presentations have been made, and an IAF leader poses a yes-no question to an official like Brand, the point is to determine whether the official is willing to make a public commitment of some kind. Will he work with the group? Will he recognize the group's authority to negotiate on behalf of the broader community? Will he declare support for the group's proposals? When these questions are posed, the official might wish to give a lengthy speech, either in order to evade the question or to explain one or more negative answers. But there comes a time when the citizens' group needs clarity on where the official stands. Is this officeholder an ally of the organization or not? There is a role in public life, as IAF groups see it, for *rituals of commitment* that clarify, for everyone involved, what relationships and commitments they have entered into.

An accountability session, like a wedding, is an opportunity not to give speeches, but rather to declare one's commitments in a way that fully clarifies a significant relationship and the obligations that flow from it. An unwillingness to say "I do," without further elaboration, when asked for a public commitment to enter an important relationship, is itself a significant act, which has consequences for all involved. But to say "I do" is to enter a relationship, to take on the obligations of the relationship, and thus to license the broader community to hold one accountable in the future for failures to meet those obligations.

The public official is free to refuse to say "I do" when asked to give a public commitment to a publicly offered proposal. The refusal can subsequently be explained at any length, in any terms, and on any occasion that the official deems appropriate. Public officials lack neither the means for explaining themselves, nor access to the media. But if officials are to be held accountable, there need to be moments when they are called on to decide what their publicly acknowledged commitments and relationships are going to be. Refusal to commit oneself to supporting a proposal, or to entering an alliance, is itself something for which one can be held accountable, which is why Brand experienced this sort of occasion as pressure. He wanted a relationship, but one in which all of the obligations were on one side and all of the power was on the other.

Elizabeth remembered a time when she was negotiating with the mayor of San Antonio on proposed legislation for promoting jobs with higher wages. "So the mayor says, 'This is the only thing we can pass. This is the only thing we can get votes for.' He got Tom

Frost [a prominent San Antonio businessman] to talk to us. And he says 'I'm here to talk to you about this legislation, and this is all that we can get passed.' Sister Gabriella says, 'No, Mr. Frost. How can you ask us to support that when it's against what we're trying to do?' We go back and forth, and you can start to see the veins around his head popping up. All of a sudden he's red. And he shouted, 'Alinsky was right. You people are the devil.'"[63]

Frost had calmed down a bit by the time the official meeting started, Elizabeth said, but as a precaution she sent messages to the leaders who hadn't witnessed his explosion, urging them to avoid confronting him. After the meeting, according to Elizabeth, "We tried to depolarize, and he went around and shook everybody's hand. He came up to me, wanting to shake my hand, and I said, 'Are you sure you want a handshake from the devil?' He said, 'Mea culpa! I'm sorry! I never should have done that! I just wanted to get something passed. We know we need your support.'"

One repeatedly cited IAF rule, which came up in my account of the Jeremiah Group, is "No permanent enemies, no permanent allies." Decent citizens' organizations do have opponents. Some of these opponents are people of good will who are not persuaded by what a given citizens' group says on behalf of its proposals. Some opponents, however, maliciously seek to crush citizens' organizations and unjustly attack the reputations of organizers and leaders. Such behavior expresses enmity, so there is a sense in which opponents of this sort qualify as enemies. Sometimes, the attacks are not only unjust, taken in isolation, but also belong to a deliberate strategy to maintain dominance. Failure to respond to such attacks inevitably leads to defeat. Niceness in the midst of such conflict is not a virtue, any more than cowardice is.

It is often prudent in such situations to "polarize" one's relationship with one's opponents by putting them on the defensive. This can be accomplished justly by publicly declaring particular individuals responsible for the attack and for whatever forms of injustice or domination are being targeted. Without such attributions of responsibility, there is no such thing as accountability. Democracy requires moments of polarization, in which the distinctions between allies and opponents and between decent and malicious opponents are clearly drawn. It is appropriate, in such moments, to declare one's intention to hold one's opponents accountable for injustice. Alinsky's advice was: "*Pick the target, freeze it, personalize it, and polarize it*" (*Rules*, 131, italics in original).

To do these things justly and proportionately, however, it is important to resist the temptation to demonize or scapegoat one's opponents, a danger about which Alinsky had little to say. Demonizing locates the propensity for injustice and domination exclusively on the opponent's side of the conflict. It explains the opponent's wrongdoing as the expression of a fixed, underlying, evil essence not shared by one's allies, rather than as the result of the egotism and self-deception from which all human beings suffer to some degree. Demonizing thus treats unjust foes unjustly, by making them out to be even worse than they are. In this way, it sets the stage for elimination of foes from the moral community—as if by sacrificing a scapegoat, one could rid the community of evil.

The idea that there are no permanent enemies, in contrast, holds out the possibility of eventual transformation of both one's opponents—even the ones filled with enmity—and one's relationship to them. In some circumstances, people become opponents of a citizens' organization because they want to maintain dominance over others and are using their power to do so. When the conflict of the moment subsides, they are likely to retain enough power to remain significant players in the political arena. It is wise to seek a just reconciliation with the other side. To count as justly achieved, the desired reconciliation cannot ignore grave wrongdoing and responsibility for it, because ignoring such things would itself be unjust.

But the point of polarizing an unjust situation is to resolve the conflict at hand, not to set it in stone. Justice is not vengeance. Fighting for justice is not feuding.

Organizers therefore also place emphasis on the importance of "depolarizing," especially immediately after major fights have been won or lost. It is to be expected that alliances will shift over time. Many organizers express admiration for business people who are willing to form alliances with citizens' organizations with which they had once fought. The struggle for recognition is hardly free of conflict, but it often prepares the ground for reconciliation. What begins with red-baiting can end in collaboration and mutual respect. Polarizing is often necessary, then, but it must be carried out in a way that avoids injustice in the present and looks forward to depolarization in the future.

The funding for job training in the Rio Grande Valley, Ninfa told me, is now coming from corporations that had once "fought tooth and nail not to give money." "At the beginning," Father Alfonso said, "there was a natural resistance in the business community, but they eventually began to understand that we're not against business. Our point is that what's good for business has to also be good for the whole economy and not come at the expense of good wages and good jobs. A culture of dialogue, of conversation, is such an important element in all of these victories." A culture of dialogue is, however, often the fruit of conflict, rightly conducted.

✻ CHAPTER TEN ✻

Organize, Reflect, and Reorganize

One day during my tour of the Rio Grande Valley, Doug Greco, the lead organizer of Austin Interfaith, asked Elizabeth Valdez whether the breakdown of the social fabric that organizers in many communities have observed over the last thirty years had also occurred in the Texas borderlands. "It's mixed," she said, "but it's getting to be that way," especially in cities like McAllen and Harlingen. "The infrastructure can't keep up, and the institutions can't keep up." Social fragmentation was now reaching the point where Elizabeth would have to rethink her strategy. No longer could she trade quite so readily on the social cohesion of Latino communities and the progressive outlook of Roman Catholic social teachings. As it reached its twenty-fifth anniversary, Valley Interfaith would have to be "reorganized."

Frank Pierson plays a supervisory role in New Mexico and Arizona analogous to the one that Christine Stephens plays in Texas, Louisiana, and Mississippi. He, too, used the term *reorganization* to characterize what needed to be done in Arizona when complacency set in among organizers and leaders there after a run of early successes. "The strength of the organizations," Frank said, is the crucial thing, "because that's the wellspring of change. We built PCIC (Puma County Interfaith Council) in Tucson in a kind of classic way, hundreds and hundreds of individual meetings, small-group meetings, listening to people, building our institutional base, pastors around the table, etc. The first large meeting we did was with a parish where we had about eight hundred people. It was very diverse. The whole point of the meeting was to get a relationship with whoever was going to be elected mayor.

"We invited both candidates," Frank continued. "One shows up, the incumbent mayor. His name is George Miller. We keep him waiting to pretty much the end of the event, and we have one question for him that the leader poses after stories outlining the core experience of families and our agenda. 'Will you work with PCIC to address these issues that are affecting children and youth in the city so that we can make a difference together?' Miller has a prepared speech in his hand, and it's about twenty pages long, okay? He throws it down on the ground, and says, 'Meetings like this scare the hell out of politicians like me. I have never seen a crowd like this in thirty years of Tucson politics. You bet I'll work with you. Tell me when you want to meet.'"

A meeting was scheduled for the following week: "Bang, just like that." But when PCIC leaders arrived, Miller seemed moody, even "pissed off." Frank suspected that the group's assertive attitude had bothered him. "We do have an attitude, okay? So we come into the meeting and he starts out. He's an older guy. He says, 'You all remind me of the Democratic Party in the fifties. It was diverse, there were large numbers of people, a mix of races and classes, and some real agenda was being talked about. I only have one criticism. I'm really pissed about something. There were no Jewish representatives in this meeting.'"

Frank and the others expected Miller to say that they should have been more inclusive when organizing the accountability session. "Instead he said, 'You know what I did the next day after this meeting? I called Rabbi Arthur Aleski, and I told that son of a bitch to get off his fat ass, high horse, low horse, or hobby horse, and get involved in this organization!'" Frank sees this moment as an important transition for IAF in Arizona, because collaboration with Miller led to a long series of important initiatives, ranging from after-school programs to job training and an effort to raise the minimum wage. The collaboration bore significant fruit for a period of about seven years.

"Then something happened," Frank said. "We got preoccupied with programs, and stopped organizing, to be honest. When we stopped organizing, we got our butts kicked, I mean badly. We're nonpartisan and we never intervene to support one candidate versus another in an election. However, in the late nineties there was a group of candidates who decided to whack away at the programmatic initiatives that we had produced over seven years of work. One by one, the initiatives came under attack." In 2004 the new mayor set out to eliminate "our crown jewel job training strategy." Overnight the program went "from half a million bucks to zero."

This move woke PCIC organizers up. They realized that if attacks on their earlier victories continued to gather momentum, the organization would have trouble surviving, and the public of accountability that had been created would have to be reconstructed from the ground up. "For ten months we were knocking on doors," Frank said. "But that campaign didn't really build the organization. It got into mobilization and sort of hollowed us out."

Mobilizing around a particular issue or for a particular electoral outcome is more like "movement" organizing than the careful, sustained broad-based organizing to which IAF is generally committed. The trouble with movement organizing is that if and when the issue being focused on is resolved or the desired electoral outcome is achieved, there is nothing much left—no continuing structure of relationships and accountability.

Renee, in discussing her work in the Astrodome, had told me that movement organizing was necessary in that crisis situation, where the Katrina survivors had been uprooted from their neighborhoods and religious communities, and reduced to atomized individuals. Once the evacuees were out of the shelters, TMO immediately got back to what it does best, broad-based organizing involving individuals in relation to their institutions. Similarly, when Brod Bagert and I were driving through the ruins of the Lower Ninth Ward in New Orleans, he had enumerated the shortcomings of the organizing that had been tried there by groups other than IAF. Because it hadn't involved dues-paying institutions and because the organizers were getting burnt out, the work was unlikely, he thought, to result in a powerful organization, let alone one with the ability to hold public officials accountable over the long haul.

Frank, like Renee, had resorted to something like movement organizing in responding to a crisis, but in this case the goal was simply to resist a concerted attempt to destroy what PCIC had accomplished over the better part of a decade. Now PCIC would have to face the fact that it had been vulnerable to attack only because it had neglected to keep up with the one-on-one conversations and house meetings that help leaders earn the entitlement to represent others. Only when it can be demonstrated that leaders authentically speak on behalf of others is a citizens' organization able to influence and contest the decisions of elites. Exercising the right to free speech adds up to little when it isn't integrated with exercising the right to assemble peaceably, to organize.

"So the situation we're in right now," Frank said, is one where "we've really gotta reorganize. We've really got to rethink what we're doing and build new relationships through allies."

Ernie told me that his rule of thumb when working with COPS in San Antonio was that it was necessary to reorganize every two to three years. When he arrived in southern California in the late 1990s to assess the health of organizing efforts there, however, he discovered that IAF projects in the area had become so complacent that they would have to be radically "disorganized" and reconstituted before progress could be made. Organizers in Los Angeles, he said, had made the mistake of going after each new issue, without doubling back to reestablish institutional footing in the communities they were serving. Their grassroots democracy had become all grass, no roots.

Ernie invited Joe Rubio to join him at a meeting with leaders in

California. In the course of the discussion, it became evident that some leaders didn't know what a core team is. Others openly resisted the idea that house meetings were really necessary. To Joe and Ernie, this meant that these people weren't leaders at all. They had lost their authority to represent others, the very authority that is the fulcrum of power within any genuinely democratic citizens' organization. They had no followers beyond their immediate circles of friends. They spoke for no one in particular, and there was no one to hold them accountable for what they said when claiming to represent this or that institution. Their citizens' groups had become clubs for do-gooders.

Ernie and Joe were encouraging the California leaders to engage in *reflexive* critical evaluation. The practice is reflexive when a group is evaluating its own performance and capacities. Participants in the group are put in the position of having to evaluate themselves. The point of the evaluations is to foster change in the group's practices and relationships, as well as in the habits and capacities of members.

Of the IAF events I attended during my travels, nearly all of them that involved more than a handful of people concluded with a critical evaluation of some sort. On these occasions, everyone was encouraged to distinguish between what had gone well and what hadn't, and answers to these questions were explicitly linked to decisions about future conduct. Critical comments were often blunt. Participants needed to learn how to speak the plain truth about how things were going, but also how to do so without being cruel or trying to score points. And they needed to learn how to hear criticism of their own weaknesses.

In an important book entitled *Elusive Togetherness*, the sociologist Paul Lichterman studied a number of church and civic groups in a single town he called "Lakeburg."[64] All of the groups were well-intentioned. They had ideals, for the most part ideals Lichterman found admirable. Their members hoped to change the world, or at least their own community, for the better. This was one of the reasons that had moved these people to gather together in groups. But the groups had distinct cultural styles, different ways of relating to themselves and different ways of relating to others. In a word, they were *organized* differently: some happily, some not. Only one of the groups, Lichterman concluded, had had much of a positive impact outside its own circle. Interestingly, it was not the group that focused primarily on offering radical criticism of the broader society and the powers that be. Prophetic voice and utopian vision, he concluded, sometimes come at the expense of becoming related on positive terms to other groups similarly concerned with promoting change.

What was distinctive about the more powerful group was, first, that its activities were largely directed to *bridge building*. Members of the group did not merely build up relationships with one another. They were less concerned about maintaining a determinate ideological or corporate identity, over against other groups, than about entering into cooperative and productive relationships with other groups. They saw the formation of alliances as essential to improving their chances of actually changing things. When meeting with members of other groups, they made it their habit to listen to them and to take into account what they learned from them.

Second, because they valued both their bridge-building efforts and their capacity to learn from their interactions with others, their understanding of themselves as a group was *flexible* without being entirely *amorphous*. This means that the group's self-understanding changed over time in response to the group's interactions with other groups, including both the Haves and the Have-Nots of Lakeburg. Flexibility in the face of changing circumstances was itself integrated into the group's identity. It was a virtue in which the group took legitimate pride.

Finally, the group was *reflexive*. The group repeatedly took stock of what it had become, what it was trying to accomplish, and how things were going. It adjusted its behavior in light of what it discovered while taking stock of itself.

Lichterman's study serves as good reminder that successful civic practices need to be understood comparatively, in relation to practices that don't work as well. By spending a year in one town, examining groups that fell at all points along the spectrum from the self-defeating, to the relatively ineffective, to the admirably effective, Lichterman was able to define some of the variables that might explain different levels of success. A number of the IAF groups I have spent time with exhibit all of the traits Lichterman ascribes to the most successful of the groups he studied.

The case of IAF in southern California is one in which organizers exhibited too little flexibility and reflexivity to right their ship when their bridge building began to go badly. But the underlying problem was a failure to maintain relational activities within the umbrella organization and its constituent institutions. Because one-on-one conversations and house meetings had atrophied, authority relations within the group began to disintegrate. Leaders and organizers were no longer putting themselves in a position to hear anything they didn't want to hear from others within the organization. So even if they had wanted to be flexible and self-critical, they would have lacked the information they needed to take into account. The main effect of the diminished authority of the leadership was a lessening of power. Because leaders didn't really speak for anyone other than themselves, their capacity to bring about the changes they desired diminished.

In this case Ernie replaced the former organizers, and essentially started over from scratch in Los Angeles County. For a full year, the new organizers concentrated on individual meetings. According to Ernie, they conducted a total of roughly fifteen thousand one-on-one conversations during that period, identifying new people with the potential to lead, learning what those people were angry about, and determining which institutions of which kinds exercised power in the relevant communities. My visit to the area gave me much evidence of the newly invigorated citizens' groups there. But to understand such groups, it is important to keep in mind something that is not part of Lichterman's study. To be an IAF group is to be part of a network and thus to be held accountable not only by individuals participating in the group and by other persons, groups, and institutions with which the group interacts in its own community, but also by the representatives of other groups in the IAF network.

The organizer, in particular, is held accountable to other organizers affiliated with the network, with some organizers exercising supervisory authority over others. The network in Louisiana assigns Christine Stephens a supervisory role in relation to Jackie Jones and assigns Jackie a supervisory role in relation to Brod Bagert. (Since the time of my visit, Brod has moved on to Baton Rouge.) Ernie Cortés has the task of overseeing organizational work throughout the Southwest IAF network. The resulting supervisory structure places a significant degree of power in the hands of the regional supervisor. Without that power resting somewhere, there would have been no one with the capacity to decide, on behalf of the network, that Los Angeles IAF operations needed to be reconstituted.

In one sense, then, the regional supervisor stands at the top of a hierarchy. It is not the case, however, that power and authority flow mainly from top to bottom in IAF. To retain the powers of the chief supervisor, one needs to acquire the authority to exercise those powers. And this can be done only by earning the respect and thus the consent of most groups and organizers in the network, just as those groups and organizers must do in relation to their institutional constituents. Once organized, any unit in the network can, if it wishes, drop out of the network, either to strike out on its own or to join a different network. The cost of doing so is loss of the guidance and sharing of information that this particular network offers. New networks have sometimes been spawned here and there around the country when supervisors have failed to earn entitlement to lead. But the longevity and growth of IAF in the Southwest region suggest that Ernie continues to be recognized as a figure with genuine authority.

No one knows, of course, how the network will cope with his eventual departure. But it has clearly been Ernie's aim all along to build a structure of leadership that can survive the retirement, illness, or death of anyone involved in it. "The trouble with charismatic leaders," Ernie once told me, "is that they die."

✳ CHAPTER ELEVEN ✳

The Compelling Force of the Ideal

The rock, the terrain upon which we struggle, is . . . a terrain of ideas that, although man-made, exert the compelling force of the ideal, of the sublime.

—*Ralph Ellison*

AT THE END of my tour of the Rio Grande Valley, while Ernie Cortés and I were waiting in the airport before boarding our planes, I asked him what is least well understood about the network of citizens' groups he has helped found throughout the Southwest. "Three things," he said. "The first is the way we connect the experience of people with big ideas. The second is the way we function as a learning organization. The third is the fact that we don't depend on a single strong individual."

Charisma often counts heavily in social settings where individuals are grouped loosely around vaguely articulated ideals. The magnetism of the charismatic leader can serve, for a time, to counteract the tendency of a weakly structured group to disintegrate and disperse. But in the leader's absence, either the group does disintegrate, or it invents a more structured way of organizing itself by giving more definition to group membership, differentiating roles for leaders and rank-and-file members to play, forming people into individuals capable of playing those roles, and articulating norms for inspiring, guiding, and disciplining conduct.

Students who leave home for school, and enter the betwixt-and-between status of late adolescence, tend to be weakly grouped and somewhat lacking in precisely articulated shared norms. Then, according to the cultural anthropologist Mary Douglas, they often "rush to adopt symbols of non-differentiation and so accentuate the condition from which they suffer."[65] For this reason the student movements of the 1960s were not only inherently prone to disintegrate but predictably ineffective in achieving the social change they called for. Weak social formations of this kind are good at welcoming strangers, generating moments of intense communal amity, and providing release from excessive social pressure coming from parents or teachers. But weak formations are not equipped to defend freedom and equality against violent attack, to survive the death or corruption of leaders, or to develop and carry out a plan of institutional reform for society as a whole.

The unemployed and the working poor also tend to be weakly grouped, unless something like ethnic identification, religious affiliation, or gang membership picks up the slack. The unemployed are dispersed in the general population. They are not gathered anywhere in particular, so it is difficult to get them organized. People are constantly joining the ranks of the unemployed, while others—sometimes very few—are rejoining the workforce. The identity of being unemployed is therefore an inherently unstable one as a focal point for organizing, except in prolonged periods of depression. The working poor have trouble gathering for other reasons, the most important of which is that working long hours at multiple jobs while barely scraping together rent and food money leaves no time for anything else.[66] The working poor are often de facto noncitizens. Their citizenship rights are merely formal. To take the time to exercise those rights would be to sacrifice the essentials of life.

What, then, should people experiencing weakened social ties do? Douglas answered this question with characteristic bluntness: "They should react strongly against non-differentiation and seek to establish clear categories and distinctions which the oppressors would be forced to recognize. They should organize."[67] This is more easily recommended than done. The current stratification of our society imposes burdens on the least advantaged that make organizing appear difficult or impossible. One reason that groups like Valley Interfaith provide grounds for democratic hope is their success in overcoming this basic structural obstacle to reform.

The remedy Ernie Cortés proposes for weakly grouped people is also a matter of organizing and seeking to establish clear categories. The organizer cannot take for granted that the institutions, associations, and neighborhoods joining a citizens' organization already exhibit the forms of sociality essential to democratic citizenship. In many cases, perhaps most cases, the face-to-face interaction that transpires within them is minimal, fleeting, and initially incapable of generating solidarity or deliberation. People neither know one another's concerns, nor have many opportunities to tell their stories to others outside their immediate circle and then hear their own concerns and identities reflected back to them. Even those who are not merely "bowling alone" are rarely connected in ways that foster collective agency.[68]

The organizer's objective is not merely to found a new coalition, identify leaders for it, and give a little advice along the way. The broader objective is rather to help people transform their culture and habits democratically. Achieving democratic sociality at the level of the group goes hand in hand with achieving democratic individuality at the level of the person. Ernie and his colleagues often speak of citizens' organizations as public universities.

The IAF slogan that Ernie is most fond of repeating is known as the Iron Rule: "Never do for others what they can do for themselves." Many of the organizers and leaders I conversed with during my travels mentioned the Iron Rule to me in explaining their own increasing sense of empowerment. The mentor or coach needs to open up space in which individuals can act and grow and speak in their own voices. They must have a degree of self-trust if they are to behave as citizens and as members of a coalition. Among the many things the coalition will need from them is the courage to criticize its own leaders and, perhaps, the full range of skills and virtues required to step into the shoes of those leaders.

Individual citizens can acquire those skills and virtues only within groups of certain kinds. Individuality is a social achievement, not what a person already has before learning to relate to others in a culture of mutual accountability. The social setting needs to be one in which group membership, roles, and norms are defined with sufficient precision to permit the group to endure, to cultivate the excellences of the people involved in it, and to bring about beneficial change in the institutional arrangements and culture of the broader political community. The definitions must be somewhat precise, because otherwise authority, accountability, and purposive action within the group would remain indeterminate, and there would be no way of knowing the difference between those outside the group who are to be treated as allies and those who are to be treated as opponents. On this point, Cortés and Douglas are saying much the same thing.

But IAF groups also include a dimension that is not captured in Douglas's social theory—the dimension Lichterman has in mind when, echoing John Dewey and Jane Addams, he speaks of the need to combine flexibility and reflexivity with a degree of stability or continuity.[69] In democratic citizens' organizations, the relevant social categories and norms must not only be sufficiently precise to have determinate content, they must also remain sufficiently flexible to be responsive to changing circumstances. New institutional units join the organization, bringing new individuals along with them. Some individuals within the group earn the trust and deference of others, while other individuals sacrifice the entitlement to trust and deference they once had. Individuals outside the group, as a result of their behavior, earn or sacrifice entitlement to be counted as allies. All the while, the ends, means, role-definitions, and norms of the group are subjected to criticism by participants and adjusted on the basis of experience.

A genuinely democratic citizens' organization differs from a rigidly hierarchical institution in several ways. One variable is the degree to which members of all ranks are in a position to participate in these processes. Another is the degree to which individuals occupying lower ranks are in a position to influence and contest decisions made by individuals occupying higher ranks. Yet another is the ease with which adjustments in the relevant roles, relationships, and norms can be made. Excessive flexibility would be indistinguishable from not having roles and norms at all, which would destroy the group's capacity to endure and act. Flexibility in these matters must strike a mean between too little and too much. Too little would produce a rigid hierarchy relatively unresponsive to change. Too much would turn the group into a relatively undifferentiated mass.

The debate over democracy goes awry when people assume that society must choose between a perfectly rigid hierarchical system and a perfectly flexible culture of freedom, the former committed to unchanging absolutes, the latter prepared to tolerate anything but intolerance. No actual society exhibits either of these patterns. There is no need to choose between them.

We misunderstand the most rigid actual hierarchies when we suppose that processes of bottom-up challenge, critical reflection, and redefinition of norms and roles do not transpire within them at all. Take Roman Catholicism as an example. The church's hierarchy nowadays often presents itself, despite the Second Vatican Council, as a timeless, top-down structure of authority centered in the indefeasible authority of the Bishop of Rome. In fact, however, the church encompasses enormous discord. Especially in the United States, where accusations of pedophilia against clergy recently brought suspicion of clerical authority to the boiling point, the reassertion of such authority tells us more about what Rome wants ecclesial authority relations to be than about who is actually entitled to deference or about who is actually deferring to whom on matters of faith and morals. Rarely are hierarchical institutions or societies as rigid as their traditionalist spokespersons and antitraditionalist critics make them out to be.

We caricature "democratic" society, however, when we view the people as an undifferentiated mass. And for similar reasons, we misunderstand democratic citizens' groups when we place them in the same category as communes and anarchist cells. To get beyond these confusions, we will need to look more closely at what has been meant at one time or another by *democracy*. Let us consider for a moment two very different ways in which the term has been used.

In ancient Greece democracy denoted direct rule by the commons, the *demos*. When the American founding fathers denigrated what they called democracy as an inherently unstable form of rule likely to permit the majority to violate the rights of minorities, they had this classical conception of democracy in mind and imagined the *demos* as an undifferentiated mass of ordinary people largely unprepared for the responsibilities of civic life. This is also the sense of democracy that modern social critics, of either a traditionalist or Nietzschean bent, tend to have in mind when they denounce democratic culture as a leveler of distinctions and as an enemy of the quest for excellence. This is not, however, the sense of democracy being elucidated in this book, for we have seen that grassroots democratic organizations are endeavoring to institute distinctions, to build up a structure of earned authority, and to cultivate excellence. Where, then, does this conception of democracy come from and what does it amount to?

When Lincoln defined democracy by contrasting it to the master-slave relationship, he took for granted that the type of polity he was dealing with, and hoped to reform, was a republic. The first modern republics were supposed to protect and cultivate a people's liberty. Achieving and maintaining liberty—in the quite precise sense of security against domination—were chief objectives of government. What made the most productive reform movements of Lincoln's day democratic, in his eyes, was that they sought to redefine citizenship, the primary locus of responsibility for political arrangements, in terms that did not entail an arbitrary exclusion. Liberty and justice were thus to become liberty and justice *for all*.

Here we have a cluster of concepts, each of which is sufficiently precise to do the socially significant work of ruling out various things. The democratic turn of Lincoln's time did not abandon those concepts. Rather, it changed how they are to be applied and what their application is now taken to imply. Conceptual change emerged out of an extended argument over how we are going to live, an argument in which reasons were exchanged, but also one in which people were struggling for authority and power, and deploying coercive force. The process resulted in more determinate conceptions of what liberty, justice, domination, and democracy are.

Far from introducing a more permissive culture, which is to say a weakening of normative constraints, the movements Lincoln had in mind when he spoke of democracy sought to expand the citizenry's conception of what a self-respecting republic needs to prohibit *absolutely* as incompatible with liberty and justice rightly understood. One can see these concepts becoming more precise and more demanding in Lincoln's own speeches and writings from one year to the next, but a similar process was transpiring on a grand cultural scale and came to the point of crisis around the time Lincoln said that a house divided against itself on matters of such great import could not long survive.

The type of polity being proposed by the antislavery reformers was a democratic republic, a republic modified democratically. It was meant to retain the basic political roles found in republics—citizen, executive, legislator, and so on—while now excluding from society anything morally analogous to the roles of master and slave. In the received ethico-political tradition, the roles of citizen and slave had been defined in relation to each other. A citizen was someone with the acknowledged authority to exercise certain responsibilities in the political sphere. A slave was someone utterly deprived of acknowledged authority, but also someone expected to acknowledge the authority of citizens and masters. Taking the roles of master and slave out of the social system, while leaving the role of citizen in place, therefore required a rethinking of what it is to be a citizen, as well as who is to be counted as a citizen. To be a citizen was no longer to possess the *authority* to stand on someone else's back.

The reforms also required revision of the basic ideal of liberty, specifically in who is taken to be its rightful claimants. The citizens of a republic were those whose liberty the polity was meant to establish and maintain; they were liberty's rightful claimants. Everyone but a masochist takes domination to be a horrendous thing to suffer under, which is why most of human history can be interpreted as a struggle to avoid it. The most common strategy for avoiding it is trying to get the upper hand: to dominate others so as to avoid being dominated. Any regime of domination, however, contains the seeds of its own destruction, because the dominated always have a reason for overthrowing the existing order. This reason is, moreover, of the strongest sort, namely that being dominated is horrendous. To seek liberty for one's own group is to seek security against domination for them. But the strategy of domination denies to others the liberty one seeks for one's own group. It thus perpetrates on others something it takes to be horrendous.

The argument against British domination of its American colonies had been that domination is not merely horrendous to experience, from the receiving end, so to speak, but also unjust to perpetrate. The reason given for deeming domination unjust was that a relationship of domination leaves one person or group in a position to exercise power *arbitrarily* over others. One cannot consistently denounce domination as arbitrary while arbitrarily excluding some human beings living in a republic from the basic role of citizenship.

The landmark conflicts in democratic republics since Lincoln's time tend to be about which relationships sufficiently resemble the master-slave relationship to be ruled out absolutely. And this question often comes down to whether the power being exercised in the contested relationship is rightly regarded as arbitrary.[70]

The classical ideal of a republic expressed the reasonable desire to institute a regime within which some people, at least, could enjoy relationships with one another that were freed from the arbitrariness inherent in domination. The compelling force of this ideal, the ethical impetus behind democratic reform over the last two centuries or so, has been increasingly widespread recognition of the arbitrariness of maintaining a polity of free citizens by dominating noncitizens at home and abroad. Republics brought before the moral imagination of humankind actual examples of citizens relating to one another by attributing to one another the authority to take equal responsibility for the political order. If such relationships exist, they must be possible. And if they are possible, then what, besides the arbitrary use of coercive force and the arbitrarily constricted application of the concepts of *citizen* and *liberty*, can keep the zone of human freedom and mutual recognition from being radically expanded?

The dominant have profited from confusion over what liberty is. Liberty in the sense of security against domination is distinct from liberty in the debased sense of an absence of constraint, interference, or influence. Lincoln, in contrast, understood that the sort of freedom being sought by the critics of chattel slavery was freedom from domination and that this sort of freedom could be achieved only if people were made secure against being enslaved by others and otherwise dominated by them. Security against slavery, or against any other form of domination, can typically be had only for those living under a society of laws, framed and administered justly, and backed up by the just and prudent use of coercive force. A society of that sort is not laissez faire about domination. It is committed, by its basic ideals, to *rule out* domination as a matter of principle and, where prudent, also as a matter of law. That means giving an increasingly determinate sense to both domination and liberty. The big question that such a society places before itself when it declares slavery a paradigmatic instance of the *horrendously unjust* is what else, besides slavery, counts as domination.

The struggle to achieve a democratic republic is, first, an attempt to make the notion of domination tolerably *determinate* without reinstituting the arbitrariness that makes domination objectionable and, second, an attempt to make this notion *concrete* in a constitution and legal system that achieve actual security against the arbitrary exercise of power. Hammering out the concepts and giving shape to the corresponding arrangements are both required for the resulting societal formation to achieve *substantial freedom*.[71] Neither of these things is possible in an undifferentiated society, where individuals are absorbed into the mass, or in an atomized society, where individuals are isolates, barely connected to one another.

Complete freedom from constraint by laws or norms is not substantial freedom. A society marked by freedom *from constraint* is in practice a society in which the strong are free *to dominate others* without fear of legal interference, effectively organized opposition from ordinary people, or even, for that matter, a guilty conscience. For the dominated, perfect freedom from constraint per se, as opposed to freedom from *unjust* constraint, is having nothing left to lose. In ethical discussion, freedom from constraint by norms would leave the dominated without moral principles to apply to the arbitrary behavior of the strong. (What business of yours is it that the captains of industry are moving their factories to some distant place or polluting your stream? Are they not free to do as they please with what belongs to them?) In the legal sphere, freedom from constraint leaves the dominated unprotected because it leaves the dominant in a position to act with impunity. In the associational context, it leaves ordinary people without the sort of group ties and differentiated roles that could generate counterpower over against the power of elites.

Substantial freedom for ordinary citizens can be found only in a society bound by, and capable of enforcing, determinate legal and ethical norms prohibiting relationships of domination. Anything less than that provides insufficient security against domination. This, by the way, is why the debates over torture and civil liberties after 9/11 are of great moment. The domestic opponents of liberty seek to eviscerate the relevant prohibitions, either by contracting the class of actions to be ruled out or by introducing exception clauses into the prohibitions to keep them from constraining the very people they were meant to constrain.

Substantial freedom for ordinary people can be achieved only in a justly administered system of just laws. Without such laws, there can be no security against such horrors as murder, rape, and domination. To strive for the creation and proper administration of such laws, ordinary people need to form groups that are capable of generating power. The members of such groups must themselves have differentiated roles to play, be willing to be governed by norms, and be willing to judge the conduct and character of others in light of those norms. The concepts of *leaders, members, allies*, and *opponents* will have to be used with some precision, as will such concepts as *domination* and *security against domination*. The whole effort is bound to fail so long as people remain loosely organized around extremely vague notions of freedom and equality.

Some people view legal constraint as inherently evil. They treat it either as a regrettable necessity, or as something one should try to dispense with altogether.[72] What attracts people to these positions in the contemporary world is that the nation-state, as it now exists, does not seem capable of framing, administering, or enforcing laws justly. It is true that the nation-state is not capable of doing these things when citizens fail to cultivate and exercise power of their own. But what if many more citizens were to cultivate and exercise power in a democratic spirit?

In any event, neither of the two antigovernmental positions just mentioned faces up to the consequences that would follow if its proposals were taken literally and accepted. When the state's capacity to tax the rich and to regulate the conduct of the economically powerful is weakened beyond a certain point, ordinary people become less secure against economic domination. This is the main lesson of the period that began with Ronald Reagan's election as president and ended—or rather, *should have* ended—with the financial crisis of 2008. We now know that a state small enough to be drowned in a bathtub is also small enough to permit elites to exercise power arbitrarily over others. If we went ahead and drowned the nation-state, in the hope that much smaller political units would serve our purposes better, what would constrain the behavior of the economically powerful in the new situation? It is wishful thinking to suppose that there will be no developers, bankers, and billionaires looking for opportunities to exploit, or that all of the relatively small polities that crop up around the corpse of the nation-state will be havens of inclusive nondomination.

Would-be masters must be constrained from behaving as they please. It will take power to do the constraining—pedagogical power in the first instance, but coercive force if necessary. Pedagogical power, including the power to inculcate commitment to norms, is something that all societies exercise over their members in the context of acculturation. If the norms empower individuals to criticize and oppose domination and the process of acculturation is carried out appropriately, the exercise of pedagogical power need not itself qualify as an instance of domination. Similarly, the use of coercive force to influence the behavior of people who would otherwise be disposed to violate the norms of inclusive nondomination need not violate those norms. On the other hand, if these forms of power are not themselves constrained by constitutional and legal prohibitions and by the counterpower of a vigilant and active citizenry, they too will be exercised arbitrarily over people. This is also something we know.

Some of my students hope that capital and empire will collapse under their own weight and usher in a new era of decentralized community, free of the need for rule and coercion. Even if this were, by some miracle, to happen, there would immediately be new elites to rein in. There would be new powerful actors seeking a dominant position in the grand scheme of things, new brigands, pirates, slave traders, tyrants, and megacompanies plotting to take over as much of the globe as they can master. The powers required to teach and enforce norms would still need to be exercised in those circumstances. Those powers will always need to be exercised—and need to be constrained by criticism and counterpower—as long as human beings are around to create and apply norms.

When Lincoln defined democracy as he did, he was using the term as shorthand for a "democratic republic." He was not proposing direct rule by the undifferentiated mass of ordinary people. Ralph Waldo Emerson's expression for the undifferentiated *demos* was *the herd*, a term of abuse Friedrich Nietzsche later picked up from him. Emerson saw the herd as a powerful and worrisome engine of social conformity. To be absorbed into the herd, or even into a small commune such as Brook Farm, he taught, is to lose one's individuality—that is, to lose one's capacity for critical resistance and for membership in effective coalitions.

The citizens of a genuinely democratic republic would not, however, be an undifferentiated mass. They would occupy roles in a social formation that includes other differentiated roles, and participate in practices in which authority can be won and challenged and in which norms can be adjusted in light of experience while retaining their capacity to rule some things in and others out. In such practices, capital and armed force, rather than having their own way, must contend with the counterpower of citizens and be constrained by the rule of law. The body of citizens ideally comprises differentiated, but related, individuals, capable of taking responsibility for themselves and of holding others responsible. When functioning democratically, the citizenry is not a herd.

Democracy, in the sense I am commending, opens up space for minority voices because it is committed both to freedom as non-domination and the avoidance of arbitrary exclusion. Neither of these things can be achieved, according to the tradition of grassroots democracy, unless a lot of ordinary people *get organized* and actually *hold officials accountable*. These are things that require action, the accumulation and exertion of power, and a cultivation of the capacity to act. The ethical substance of grassroots democracy is to be found in the socially differentiated practical engagements where, as Emerson put it, the spirit or "genius" of democracy is "transformed into practical power."[73]

✳ CHAPTER TWELVE ✳

Face-to-Face Meetings

THE GREAT DEMOCRATIC reform movements have all exhibited commitment to the basic roles, ideals, and institutional formations of a democratic republic. There is also a good deal of continuity in this tradition at the level of organizational practice. We distort the ideals when we disconnect them from the practices in which they are embodied. Many of the activities and structures that can be found today in groups like Jeremiah and Valley Interfaith have antecedents in a tradition of reform that reaches back into the middle of the nineteenth century.

Lincoln couldn't have emancipated the slaves had there not been a shift in American abolitionism, around the year 1830, from an elite movement centered around Philadelphia lawyers to a grassroots organizing effort that encompassed nearly all of New England. "Without the organization of abolitionists into societies," wrote William Lloyd Garrison in 1832, "the cause will be lost." By societies, he meant citizens' organizations like the New England Antislavery Society. What in those days was called "rambling about" is now called the neighborhood walk. Abolitionist organizers from 1830 through the 1850s followed paths leading from door to door first trod by preachers and traveling salesmen.[74]

The resulting face-to-face meetings are now called one-on-ones or relational meetings, and they were essential components of each of the major democratic reform movements in U.S. history. Feminist organizers like Alice Paul, Lucy Burns, Margaret Hinchey, and Rose Winslow borrowed tactics from the labor movement and developed increasingly extensive networks in the early decades of the twentieth century. Their "parlor meetings" were precursors of what IAF groups call house meetings.[75] Three of the most renowned civil rights activists of Freedom Summer in 1964 in Mississippi—Ella Baker, Bob Moses, and Hollis Watkins—were all virtuosi of face-to-face organizing and insisted that without interactions of this kind there could be no such thing as change from the bottom up. The criticisms that Baker and Septima Clark then offered of reliance on top-down, charismatic leadership are similar to what Ernesto Cortés now says on the same topic.[76]

Why insist on the importance of face-to-face interaction? One answer, already mentioned at the end of chapter 3, developed in chapter 8, and reinforced by the testimony of Ernie Cortés and Frank Pierson in chapter 10, is that when organizers take shortcuts and rely too much on more distant forms of interaction, the organizations become less powerful. They become less powerful because the people who claim to lead them have done less to earn the entitlement to represent those on whose behalf they speak. This is a weakness that governmental and corporate officials sense at once, and exploit to their advantage. Ernie calls the power that resides in a citizens' organization *relational* power, by which he means power that depends on the *quality* of the interactions among people, rather than on things like guns and money. Face-to-face interaction matters in large part because it is the main context in which representative authority in a democratic organization can be earned.

The history of the great democratic reform movements supports this explanation. Before 1830, abolitionism was an elite movement with little internal structure and little power. After 1830, when face-to-face interaction gradually became its organizational basis, abolitionism acquired considerable strength. An example exhibiting the opposite trajectory would be the transition from the work of Baker, Moses, Watkins, and their associates in the early 1960s to the media-oriented leadership style of Stokely Carmichael when he became chairman of the Student Nonviolent Coordinating Committee in 1966, at which point face-to-face organizing in the South had already drastically declined.[77]

Contemporary IAF shares the Baker-Moses-Watkins commitment to face-to-face organizing, but as we have seen, it distinguishes itself from movement organizing in two respects. First, movements tend to be centered on single issues. The civil rights organizers knew that Jim Crow segregation was the main issue they were dealing with. Their objective was to get people mobilized to join the struggle.[78] Second, what movements seek, fundamentally, is resolution of the main issue. They might not win everything they are fighting for, but there comes a time when the fight ends, the organizing stops, and the formerly mobilized forces get on with life. With a bang or a whimper, the movement ends. IAF groups, in contrast, are meant to deal in some way with whatever concerns emerge in face-to-face discussion. Not all concerns can be addressed at once and some are viewed as unwinnable for the time being and go on the back burner. But many are addressed over time. The citizens' organization is designed to last as long as there is a need to influence and contest decisions about what the public arrangements and policies are going to be—that is, for the long haul.

The cases of slavery, patriarchy, and Jim Crow show that single-issue movements have often made extremely important contributions to the struggle against domination. In our day, IAF is no substitute for organizations devoted exclusively to the issues of pollution, unequal pay for women, homophobia, militarism, or torture. But IAF has its own role to play in our political culture and its own way of developing the practices of face-to-face political interaction.

It is one thing to be approached by an organizer who already knows what *the issue* is, another to be approached by someone who ultimately wants to discover what *your concerns* are. When I was drafting this chapter, a representative of an environmentalist group came to my door. I had received many such visits before from representatives of the same group, always around dinnertime. The first time I listened patiently to the organizer's carefully scripted description of the issue the group was working on at the moment. There was a bill before the state legislature that needed to be passed. It was important for this and that reason. He was recruiting me to sign the petition, give my e-mail address, and make a donation. I did all of these things. Shortly thereafter, my e-mail inbox began to fill up with similar pleas. Every few months there would be another visit to my door. I would hear about another issue and receive another plea for a signature and a donation.

Even though I considered it a good thing to have this group putting pressure on the legislature and trusted its leaders to select issues and tactics wisely, I didn't want to keep on repeating this particular sort of ritual on my front porch. Never had he or his coworkers asked me what was going on environmentally in my town or county, or why I was interested in their group. They already knew my role, just as they knew the issues. I was tired of being treated as nothing more than a source of signatures and donations. So I cut off the conversation. As he walked away, he snidely said, "I'm sorry I wasn't more persuasive," but he was actually sorry that I wasn't good enough to be persuaded by his carefully packaged presentation.

Ella Baker and Bob Moses did a much better job of connecting with people than that, but they were mobilizing people around a cause that had already taken shape. The initial one-on-one conversation in broad-based organizing tends by comparison to be open-ended and exploratory. What most people have, at first, is a jumble of concerns and emotions. They express their concerns and emotions in stories about what is going on around them. One of the organizer's primary goals is to get people telling those stories. Organizers from the environmentalist group never asked me for my story. They wanted to give me theirs.

Rarely do the stories initially elicited by the broad-based organizer explicitly employ concepts like injustice or domination, or identify something explicitly as *an issue*, but they do often reveal underlying passions like grief and anger. Something horrendous has happened. There is a story to be told about it. The person telling that story is upset. A young person down the street was shot and killed. The children have to walk by prostitutes and drug dealers on their way to school. The gangs are taking over. When it rains, the outhouses overflow. The restrooms in the schools are disgusting. A child was run over at the corner that has no streetlight. A house is floating in the middle of the street. The hospital is hiring nurses from abroad while the locals go jobless. A Katrina survivor in the Astrodome can't locate his mother, and now his cell phone is being cut off.

The story expresses the passions. By listening empathetically, a good organizer experiences in his or her imagination what the story describes. There is, however, something else going on in the face-to-face encounter because the passion of the story is not only in the story being told, but also in the face, hands, posture, and voice of the one speaking. If I hear the story repeated, in the absence of the storyteller, the story itself has to carry the entire communicative burden. The presence of the storyteller would be worth a thousand words.

For the most part, we experience the emotions of other people directly by being in their presence. The philosopher Ludwig Wittgenstein said that we *see* emotion:

> We do not see facial contortions and *make the inference* that he is feeling joy, grief, boredom. We describe a face immediately as sad, radiant, bored, even when we are unable to give any other descriptions of the features.—Grief, one would like to say, is personified in the face. This is essential to what we call "emotion."[79]

Wittgenstein arrived at this conclusion by reflecting on how we actually use the language of emotion. Independently, but around the same time, philosopher Maurice Merleau-Ponty referred to *living in* "the facial expressions of the other, as I feel him living in mine."[80] There is now plentiful empirical confirmation of what these philosophers were saying. We do experience the emotions of other people in the way Wittgenstein described as immediate, and this happens above all, but not exclusively, when they are physically present to us.[81]

Moreover, we now have a reasonably clear conception of how emotions travel from one person to another in the face-to-face encounter. In the early 1990s, scientists studying the brains of human beings and other primates discovered mirror neurons. These are cells in the brain dedicated in part to the tasks of *taking in* and *partaking in* the emotions and actions of other people. They are fundamental components of the neurological equipment that *connects us directly* with the emotions of other people who are present to us. It is as if the emotional energy were *conveyed* from the other person's body to mine. I *incorporate* a neurological model of the other person's emotion. I take it into my body. Our neurological systems are, so to speak, *plugged into* each other when we are meeting face to face.

The italicized words in the previous paragraph are metaphors designed to highlight what neuroscience is telling us about face-to-face interaction. In the middle of the twentieth century, mainstream philosophy and empirical psychology were both still caught in a picture according to which the emotions of other people are not accessible to us except as a result of our intellectual activity of trying to explain what those people are doing and saying. This picture was itself elaborated in metaphors: emotions are *inside of us*, directly accessible only to the person having them. When we are face to face with other people there is always a *gap* between our *inner lives* and theirs, which is bridged, if at all, by our attempts to infer what is going on within them on the basis of their overt behavior. Wittgenstein and Merleau-Ponty were trying to break free from this picture when it was still widely accepted. The discovery of mirror neurons has led most scientists studying the human brain to conclude that these two philosophers were on the right track.

When the person before me is grieving or angry or horrified by something, and my neurological uptake is functioning properly, my perception of the other person's emotional state activates the same cells and circuits in my brain that are activated when I am grieving, angry, or horrified. This does not necessarily mean that I am favorably disposed toward the other person. Neither does it mean that my response to the other person has nothing to do with my previous acquisition of a particular culture's emotion concepts. But it does mean that face-to-face contact with the members of a community gives an organizer a kind of access to their emotions that he or she would not be able to get by reading a text message or the results of a survey. Meanwhile, the community members are gaining the same kind of access to the organizer's attitudes. If the organizer exhibits confidence, compassion, anger, and hope, the person being addressed can *take these attitudes in* by modeling them neurologically—at least in the case of attitudes that have some analogue in the person's prior experience.

The initial one-on-one meeting already begins a process of establishing emotional connection between organizer and community members, as well as the more obvious inferential process of trying to figure one another out on the basis of observation. The house meeting retains the emotional contact of face-to-face interaction and the element of storytelling, but because it includes as many as a dozen people, it works somewhat differently and fulfills additional functions.

Unless the circumstances are unusual, as in the Astrodome after Katrina, organizers assemble house meetings only when they have already conversed with many people in the community one-on-one. Those preliminary conversations yield a great deal of information about which concerns are widely shared by members of the community and about which people in the community show leadership potential. Few people attending their first house meeting know such things. Some of them, however, will find themselves tapped, perhaps for the first time in their lives, to lead a group discussion. They are given a responsibility of leadership and the presumptive authority to fulfill that responsibility.

It might be that the same stories told in the one-on-ones will make their appearance again here. But now there are more people listening, so the emotional resonance of the stories can be greatly amplified. One person, demonstrating the courage to expose his or her concerns and emotions to others, begins to acquire a sense of selfhood in their eyes.[82] This in turn is reflected back to the one speaking. The story visibly moves others in the group, who then take a similar risk of self-exposure.

Each of the stories comes from someone in particular, but as the session unfolds, one story and then another will echo a story that came earlier. Initially there might seem to be a series of disconnected individuals, relating stories about particular events they have experienced. But, with any luck, two sorts of connections will begin to take shape: emotional connections among the individuals who are mirroring one another's concerns, but also thematic connections among the stories, a number of which now appear to be about something more than the particulars referred to explicitly in them.[83]

Ideally, something is already happening to the people participating. It might be that Carmen, by engaging in this sort of discussion for the first time, begins to have a sense of herself as a public being, not merely identified with her roles as daughter, mother, and wife. When she speaks, others listen. They are moved by what she says. She is moved by what they say. Someone tells her that she speaks powerfully and wisely. Someone else tells her that she is courageous when she stands up for her family. She has told a story from her own experience, and exposed her concerns and emotions to them. Now she is receiving an image of herself back from them. Over time, people outside her circle of family members and personal friends not only defer to her judgment, but explain to her what, in their eyes, her story and identity are.

Meanwhile, in somewhat different ways, a process of mutual recognition is transforming other participants. Lupita is not Carmen. She has a different story to tell, and others in the meeting push her to tell it. She will never be the leader Carmen is, but she is now a person these others treat as having the authority and responsibility to speak and act within the group, and she is someone for whom they are increasingly prepared to make sacrifices. Lupita is one of us. Lupita is also Lupita. To be incorporated into this group, if all goes well, is not to be absorbed into an undifferentiated mass. It is to acquire self-trust as one concerned citizen among others.

Some convergence of concerns within the group is likely to become increasingly evident. It might be something as obvious as this: one story about an outhouse that overflows when the rains come leads to several other stories along the same lines, and someone remarks on the common subject matter. The outhouses are a problem throughout the colonia, not only in Lupita's yard or block. Each teller of those stories might have entered the meeting thinking of this matter as a personal concern, but it is starting to look like a community's concern.

Someone in the meeting might tie together several stories in a somewhat more abstract way. The school principal, the sheriff, and the Anglo businessmen on Main Street are all treating us as if we didn't belong here. The developers are taking the city away from us. The Red Cross is not treating us as human beings. If the discussion gets too abstract, an organizer might need to bring it down to earth a bit. Brod Bagert told me that there are a lot of people in the churches who want to talk endlessly about justice, but have trouble responding to particular problems and the individuals who have them. "We aren't here to talk about justice," Brod says. "We're here to talk about what the school system is doing to Mrs. Toussaint's disabled daughter."[84] A remark like this is meant to steer the discussion back into a zone that is neither completely abstract, and thus inattentive to the particularity of the stories being told, nor so focused on the distinctness of each story that no connections among stories can be made explicit.

Without some conception of how multiple stories hang together, the citizens' organization cannot identify issues to be researched and considered as possible causes of action. An *issue* is a *contestable matter of concern*, on which the group might consider *taking action*. An ideal issue, from the vantage of political action, is not only sufficiently well defined to be contestable, but also important and winnable. A group's ability to think in terms of issues is itself often an achievement, a result of extensive discussion.

When I visited Houston, Renee Wizig-Barrios had gathered together about a hundred parents and teachers associated with various schools in the greater Houston area. After a few leaders and organizers welcomed the group and told some stories about public education, we broke into house meetings of about ten people each. The leaders of the meetings I attended started things off by asking the people participating to say something about who they are and what they want to see changed in the schools. These questions elicited stories. The storytellers described having been born in a particular place, growing up under certain conditions, and moving to the community they now live in. They also referred to turning points in their lives, such as the death of a parent, the birth of a child, the loss of a job, an illness they have suffered, or a child's disability. Most of the stories then homed in on some event that the storyteller found upsetting and concluded by declaring this the kind of thing he or she wants changed.

Stories presented in this way are examples in search of something to exemplify. The kind to which the case belongs will eventually need to be specified, and this will involve hammering out a concept. The concept groups together cases that are similar in certain respects felt to be important. To have such a concept in hand, as a group, is to have some shared expectations concerning the cases to which the concept should be applied and concerning what follows from rightly applying the concept to something.

In the house meetings at Wicker Elementary School in New Orleans, many people were concerned about truancy, but then eventually zeroed in on the topic of *disgusting restrooms in the schools*. This concept already gave some definition to the group's thinking. The concept of a disgusting restroom applies only to restrooms, not to classrooms or playgrounds. As the discussion continued, the group needed to specify more precisely what it was about the restrooms that they wanted changed. "What do you mean by 'disgusting'?" someone must have asked. To classify a restroom as disgusting implicitly authorizes an inference to the conclusion that it ought to be changed, but which restrooms are we talking about here, and what about them needs to be different?

Effective house meetings move toward increasingly precise application of value-laden concepts. They also tend to shift attention toward what *ought* to be changed and away from what *I am upset about* and what *I want*. If I say that something is *bad* or *wrong*, that it *needs* to be changed, or that it *ought* to be changed, I have put forward an evaluative claim. What I have expressed isn't merely a want or desire, but a commitment *that* such-and-such is so. In expressing the commitment, I authorize you and others to adopt it, and create room for the possibility that you will reject it. If I accept the commitment and you reject it, we are in conflict. Evaluative claims can be incompatible with each other. They can also have implications. Claims function as reasons for other claims and reasons can be requested for them in turn. To give a reason for accepting a claim is to make another claim.

The shift, in the course of a house meeting, from expressions of desire to exchanges of evaluative claims assumes that everyone in the discussion has the authority to propose, reject, and challenge claims as they see fit and to request reasons from others for the claims they have put forward. "What do you mean by that?" is one question that gets posed in response to a claim. Another is, "Why should I believe that?" Yet another is, "So what?" In other words, "What follows if you're right?" The house meeting, like all subsequent forms of democratic interaction the group will undertake, is a realm of claims, questions, and reasons that individuals direct to one another in the second-person, as well as a realm of concerns and passions expressed in the first-person.[85]

One of the most important features of a house meeting is that it gathers together people who are at least somewhat upset about how things are going and interested in seeing them changed. It is not merely a random collection of individuals. The discussion is tilted in the direction of change, and it is insulated from both the gaze and direct influence of people who seek to resist change. In the Houston sessions I attended, there were no school superintendents or union presidents trying to intimidate others from expressing concerns or trying to determine in advance how certain concepts would be used. By treating one another as authorized to express concerns, apply concepts, and make inferences, participants were jointly exercising authority over their own feelings, thoughts, and words.

All of the great reform movements have gone through phases in which somewhat insulated face-to-face discussion within small groups was required to establish a rectified way of speaking and thinking about the matters being contested. The feminist consciousness-raising groups of the 1960s and 1970s are a good example of a kind of insulated discussion that has given the agents of social change the emotional reinforcement and conceptual agility required to break with the status quo.[86] House meetings like the ones I sat in on in Houston are of interest in part because of what they have in common with groups that have insulated themselves in this way in the past. But house meetings are also of interest because of their distinctive features.

Within groups like Jeremiah and TMO, house meetings belong to the endlessly repeating cycle of organizing, acting, reflecting, and reorganizing described in chapter 10. This has three important implications that contribute to the distinctiveness of broad-based organizing. First, the more insulated phases of small-group discussion are relatively limited in duration. Second, they recur as the encompassing citizens' organization moves through the organizing cycle and seeks to renew itself by engaging once again, from time to time, in face-to-face interactions of this sort. Third, house meetings are constituted in a way that orients the group toward public action. They therefore have the benefits of the self-enclosed sect without the drawbacks. The concerns, proposals, and reasons that emerge within the small group will soon have to go public. When this happens, the concerns, counterproposals, and reasons of *other* groups will have to be responded to.

Issues, I have said, are contestable matters of concern. The point of framing an issue, instead of leaving a concern only vaguely defined, is to prepare to take public action on it, in the understanding that the group will be contesting powerful and influential people who will want to block what the group proposes. In an initial house meeting, what it would be like for the citizens' organization *to take action* might not yet be in view. It is when an issue has been defined, a proposal for dealing with it has been formulated, and a strategy for implementing the proposal has been sketched out that the group must begin to anticipate the demands for reasons that will be forthcoming from people outside the group in the broader community. This is when the more abstract vocabulary of the democratic tradition enters more fully, and appropriately, into the discussion. Issues must be framed, and proposals must be defended. The language of framing and defending is more abstract than what one hears in the first round of house meetings. There will still be a role for stories at these later stages, but it will mainly be to illustrate the concerns that led the group to select a particular issue and fight for a particular possible solution to it. The stories are now serving primarily as examples of something, rather than as vehicles of self-exposure. They exemplify the kind of thing the group proposes to change, but at this later point in the process, the substance of that kind can itself be articulated explicitly.

The upward flow of concern and the transformation of concerns into evaluative claims can be interrupted, as we have seen, whenever one-on-ones and house meetings are neglected. The process can also be corrupted when organizers convey the wrong attitudes to citizens in the meetings they do hold. If organizers or leaders come across as manipulative, they are unlikely to succeed in eliciting the concerns of participants and winning their trust. Manipulation of the process treats them as instruments of the organizer's will, and thus tends to involve the imposition of the organizer's concerns, claims, and proposals on the community he or she is trying to organize. Most people have a nose for manipulation in the context of face-to-face interaction. If they sense that the organizer is manipulating them, they are likely to withhold their trust, in which case the organization will rapidly lose power. Furthermore, if the organization's official definition of an issue and its proposals for addressing it do not jibe with what actually transpired in the house meetings, the leadership's authority will rapidly diminish for that reason.

The quality of the emotional connections being forged and the intent of the organizer are therefore essential to the process of earning the authority to lead. Good democratic organizers tend to exhibit a number of distinct traits: confidence, hopefulness, practical wisdom, tempered anger, a commitment to justice, the courage to persevere in a tough fight, the willingness and ability to listen to what others are saying, an aptitude to care noninstrumentally about the people being listened to, and a capacity to mirror, empathize with, and help conceptualize the concerns that ordinary citizens are expressing. When Alinsky wrote that the ideal organizer "suffers with" the people and "becomes angry at the injustice" their stories personify, he was calling attention to the role of empathy.[87] I am suggesting that empathy is one of several key factors.

I want now to turn for a moment to two conditions in which a person's neurological uptake does not function optimally. Both of them are interesting, for the purposes of the present analysis, because of what they help us see about human interaction not affected by such conditions. The first is called Moebius syndrome, which prevents individuals from moving their faces. Because their faces do not express emotion, people with this syndrome do not already possess engrained templates, so to speak, of the neurological pattern underlying the facial expression of grief or anger. As a result, when they are face to face with a grieving or angry person, they do not simulate the other person's emotional state in their own brains. "This inability," writes neuroscientist Marco Iacoboni, "breaks down any form of emotional interaction and makes impossible a deeply felt understanding of others' emotions."[88]

The second condition is autism, which appears to affect the mirroring function of the brain more directly. The autistic child can infer that another human being has certain emotions and intentions, and is therefore likely to behave in a certain way. But the noninferential connections with other people's emotions and intentions are missing or drastically diminished. Autistic children do not suffer with another person, become angry at the injustices described in that person's story, or in general, model the emotional states of another person in their own brains. Something about their mirror neurons—or about the circuits connecting those neurons with the insula and the limbic system, or about some more complicated brain function that relies on those circuits—causes these kids to interact with others in a relatively abstract way.[89]

The lives of autistic children, like the lives of people with Moebius syndrome, show us what it is like for family and friends when one person's social mirroring is reduced or eliminated. The effects on the social network in which the child lives can be extensive. These two conditions are therefore apt metaphors for what happens to democratic society when the practices of one-on-one interaction are neglected. In effect, political society itself lacks the emotional connections that bind people together at the most basic neurological level—not, however, because its members are unable to move their faces expressively, nor because of the state of their mirror neurons, but simply because citizens are no longer doing what their faces and brains equip them to do.

I am not suggesting that there is no place in democratic life for forms of communication less direct than the one-on-one or small-group meeting. There are many ways of connecting with other people that do not involve face-to-face encounter, and some of them permit a kind of neurological mirroring to take place. What you hold in your hands is a book. Many of the stories recounted in it are meant to simulate for the reader the experience of a one-on-one or small-group meeting. My hope is that what was said to me, when passed on to you in this edited form, will retain its power to convey the emotions of the people with whom I have been interacting. Similar communicative work can be done in documentary films and in digital video, both of which media have the additional advantage, over the written word, of presenting the voices of people aurally and their faces visually. It would please me if there were many more works, in all of the relevant media, directed toward the aim of conveying the concerns of ordinary citizens to a wide audience consisting of other concerned citizens. A YouTube video of an irate protester heckling a politician is not what I have in mind. Neither is reportage in the "Ain't it awful?" mode favored by most documentarians.

I am suggesting, however, that ordinary citizens are unlikely to acquire enough power to rein in the new ruling class without a good deal more face-to-face organizing than we have now. A recurring theme in my discussions with organizers is their worry that the communicative benefits of the digital age are tempting many people to neglect the forms of face-to-face interaction that every successful grassroots organization developed so far has engaged in. Once, while traveling with half a dozen organizers in the Rio Grande Valley, I realized that I was the only one in the van not at that moment on a cell phone. A few years from now, their successors might all be using laptops or Twitter for the same purposes. If those tools make it easier for them to schedule the next one-on-one or small-group meeting, then so much the better. If, however, using the tools begins to replace such meetings in the life of citizens' organizations, the consequences are likely to be undemocratic.

✻ CHAPTER THIRTEEN ✻

The Passion of St. Rose

When an alien resides with you in your land, you shall not oppress the alien. The alien who resides with you shall be to you as the citizen among you . . . for you were aliens in the land of Egypt.

—*Leviticus 19:33–34*

ERNIE CORTÉS APPOINTED a number of new organizers during the reorganization of IAF in California. One of them was Daniel May, who had been on the job for about three years when he took me on a tour of the area in the summer of 2006. Daniel worked in the part of L.A. County known as the Southeast, which includes a collection of small cities that used to be white and working class in makeup but have recently become largely Latino, poor, and undocumented. The most densely populated of the cities there is Maywood, where at least thirty thousand people are packed into a mere 1.4 square miles. The most vibrant institution in Maywood is Saint Rose of Lima Catholic Church, whose priest, Father David Velasquez, arrived there in 2003. One of Daniel's first one-on-one meetings in Maywood was with the newly arrived priest.

In that meeting Father David made clear that organizing was not his main priority. "He told me," Daniel said, "that running St. Rose was like trying to manage several congregations that shared a building: the prayer group, those actively involved in all the other ministries, and everyone else who just came to Mass. He didn't see organizing as a way of addressing what he saw as the fundamental challenges in the congregation."

Father David did give Daniel the names of parishioners who might want to give some time to organizing. When Daniel followed

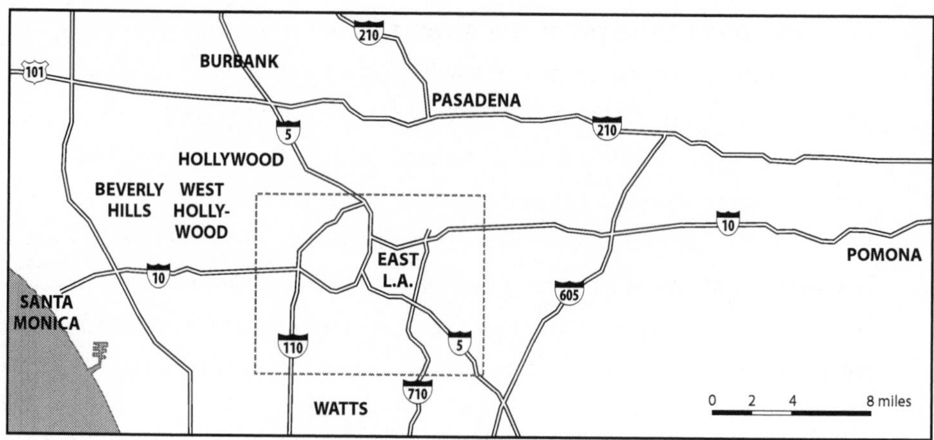

Map 13.1 Los Angeles County

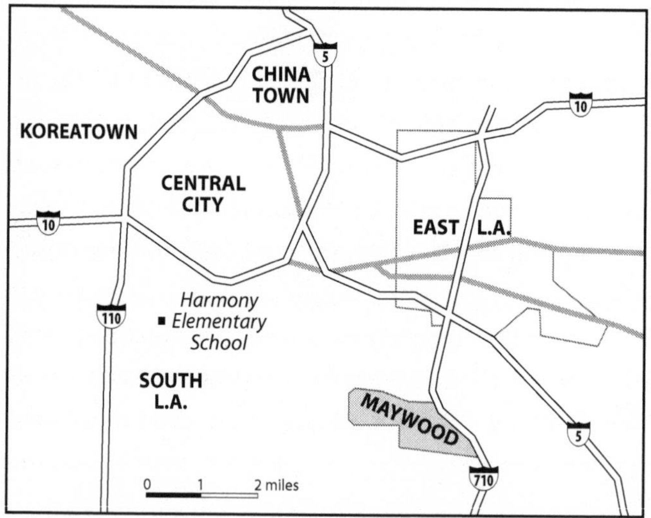

Map 13.2 Central Los Angeles

up, he asked them what they wanted to see changed in the neighborhood. Many of them told stories about the topics Daniel expected to hear about, including schools, safety, and jobs. But the most pressing concern seemed to be about a particular form of harassment that had begun to tear apart many Maywood families.

The police had begun pulling over drivers, nearly all of them Latino, impounding the car of any driver without a license. Recovering an impounded car from the towing company after the mandatory holding period of thirty days would cost around twelve hundred dollars. The per capita annual income in Maywood is less than nine thousand dollars. Loss of transportation typically resulted in loss of a job, which in turn often meant a family's eviction from its housing. In a city whose population is rumored to be divided almost equally between undocumented residents and U.S. citizens, the catastrophic effects on poor families spread rapidly through the community.

In an account of the impounding controversy that he was kind enough to write out for me shortly after my visit to Maywood, Daniel reported that checkpoints were set up twice a week for four-hour periods. "In the early nineties, the California Legislature passed a law declaring that undocumented immigrants could no longer receive driver's licenses. A couple years later, they passed a law saying that anyone caught driving without a driver's license would have their cars held a mandatory thirty days. The checkpoints stopped thousands of cars, and every night hundreds would be towed. Tow trucks lined the street, and dozens of police officers milled around, many getting lunch from the food truck that parked beside the checkpoint. It was a circus, with neighbors congregated across the street watching and families who had their cars taken lined along the street, children crying and mothers sitting dejected on the curb."

It might seem puzzling that the police department in a city with a nearly 97 percent Latino population would be profiling Latinos. Almost all of the Maywood residents who were not undocumented were related to someone who was. But undocumented aliens cannot vote. And with extremely low voter registration among those otherwise qualified to vote, the owners of local businesses had little trouble dominating the city council. The population was poor, but what money it had flowed directly into the cash registers of the businessmen, who faced little opposition when they sought to translate economic power into political power. Daniel quickly came to think of the Maywood city council as the political arm of the local business community. Why, then, this particular means of extracting money from the poor? Only a little research was needed to uncover the likely explanation. The towing company that was making huge profits from the impounding scheme was not only a thriving business in the area, but also a major contributor to successful city council candidates in Maywood and other cities in Southeast L.A.

Anna Eng, another organizer with whom I toured sections of Los Angeles County, told me that the practice of impounding the cars of undocumented drivers had been adopted by a number of municipalities in the area. There had been complaints, but no one had succeeded in bringing the issue to public attention. In cities with an ethnic makeup unlike Maywood's, impounding might well have enjoyed a degree of public support.

Daniel's supervisor was Sister Maribeth Larkin, a veteran of IAF fights in the Rio Grande Valley and thus someone familiar with police harassment of undocumented immigrants. A *Los Angeles Times* profile once referred to Maribeth as "a Catholic nun who walks with the tilt of a general," but she describes herself as shy by nature. Her job, she told the *Times*, is simply to help other people "exercise their own power, to organize themselves, and confront injustice. All I do is identify talent and mentor people."[90] In this instance her task was to give Daniel a firm push. As he expressed his outrage at the impounding scheme for what seemed to Maribeth like the hundredth time, she blew up at him, saying that the issue existed only in his head. "If it's an issue, go make it an issue," Daniel remembers her saying. "If it's not, just shut up about it!" Evidently, Maribeth's mentors had at some point induced her to overcome her shyness.

Daniel got the point. In a church not far from Maywood he gathered a group of leaders from Southeast L.A. He told them what he had learned from his one-on-one meetings and from looking up the list of campaign contributors. The issue appeared to have legs. The community was already angry about it. It was clear which political officials needed to be held accountable for the scheme and which business people were profiting from it. And the issue seemed winnable, so it would probably be a good way of generating confidence in the community's capacity to bring about change democratically.

Sal Valdez, who represented Saint Alphonsus Church at the meeting, pointed out that something was missing: "There's no one here from Maywood, Daniel!" The reason was that the organizing process had barely begun there. St. Rose would have to become a major player if the process was going to get anywhere, but Daniel had had time only to get his foot in the door. He had a few contacts, but none of the St. Rose parishioners had yet done their own one-on-one meetings with other parishioners or residents. They had not been to a training session. There had been no house meetings. No core team within the parish had been formed to take responsibility for moving forward. Father David had not even made a firm commitment on behalf of St. Rose. Still, Daniel was persuaded that if leaders elsewhere on the Eastside raised the issue, Maywood would rapidly discover the value of developing a political outlet for its anger.

It was not long before Daniel received a call from Father David, asking to meet again. He was now prepared to commit St. Rose to the process. Two priests, one from Huntington Park, the other from Cudahy, had told him that it was his responsibility to use his authority as a pastor for the good of the community. He thought they were right. Now a core team of leaders could be formed.

One warm summer evening I ate dinner with Father David in his quarters at St. Rose. I found him a humble and soft-spoken man. He had grown up in Mexico, and his previous assignment had been in Ventura, California. His Mexican roots taught him the value of keeping families and communities together, especially under conditions of poverty. But nothing he had done in Ventura, where the population was almost 80 percent white and relatively well off, prepared him for his present post. When I asked him why he decided to enter the fray over impounding, he replied that it was his responsibility as a priest "to take care of my brothers who are suffering." What the police were doing was not the right way to handle illegal immigration. He didn't know how to solve the larger problem, but he knew that dragging his community deeper into poverty was not going to help.

Once the core team had been formed, it seemed wise to ask for a meeting between leaders of LA Metro, as IAF's southern California branch was then called, and the chief of police, Bruce Leflar. Leflar agreed to the meeting, but then backed out. When Leflar appeared at a city council meeting, one of the leaders confronted him and offered a choice. Either he could reschedule, or the leaders would lean on their connections with the *Los Angeles Times* and bring a reporter with them to the next city council meeting. Leflar rescheduled the meeting, but when Daniel, another organizer, Father David, Sal Valdez, and two other leaders arrived at the police station, the chief gave them a choice. He would meet with four of them, not more. Either they would accept this restriction, or they could go home.

The group met briefly outside the station and decided reluctantly to accept the chief's restriction. Daniel and one of the leaders would remain outside, while the others went in. Daniel was disappointed, but the leader who had been excluded was furious, and stormed off when the others entered the station. Over the next days he didn't answer Daniel's phone calls, but when a week had passed, he called a meeting to apologize. "I did not do my duty as a member of the organization," Daniel remembers him saying. "I never should have let that meeting happen. I'm part of this organization because of the way we operate, because we don't let officials dictate the terms of the debate for us." The right way to proceed, he said, would have been to refuse the chief's terms "and then go and build the power necessary so that they are begging us to meet with them."

Father David saw things differently: a meeting that included four community leaders was better than no meeting at all. But the meeting proved unsatisfactory. The chief told Father David and the other leaders that there was no real issue at stake. Aside from them, no one had complained. This response made clear that the chief did not recognize the negotiating team as anything more than self-appointed do-gooders. They had not established themselves as speaking for the broader Maywood community, and until they did, they lacked the authority to negotiate. The chief, as long as he held office, did what the city council directed him to do, and he had power to administer the law as he saw fit. He saw no reason to abandon the impounding program.

If the group were going to get anywhere, it would have to generate some power of its own. One way to do this was to establish its entitlement to represent the sizable segment of the population that had been angered by the checkpoints. Another way was for the organization to use its influence to bring other powers into the mix. Neither Father David nor Daniel sought, however, to put the chief and his associates in the position of needing to beg for a meeting. Their aim—at least, the aim they expressed to me—was to level the playing field, not to reverse the existing relation of domination.

Fabian Nuñez, who had recently been elected as the area's representative to the state assembly, agreed to meet with the core group and expressed interest in pursuing the issue. He was willing, as Daniel put it, "to lean on the city council." Daniel also approached Frank Del Olmo, the managing editor of the *Times*, and gave him an overview of the situation. After doing some poking about of his own, Del Olmo wrote an opinion piece for the Sunday paper entitled "Maywood's Mean Money Machine," according to which 180,000 cars had been stopped in Maywood's checkpoints in the previous year. Del Olmo termed the policy a "draconian" program of "holding cars hostage." The article sympathetically described the plight of Flor Cervantes, a woman who had recently been stopped in a Maywood roadblock while driving her two children. It also put a spotlight on the financial benefits of the scheme, both for the City of Maywood, which figured to collect $250,000 a year in fines and for "Maywood Club Tow, which has the contract to handle Maywood's lucrative impound business."[91]

When the piece appeared, the city tried to cut a deal that would allow the checkpoints to continue, but in modified form. The citizens' group continued to press for a moratorium, but accepted the city's action as a first step. All the while, the organizing in Maywood proceeded apace, with community interest fueled by the publicity. LA Metro sponsored an "action" in the parking lot at St. Rose early one summer evening, with fourteen hundred people in attendance.

Father David opened the event with a prayer, in which he outlined the responsibilities of government and church in such matters. It is the city's responsibility, he said, not to take cars away from the people, but to help them get their cars back, so they can get to work, earn their bread, and take their children to school. The city is responsible for the well-being of everyone living in Maywood. And it is the church's responsibility to make sure this happens. According to Daniel, a speaker representing a teachers union alluded to Lincoln: "The history of this country is the story of making our reality match our ideals. And that is what we are doing tonight—seeing that democracy of the people, for the people and by the people is a possibility today, even in Maywood."

Then a number of people told stories to illustrate the effects of impounding on the community. "One mother spoke of saving her tips for a year working as a maid at a hotel in order to buy a car, only to have it taken in a checkpoint. A teacher spoke of a student whose father had tried to take his own life after he lost his job when he couldn't get there on time after his car was taken. During those stories," Daniel wrote, "it was so quiet you could hear the breath of audience members."

The citizens' group had now established its capacity to mobilize Maywood residents in large numbers and to use its influence to bring political and media pressure to bear on city officials. The group had also established its authority to speak for Maywood residents in public settings and at the negotiating table. City officials reacted by declaring a moratorium on the systematic twice-a-week checkpoints. But other signs were more troubling. The city was still towing cars aggressively, albeit more randomly. One of the cochairs of the public meeting and another leader woke up one morning after the meeting to find that their tires had been slashed. A message was left for the cochair on her church's answering machine, threatening her with "persecution" if she continued in her role. Another leader's house was placed under police surveillance. His brother's car was impounded.

For more than one reason, then, it was clear that the Maywood establishment now recognized the local branch of LA Metro as a force to be reckoned with. Yet no lasting resolution of the issue had been reached, and the community continued to feel both apprehensive and angry about the entire affair. The modest victory of the moratorium infused the fledgling organization with energy and confidence. One-on-one conversations and house meetings continued. The parishioners at St. Rose became more involved and learned much from their more experienced counterparts in neighboring cities.

It is significant that the broader attempt to reinvigorate IAF organizations in southern California had already begun to bear fruit by the time that the impounding controversy emerged in Maywood. As Anna Eng stated emphatically to me, without support from the now reorganized citizens' groups in neighboring municipalities, the new effort in Maywood would have fallen flat. A year after the original public meeting at St. Rose, IAF in Los Angeles dropped the name LA Metro, reincorporated itself as One LA, and held a founding assembly for twelve thousand leaders from affiliated institutions in the area. Of those leaders, about five hundred were from St. Rose. Father David was a featured speaker at the convention. "We had enough of the checkpoints in our city, and we stopped them!" he told the crowd. This was in the summer of 2004. St. Rose had come a long way in a short time.

But frustration within the parish was growing. "Every police officer is a checkpoint," Father David told Daniel. More and more parishioners complained that they were getting stopped for violations they hadn't committed, and would then lose their cars for a month. The group decided to pressure the city to release impounded cars after a single day. It was time to plan another public action.

The mayor pro-tem refused to meet. Two other officials, including the mayor, agreed to do so in November, but then came to the meeting forty-five minutes late. Their line, according to Daniel, hadn't changed since the summer: "We're just following the law." The group asked them to look into what other cities were doing and requested a follow up meeting. When neither official was prepared to commit to meeting before January, the atmosphere became charged. One official said he had "other commitments." Daniel, who had kept his mouth shut until that point, remembers saying, "I think that shows a lot about what your priorities are." The official then leaned across the table in a way Daniel took to be threatening, and said, "You don't know anything about me, or about my culture! I'm a father, and a Latino, and you're damn right I have other priorities!"

Leaders within the St. Rose parish were unsure how to press forward and held an internal meeting of roughly five hundred people, which broke out into about fifty "house meetings." People swapped stories about how police harassment had affected them. These meetings solidified the leadership's view of what had been going on during the so-called moratorium and began to shape participants' anger into something that could fuel constructive action.

"Three weeks later," Daniel reported, "we held a *posada*, the Catholic ritual where [parishioners] parade around the neighborhood in the week leading up to Christmas in reenactment of Mary's search for a place to have the child. Around four hundred people walked to the council chambers holding candles, with dollar bills taped onto their backs to symbolize the fact that the city was making money off the backs of the residents. Only a hundred and fifty or so could get inside. Veronica Guardado spoke at the council meeting, [saying] that we wanted an end to the thirty-day holds and that we wanted to meet with all the council members. And then we left."

Council members would be up for reelection in 2005, but they didn't budge. Despite the hundreds of people who had participated in public actions, the citizens' group had not yet demonstrated its ability to register and turn out voters, so council members saw no reason to give ground. It was gradually becoming clear that preparing for the city council election in Maywood would be the major task of the year for One LA's leaders from the Southeast.

In the summer before the election, about twelve hundred people, by Daniel's estimate, attended a major action at St. Rose. A number of public officials—from the state legislature, the U.S. Congress, other city councils, and county law enforcement—expressed support for One LA. The group's next objective was to canvass the entire Maywood community in the hope of registering, motivating, and informing voters.

A few hours after my dinner with Father David, I sat with Veronica Guardado at a picnic table in the St. Rose parking lot. She told me that throughout the election year, she herself was unconvinced that her friends and neighbors could be counted on to take action when the chips were down. She remained skeptical even after participating in door-to-door canvassing in her neighborhood.

"The community is going to accomplish something like this?" she said. "Okay, right! I've lived here long enough to know that you just can't depend on people to get involved. They will tell you that they'll come to a meeting, but then they won't show up. They'll tell you that they're going to vote, but then it won't happen. You could hear all the same old arguments we've always had among ourselves." To Veronica's surprise, however, hundreds of new voters were registered.

The plan was to invite all candidates to an accountability session and to ask each of those who attended whether he supported the proposal to end thirty-day holdings. The group would then distribute a scorecard, showing who had attended, who had not, who had agreed to the proposal, and who had not. No candidates would be endorsed by the organization. But this self-restriction caused some members of the Maywood core team more than a little anxiety. What if one or more of the incumbents attended the accountability session and said yes? Given their previous behavior, how could they be trusted? Equally important, how could Maywood citizens avoid confusion without a clear directive to vote against the incumbents?

Daniel tried to offer reassurance. IAF groups had been in similar situations many times before. Each candidate's publicly stated commitment could be measured against his behavior on the council. If a majority of the incumbents agreed to the proposal, One LA would have its victory before the election. This would be clear evidence of recognition from the city establishment, and it would further empower the community to hold the establishment accountable in the future. If a majority of the incumbents did not agree to the proposal, the people of Maywood would understand what the scorecards meant, and vote against the incumbent slate. The community was now angry enough and sufficiently well informed to behave prudently. Veronica went along, but retained her doubts. Another leader stormed out of a meeting, protesting that the strategy was doomed to fail. As Daniel saw it, in late summer and early fall, "the core team was in shambles." The organization's weekly walks were not eliciting enough participation from the community to shake up the council.

While the previous summer's public action had not done enough to motivate the community, the other side finally reacted. With a month to go before the accountability session, a dozen or so protesters, most of them teenagers, assembled in front of St. Rose, carrying signs accusing Father David of sexual abuse and One LA of protecting abusers. Some of the protesters distributed a flyer with quotations from a recent *L.A. Times* article alleging that five abusers had served at St. Rose.[92] The alleged abusers had departed St. Rose before Father David arrived there, but the flyers insinuated otherwise.

Father David told me that when members of his parish came to tell him what was going on, he replied by saying, "I am your priest. I will not raise a finger in this matter." In fact, parishioners immediately came together in anger against what struck them as a blatant lie, intended to discredit the most authoritative figure involved in the citizens' organization—the closest thing Maywood had to a Carmen Anaya. That the teenage picketers were thought to be gang members hardly enhanced the credibility of the charges they were making, but it did raise worries about physical intimidation.

As Daniel remarked to me, "Sometimes your enemies do your work for you." Suddenly, the numbers participating in neighborhood walks increased significantly. "I learned what Alinsky meant by political jujitsu, when your opponent's idiocy is your greatest asset. That protest organized the church behind the fight in a way we never could." By overreacting, the Maywood establishment had shown its willingness to lie and slander to maintain its power, turned Father David into a martyr for the One LA cause, and motivated the community to come to his defense.[93]

The accountability session was set for the evening before the election, with St. Rose as the location. Invitations went out to all candidates, stipulating that anyone who wanted to participate needed to attend a preparatory session. The incumbents didn't respond. But there was a significant complication. Gil Cedillo, a member of the state legislature widely respected in the immigrant community, sent a letter to all of his constituents in Maywood, endorsing the incumbent slate. Evidently, the incumbents had done a favor for him, which he was returning. Members of the core team worried that their organizing would now come to nothing.

The church was filled to capacity on the big night. There were reporters present, as well as a few TV cameras. "When the leaders took the stage," Daniel wrote, "a roar erupted through the church that I will never forget." The chair of the meeting explained the agenda. When it was time for the candidates to come to the front, the leaders faced a dilemma, because the incumbents were among those walking forward. The chair explained that the incumbents had not met the conditions for participating, given that they had neither formally accepted the invitation to participate, nor attended the mandatory prep session. There were only a few supporters of the incumbents present, but they protested vociferously. At the chair's prompting, the crowd drowned out the protests by chanting "One LA!"

With incumbents and their opponents alike standing before the crowd, the chair put the key question only to the opponents, who responded by signaling their support for ending thirty-day holding. The tension in the room was palpable. The campaign manager for the incumbents, Sam Peña, was in the back of the church with a few supporters, gathering around him anyone from the media who would listen. He said that the incumbents had been invited to attend, but were now being humiliated and arbitrarily excluded. When the meeting ended, according to Daniel, Peña threatened to sue the church for revocation of its tax-exempt status.

"Outside the church it was a melee," Daniel recalled. "People were screaming at each other, with the incumbent slate hollering at our people and many of the church congregants hollering back. The news cameras swarmed as I tried to pull off as many of our leaders as I could and get them into a hasty, chaotic evaluation. I talked with Ernie later in the evening from the church parking lot, and he chewed me out for allowing the leaders to prohibit the incumbents from speaking. 'You're teaching them to be over principled!' he hollered. 'They're Melians! They have to be more flexible! They have to learn that they got to deal with power whether they like it or not.'" Daniel conceded the point. "Well," he remembers Ernie telling him, "you'd better win!"

For many readers, this cryptic reference to the ancient Melians will require some explanation. Melos is an island in the Aegean Sea. Those who lived there in ancient times, the Melians, tried to maintain neutrality during the Peloponnesian War. In 416 BCE they were attacked by the Athenians and massacred when they refused to surrender. The Greek historian Thucydides illustrated what he took to be their fatally uncompromising attitude toward Athenian power in "The Melian Dialogue," which imagines a debate between Athenians and Melians shortly before the massacre.[94] IAF often has leaders read or enact the dialogue in training sessions to bring home to them the fatal consequences of an excessively rigid approach to political conflict. Ernie was telling Daniel that the Maywood leaders should have demonstrated their own flexibility and permitted the incumbents to speak. Not doing so made the leaders vulnerable to Peña's charges and placed at risk everything that had been gained when Father David was attacked. The incumbents had outfoxed them.

Preliminary indications the next day were good. Many voters told Daniel that someone from One LA had reminded them to vote. One woman told him in Spanish that she had called everyone on her list. When the absentee ballots were counted, the incumbents were already trailing a bit, and it was clear that Peña's candidates were going to lose. When the initial results were posted, it was time to begin depolarizing. Daniel and one of the leaders approached Peña, offering to shake his hand, but he refused.

Instead, according to Daniel, Peña told him: "I'm not shaking your hand, not tonight. And Daniel—the police are looking for you. You're a wanted man in this town. You're wanted for assault." Daniel wondered what he could be wanted for. "You already know. Don't pretend like you don't." The chief of police later told Daniel that there was nothing to it. A few more troubling signs of intimidation were directed at Daniel and Father David, who received threats on the church answering machine and had to replace some windows that were broken by rocks thrown from the street.

But the real news was that a major victory had been won. Almost a thousand new voters had turned out, and the incumbents had been trounced. Sam Peña remained on the council, but no longer had enough votes to have his way. The new council's first act was to end thirty-day holds. It later made national news by refusing to enforce some provisions of the Comprehensive Immigration Reform Act of 2006. Leaders such as Veronica meet regularly with the new council members, but the rule is still "No permanent enemies, no permanent allies." Holding public officials accountable is something that can be accomplished only by maintaining independence from them. When I visited, Veronica, Father David, Sal Valdez, and others had begun meeting with leaders from other groups throughout the state to develop a more reasonable approach to immigration reform. At the local level affordable housing was emerging as a common concern, which is hardly surprising, given the population density and basic living conditions in Maywood. When I was about to leave the city, Veronica stopped me for a moment, opened her wallet, and pulled out the stub of the ballot she had cast. She carries it with her as a reminder of the power she holds in her hands.

✻ CHAPTER FOURTEEN ✻

Blood and Harmony

A FEW BLOCKS AWAY from St. Rose is a section of the City of Los Angeles that has become so emblematic of gang violence and ethnic strife that officials have formally changed its name: what used to be called "South Central," and thus shared its name with a 1992 movie about the Crips, is now officially known as "South Los Angeles." Locals still refer to the area by the old name, and I will follow their lead here. South Central has approximately 1 million residents. The population density is half that of Maywood, but almost 6 times that of Los Angeles as a whole. As a result of immigration, Latinos now make up more than half of South Central's population. In the period since 1980, the African-American population has shrunk from 64 percent to less than 40 percent. Tension between Latinos and blacks is high.

During the week before Anna Eng took me to visit Harmony Elementary School in South Central, six murders had been committed in the immediate neighborhood of the school. Three of them were allegedly the work of two men, probably gang members armed with assault rifles, who got out of their car and fired more than thirty rounds into a Latino man, Larry Marcial, twenty-two; his nephew, ten; and their neighbor, seventeen. The twelve-year-old brother of the ten-year-old was also hit. Gangs had become a dominant form of organizational life for the young in the 1970s. When crack cocaine became the local drug of choice, beginning in 1982, gangs found the drug trade so lucrative that they were able to acquire massive arsenals of weaponry of the sort used in the Marcial murder.

As a teenager in Trenton, New Jersey, I belonged to a civil rights organization. Membership was open only to pairs who were committed to attending meetings and organizing as a team. But there was an important restriction on what the pairs had to look like: each pair had to include two races. To join, I needed to find someone of a different race who was willing to join with me. In other words, the rite of initiation involved befriending someone unlike myself. This requirement threw me and my partner, Alonzo Younger, into one another's lives. It meant that his friends and family would need to come to terms with me and that my friends and family would need to come to terms with him. Each of us discovered a great deal about what life was like for the other. In a racially tense community during a time that included the King assassination and a riot in Trenton, we found ourselves in circumstances where it took courage to be seen together. For me, that meant getting a taste of the racism being directed against my partner. It also meant learning much about divisions and traditions in the black community that I had known nothing about. The friendship that developed with my partner mattered enormously to me, as did the sense of belonging to a larger group committed to bridging the racial divide.

The black and Hispanic gangs that dominate the streets of South Central are highly dedicated recruiters, with especially powerful incentives, positive and negative, to offer to recruits. Most young people do not like being isolates. To join a gang is to belong to something. Belonging confers identity, which is signified in gang colors and gestures. Your fellow members are your friends, and you can count on them to have your back. One rite of initiation for a person entering a gang—on analogy with becoming a "made man" in La Cosa Nostra—involves harming someone unlike himself. Joining a group in this way is as unlike the rite of initiation I had undergone in Trenton as an experience could be.

The identity-conferring activity is also character-conferring. It begins to create in the new member a disposition to behave in a certain way toward others in the future. In my case, the group was inculcating in me a habit of bridge-building, so that the identity-conferring boundary around the group was already rendered permeable in the very act of defining it. In the gang member's case, the group is not only inculcating habits that direct violence across the group boundary, but also rigidifying that boundary. For the insider, the group boundary marks the difference between people who can be trusted and those who cannot and between people for whom risks are undertaken and those on whom harm may be imposed. The violence directed at outsiders reduces the surrounding community to a condition of terror, thus further contributing to the destruction of civic culture. Gangs emerge in response to a disintegrating social fabric and then exacerbate the unraveling that gave rise to them.

The point of my visit to South Central was to meet with Robert Cordova, the principal of Harmony Elementary and a leader active in One LA. Harmony is a feeder school for Jefferson High School, which has long had a reputation for violence. The black enrollment at Jefferson has fallen to less than 10 percent, the remainder being Latino. A year before my visit, a riot at Jefferson High had made national news. A more recent report put the Jefferson High dropout rate at 58 percent.[95] Robert is trying to figure out how to change the way one school works but understands that his efforts depend on the willingness of other South Central institutions to cooperate with his.

A number of churches in the area have become affiliated with One LA. Like Claiborne Avenue in New Orleans, South Central used to be a primary locus of black culture in the city, the home of many thriving African-American businesses, jazz clubs, and churches. Relatively little of that cultural infrastructure remains. Because Latinos have become the majority of the population, some of their own institutions are growing stronger. However, as Robert put it, "50 percent of the population can't prove they live here," which makes them reluctant to enter into public relationships outside the church.

Robert has put a lot of work into creating a "community of learners," in which administrators, teachers, and parents all feel jointly responsible for what the school is accomplishing. It was IAF training, he said, that changed his conception of himself as an administrator. "It forced me to clarify my story. It was more helpful to my work here than my master's training. It's not just that it helps me when I'm out in the community." Like Brod Bagert, he was forced to confront the fact that he had not been listening to people in a serious way. "Can you listen? The fact is, I never listened," Robert said. "I had an open door, but never really was thinking that every parent has something to teach me. Now I think of myself less as an administrator, more as a leader. A leader has to be inspirational."

Some of the teachers at Harmony were as suspicious at the beginning of the organizing process as Connie Maheshwari's teachers were when she initiated a similar process at Sam Houston Elementary in McAllen, Texas. When Robert first organized a meeting between parents and teachers, only seventeen of his forty teachers came. But despite having to deal with a bureaucracy above him that is often uncooperative, Robert feels that he is making progress, both in hiring better teachers and in working with the teachers who are there. "If you're a teacher, you need to find out who you are, what your strengths and weaknesses are. The school needs to help you become a better educator. Some teachers aren't willing to accept help. I try to coach the ones who receive below-standard evaluations, but in some cases it took two years to learn that they just wouldn't take help."

"The biggest challenge," Robert said, "is building the capacity of the parents and teachers to believe." Robert has found it easier to make headway with the Hispanic parents than with their African-American counterparts, who have what he calls "very low involvement." "Things have been bad here. Trust has deteriorated. It's tough to get through the anger. I go door to door, trying to talk to parents. One of my goals is to be invited someday into one of the African-American homes, but it hasn't happened yet. I can get on the porch, but not in the front door. That's where I've been least successful." During the week of my visit, Robert was paying a price for his decision to hold a memorial service for the recent murder victims, three of whom had ties to Harmony Elementary. "Some of the black moms were upset that a big deal was being made about Hispanic deaths when blacks were dying all the time."

"One person told me, 'This is not my concern anymore. I'm getting out.' At one meeting, an African-American parent said, 'If I hear one word of Spanish, I'm out of here. I ain't hearing any of that.'" It will take many small steps to build bridges across divisions of this kind, but there are ways to inspire at least a little trust. The African-American community's "history with the police is way bad," said Robert. "Our core team is working on the relationship with the police." The citizens' group has already had some success in campaigning for street signs and streetlights. These are crucial steps, he thinks, in reclaiming the streets. If ordinary people can reclaim the streets, other things become possible.

Are there enough institutions involved? Robert hopes to get more businesses to participate in the organization. Later that day, I toured the area with Daniel May, who said that there were four Catholic parishes in South Central taking an active role in the attempt to restore trust to the community. As we passed one of the churches, Daniel remarked that the new pastor there is rumored to be associated with Opus Dei, a Catholic organization with a rigorously conservative social agenda. "All he wants to talk about is abortion," Daniel said. "I'm worried that we're going to lose that one."

✻ CHAPTER FIFTEEN ✻

Fathers and Sisters for Life

As a Roman Catholic, the Opus Dei priest mentioned at the end of the previous chapter must be mindful of Pope John Paul II's 1995 encyclical letter *The Gospel of Life*, which calls for "the establishment of a new culture of life."[96] The encyclical contrasts the culture of life with its opposite, a "culture of death." The latter is said to be "a veritable *structure of sin*" in which abortion and euthanasia are tolerated rather than strictly prohibited under law (22, italics in original).

Many Roman Catholics associated with IAF accept the Vatican's position on the sanctity of life, but express concern that some priests and bishops may be narrowing their vision of what the church's tradition of social teaching requires. Sister Christine Stephens once told me that she had recently "sat through three Sundays of anti-abortion sermons." In the most recent one, a deacon said that "we are called to be concerned about the unborn, the sick, and the aged. And I thought: What happened to the widow and the orphan and the poor? All of a sudden it's narrowed down to the unborn, the sick, and the aged. I'm a faithful daughter of the church and I'm against abortion, but I swear to God, it's driving me nuts."

Sister Christine's complaint was not with the papal encyclical itself, but rather with those in the church who have taken John Paul's call for a "*great campaign in support of life*" to involve a shift in focus away from the venerable tradition of Catholic social teaching on just treatment of the poor (168, italics in original). That *The Gospel of Life* was not intended to jettison that tradition can be inferred, she thinks, from John Paul's blunt claim that "the selfishness of the rich countries" needs to be unmasked. John Paul also rejected "economic models" that "aggravate situations of injustice and violence" (32–33).

It is entirely legitimate, Christine thinks, for the church to sponsor political initiatives on particular issues, such as abortion and euthanasia, provided that the full scope of church teaching is not obscured in the process. But the "Gospel of life" issues include capital punishment and war, no less than abortion and euthanasia. Pastors who focus on the latter two issues at the expense of the former tend to give a severely constricted impression of what church teaching entails. They also risk playing into the hands of politicians who are trying to distract attention from the dangers of militarism and plutocracy. In the United States the Republican Party has benefited heavily from a narrow preoccupation on the part of some pastors and bishops with abortion.

The Gospel of Life reaffirms the Vatican's commitment to "the democratic ideal," understood as an affirmation of "the dignity of every human person" (36).[97] Citizens' organizations, from Christine's point of view, are embodiments of that ideal, because they provide an institutional setting in which individuals can demand and express respect for human dignity. One-on-one and small-group meetings are contexts in which the church and the broader political community can become conscious of the concerns that individual citizens and church members in fact have. Church doctrine calls attention to the abstract value of dignity, but concrete interaction of the right kind is needed to honor the dignity of actual adult persons in their particularity. The single-issue initiative, undertaken at the behest of church officials on the basis of traditional teaching, must be supplemented by practices in which the concerns of the community percolate up from below.

One stop on my tour of the Rio Grande Valley was in Las Palmas Colonia, near Harlingen, where I met with Father Pat Seitz, a local priest. He recounted his stories about recent victories in the area. After months of negotiating with the U.S. Postal Service, Las

Palmas residents can now have mail delivered to their homes. Streets have signs, which allow the postal workers to find them. Sewer pipes are being installed, thanks to a grant of half a million dollars. When that process is complete, the streets will be properly paved. In Elizabeth Valdez's words, Father Pat had been given "a hard time" by parishioners focused mainly on abortion. They wanted to know why he gets the church involved in political controversies over postal services, streets, and sewerage.

"I told them," Father Pat said, "that in years past the church has always been involved in social justice issues. We were just getting ready to support American Pro-Life, and I said, 'We've asked you before to sign petitions against abortion and you signed them. And we sent them to Washington. So we're involved in politics, aren't we? The same is true when we did it during the civil rights movement. Years ago in the Valley, we had some of the same issues of civil rights, and I said we can't stand for that. We have to be willing to take a stand. Everything's political. We have to live with the church teaching.' So that was the way that I handled it, because I've got a very conservative congregation. At one time they protested against Valley Interfaith, and I got a little too angry with them. It was a big mess: a trip to the hospital, anxiety, so I learned to control it a little bit better."

Just as IAF pastors and organizers differ from their counterparts on the religious right, they also differ from proponents of liberation theology, a movement with intellectual roots in the Christian-Marxist dialogue in Europe during the 1960s. Among Roman Catholic priests, the movement was especially influential in Latin America in the 1970s, before the Vatican disciplined its leaders for partisanship and excessive reliance on Marxism. Ernesto Cortés once told me that the liberation theology movement had essentially invited Vatican censure by allowing its own version of regularized house meetings, the so-called base communities, to develop into a second church within the church. Whatever the merits of this alternate form of ecclesial polity might be, it should have been obvious, he thought, that the Vatican would feel bound to uproot it. Cortés has been careful to shape IAF practices in a way that would not invite the church to respond negatively. He, Sister Christine, and others in their sphere of influence are also much more eclectic in their theoretical commitments than the liberation theologians were. Red-baiting notwithstanding, IAF is not a network of Marxist cells. Books by economists, sociologists, historians, theologians, philosophers, and political theorists of various sorts circulate through the network. Organizers appear to borrow ideas and explanations from whatever books seem to shed light.[98]

Sister Judy Donovan was once the lead organizer of Valley Interfaith in Texas and now serves as the lead organizer of the IAF projects in northern California. Before joining the network, she worked in Brazil, where she became involved in rural base communities. Peasants who had become organized under her influence confronted landowners, only to be arrested and defeated: "That was a real epiphany for me in thinking our analysis is wonderful and our theology is beautiful and, you know, we're on the side of goodness and light. But so what? Goodness and right fail all the time. There had to be a way to put our words of faith into action or, you know, what does it matter?" Judy came to see liberation theology as excessively abstract and idealistic. IAF organizing attracted her in part because of its pragmatic orientation: "It's a way of taking all that idealism and ideological bent and actually testing it and being able to do something with it and directing it and having a community that holds me accountable to doing that."[99]

In Brownsville Monsignor Heberto Díaz told me that when he was young, he was once assigned the task of driving Bishop John J. Fitzpatrick to a meeting. They were on back roads and then on a military highway that went through one of the colonias, which meant that he could see the conditions with his own eyes. "From that point on," Monsignor Díaz told me, "I realized that the most important job of a priest in a community like this is what the church calls the preferential option for the poor, to really do things to help the people, our people, my people in this area—to grow in education and have all the things that they need to live a happy and prosperous life. All through high school, I didn't have problems with electricity or sewerage or things like that. It was a shock to realize that even in the eighties people didn't have essentials. It was an eye-opener for Bishop Fitzpatrick to show me all of that. That's what began my journey to being more involved." For Monsignor Díaz, it was a church official of high rank who changed his outlook. It can matter enormously who holds high office in the churches, above all in the Roman Catholic case, where hierarchical distinctions are strong.

I heard much about Bishop Fitzpatrick during my travels in the Valley. One story had to do with his decision to have the Diocese of Brownsville sponsor public radio and television stations so that citizens in the Valley could have access to better sources of news and commentary. Another story had to do with an episode of freezing temperatures that destroyed local crops late in 1983 and put thousands of farm laborers out of work. Someone got the idea of hiring the laborers to clean up the mess.

"We had this detailed proposal," Ernie Cortés told me. "We had the support of everybody in the Valley: mayors, county commissioners, city councils, school boards, everybody." But Tom Pauken, who had run two unsuccessful campaigns for a congressional seat, attacked Valley Interfaith, and the Reagan White House became reluctant to support the proposal. "We pulled together a huge press conference of all the priests, who said we asked the Reagan Administration for bread and they sent us a political scorpion," Ernie explained. Pauken countered this move by putting together a group of influential "right-wing Catholics," and approached his priest, asking him to be a part of it. The priest went to Bishop Fitzpatrick, who, being unaware of what Pauken was trying to achieve, gave the priest permission to join Pauken's committee. Ernie and some others associated with Valley Interfaith met with the bishop to explain what Pauken was doing.

The bishop then arranged a meeting with Ernie and the priest. Bishop Fitzpatrick told the priest, "You know, I didn't know this guy was trying to kill Valley Interfaith. An attack against Valley Interfaith is an attack against me. Father, you can do what you want to do, but I just want you to know that." The priest responded by saying that "we've got to mediate between the rich and the poor." The bishop said, "No, Father, we're supposed to listen to the rich and listen to the poor. But if push comes to shove, we have to stand with the poor." According to Ernie's recollection, the priest said, " 'Well, Bishop, I'll do whatever you tell me to do.' And Bishop Fitzpatrick says, 'Are you sure?' 'Yes. Yes.' And the bishop said, 'Well, here's your letter of resignation from the committee.' "

Ernie stayed behind after the priest left, and said, "Bishop, you were magnificent! I've never seen a Catholic Bishop do that before!" Bishop Fitzpatrick responded, "I had to: I was guilty."

When Bishop Fitzpatrick celebrated a Mass inaugurating Valley Interfaith, Father Carlos Zuniga was in ninth grade and living in McAllen. Memories of the Mass stayed with Father Carlos over the years, and he followed the activities of Valley Interfaith in the papers even when he was living elsewhere. Now that he has returned to the area, he has decided to get involved—though only after overcoming some doubts, according to several organizers. "The Gospel," Father Carlos told me, "is about the good news that the Son of God came to this world and changed the world. And the Gospel is about liberating and transforming. And I always keep in mind what St. Francis of Assisi said in the twelfth century: 'Preach the Gospel. And, if necessary, use words.' And I think that in itself carries the essence. In other words, do it by action. I think that should be the model of Valley Interfaith."

"The priests, they listen to the other priests," Christine said, "like

Alfonso and Jerry Frank. That's what we get with these young guys. They're not coming out of the seminary with this in their gut. They're only getting it from the guys who have it in their gut. They're not getting anything on social justice." The average age of priests in the Valley is said to be the youngest in the country. According to one Valley Interfaith participant who asked to have her name withheld, "The young priests are coming in very spiritual. For them it's a very narrow concept of spirituality. It's a relationship between me and God, and it's charismatic. And there are some that are very prolife, and use that as an excuse to keep away from the organization."

One reason that Father Alfonso is able to serve as a role model for the young priests now working in the Valley is that he shares their strongly prolife commitments and their attraction to the more charismatic forms of Catholic worship and spirituality. "It is a process of conversion for the pastor, as it is for the people," he told me. He had spent a long time in his previous parish, which allowed him and his parishioners to "evolve together in a certain way. It was something fluid and organic." His current parish, St. Joseph the Worker in McAllen, was already involved in Valley Interfaith when he arrived. He initially thought that this history would allow him to make rigorous demands on the parish, but some parishioners let him know that they didn't like what he was doing. Ethnically, the parish is fairly homogenous, but there are economic differences that affect how parishioners see themselves. He became frustrated, but then "backed up a little bit" and worked harder at listening. The important thing to realize is that "the process of conversion is an ongoing thing" for both the pastor and his flock.

"You have to speak with a congregation and speak about principles of involvement," Father Alfonso said. "What is the tradition of our faith? What is the social doctrine of our faith? I tried to integrate that with the sense that it is part of our spiritual life. Spiritual life is what we do all of the time. It's what happens at school. It's what happens at work. It's what happens with family. They're all connected, so that we were very fortunate to have lots of church documents that support that kind of a teaching—the social doctrine of the church."

Liturgy is at least as important to the spiritual dimension of politics as doctrine is, because of its capacity to knit the parish together and to connect parishioners with the broader community. "It's a matter of helping people to be connected with one another. In our liturgies we tried to be very specific about being culturally sensitive to our people. Most of our people are Hispanic with a close connection with Mexico. So we try to do lots of stuff that is cultural." Father Alfonso brought along photographs to show what he had in mind. One of them depicted a procession in the church involving "all of the organizations," including Valley Interfaith, "that are part of our neighborhoods." Other pictures showed the preparations for annual celebrations in honor of the Virgin of Guadalupe, the patroness of Mexico. *Los Matachines*, known as soldiers of the Virgin, dress in traditional Aztec costumes and dance in the Virgin's honor. Related cultural events are staged in local schools. "It's not just churches. It's creating a sense of community with churches and with our business people and all that."

Another photograph pictured a prolife liturgy. It is important, Father Alfonso said, for his parish to keep in mind the full range of Catholic teaching. His parish's public engagement isn't exhausted by its involvement in Valley Interfaith. He is anxious to counteract the "stereotype" associated with Valley Interfaith in some people's minds. "We aren't just about making trouble for the mayor or whatever they think we're doing. We're authentically Christian and authentically very spiritual. And what motivates us in the public arena is our faith. When we go to the commissioners meeting—before we do that or before and after—we take some time to pray on the steps or wherever we may be and we celebrate." Prayer and liturgy give parishioners "a vision, a prophetic vision." "As you go into the trenches, you need something that's very deep to sustain you in the fight. For us to remain in that work we have to come back to what transcends us, that kind of corrects us and our roughness. Part of a priest's job in a Catholic church is liturgy, the cultic aspect of life. But accountability sessions are liturgies, too." What appears secular in the eyes of the average citizen has a sacred dimension in the eyes of the church.

"Liturgy," Ernie responded, "is the work of the people."

"Right," Father Alfonso replied, "it's a public work."

"Where were you in 1974?" Ernie asked.

"I was in seminary," said Father Alfonso. "At that time COPS was coming into its own, and that's the first time that I saw the church in a very big way being active in the public sector."

Ernie wondered whether Father Alfonso remembered the one time they had met in 1974. "No," Father Alfonso said. "Oh my goodness, refresh my memory." Ernie wanted to tell the story for the benefit of the younger priests and other leaders who were present.

"Well," Ernie said, "I remember doing the meeting because I was told this was someone I ought to meet with, because he was doing experiments with liturgy and music. And you had this gift of liturgy and music and social justice. But your reception was very cool at the time. I just want you all to know that people don't always start where he is now. So if you don't think you're where he is now, you know God has opportunities and preparations and moments for you, too."

"Well, I'm glad you say that," Father Alfonso said, "because it is a process of conversion or growth or maturity, whatever word you want to use. You know what I am, and hopefully I'm still growing and still learning."

"I can testify," Ernie said. "You have grown significantly even over the last two years."

"And one of the reasons why," Alfonso said, "is I am an introvert. Public stuff was not what I dreamed about when I entered the seminary. It was a spiritual experience that kind of broke through my private life and made me aware that there was something beyond me and more powerful that drove me and inspired me. That's when I started to want to share my faith with other people. One day a guy in a prayer meeting said, 'You know, it's fine you guys pray in there, but I'm going to jail and no one is going with me.'"

Father Alfonso recalled making a presentation on behalf of Valley Interfaith before a commission. In the middle of the presentation, the commissioner running the meeting began to ignore him. Afterward, in an evaluation of the session, Sister Christine told Alfonso, "Never let people disrespect you in that way!" That remark had a big impact on him. "I feel sometimes that those people are not respecting my parishioners. You know, when they think that they're better than we are. They treat us like they're Daddy and we're like children. How insulting that is! And how un-Christian that is! We do them a favor when we tell them that this is not right. If they want to be respected they also have to know that we want to be respected. Jesus, the only time he spoke back according to our tradition, is when they struck him. He did teach us to turn the other cheek, but when they did strike him, he said, 'Why did you hit me?' You know, he did not stay quiet."

✻ CHAPTER SIXTEEN ✻

Pastors and Flocks

ONE OF THE MOST COMMON charges against IAF groups is that they blur the line between religion and politics. Political opponents like Othal Brand use the charge to undermine the legitimacy of citizens' organizations. But the charge also arises within parishes and congregations debating whether participating in a citizens' group is appropriate. It is a charge that pastors, in particular, cannot ignore. How, then, do they answer it?

We have seen that organizations like Jeremiah and Valley Interfaith rigorously avoid endorsing candidates, affiliating themselves with political parties, and donating money to campaigns. Their political goal, the participants say, is not to run for office or to take over government. They have no interest in holding political office. Their aim is to influence and hold accountable officeholders who are deciding the fate of the community. IAF organizations are self-consciously nonpartisan. In their view, the separation of church and state requires rigorous respect for the line between partisan and nonpartisan political involvement. It also requires a manifest and consistent commitment to the common good.

The framers of the First Amendment of the U.S. Constitution understood that the legal imposition of a state religion on a religiously diverse population would be a form of domination. Many of the framers had experienced religious domination firsthand, and were therefore strongly motivated to secure themselves and their heirs against it. All of the IAF groups discussed in this book strongly endorse this constitutional provision. The common good they seek is a polity in which no religious group—nor any other kind of group—dominates others. The reason that a commitment to pursuing the common good in this sense needs to be *manifest* and *consistent* is that otherwise other groups in society will have reason to suspect that the intent of the citizens' organization is to impose its religious outlook on others. The commitment is manifest if it is made apparent in the public statements and behavior of the organization. The commitment is consistent only if statements and behavior that implicitly or explicitly express the desire to dominate are strictly avoided.

In the next chapter, I will be looking at vagaries surrounding this conception of the common good, in particular, the senses in which it is secular and the senses in which it isn't. In the present chapter, I want to look more closely at the reasons pastors and lay leaders give for drawing the line between partisan and nonpartisan political involvement as they do—in particular, when deciding whether to bring their institutions into IAF groups. These reasons have to do in part with religious conceptions of pastoral responsibilities, but also with concerns related to freedom of religion, freedom of expression, the right to assemble peaceably, and the right to petition for the redress of grievances. Taken together, these provisions in the Bill of Rights give citizens' organizations the license to do all of the things we have seen them doing in this book. When citizens with religious commitments assemble peaceably, they are entitled to express those commitments publicly, both in their public actions and in the reasons they offer for their public actions. Their grievances are, as we have seen, sometimes born in grief and anger, passions that are connected with their deepest concerns, some of which are acquired and cultivated in religious communities and practices. If you asked these people to check their religious commitments and deepest concerns at the door, on their way into the public arena, they wouldn't know how to do that. The separation of church and state does not go through the heart of the believer.

The First Amendment does not prohibit pastors from engaging in politically consequential activities. They are citizens, so they must be given some room to act as such. All pastors make choices that have political effects. The effects can be easy or hard to notice, intentional or unintentional, good or bad. They can result from intervening actively or from trying to mind one's own business. Whatever the proper relation of religion and politics might be, it cannot require pastors to refrain from affecting the political lives of their communities. Ministry matters—politically, as well as in countless other ways. A wise pastor understands how.

Bishop T. D. Jakes once described himself as "a pastor, not a politician."[100] By framing the issue in this way he implicitly equated political engagement with running for, and possibly holding, public office. By reducing the former to the latter, he rendered the political effects of his own pastoral work invisible. Pastors, he implied, have their own work to do, work that pertains entirely to a sphere distinct from politics. This is a thought in which many pastors take comfort. They have homilies to write, eulogies to deliver, confessions to hear, patients to visit, Bible schools to run, charities to administer, and budgets to balance. Let the politicians dirty their hands in struggles over candidates and public policy. Let political parties foment public acrimony and then try to control it. A pastor has enough to do without getting involved in such matters.

Pastors are already involved in such matters. The unintended consequences of their choices involve pastors in political affairs even when the intended consequences of their choices do not. Consider Bishop Jakes' conduct in the Astrodome, where he told Katrina survivors that God would provide. No one suspected that he was preparing to run for political office. But the IAF minister who commandeered the microphone from him did suspect that Bishop Jakes' message implicitly reinforced the dominant position of economic and governmental elites *over* the Katrina survivors. By merely consoling the survivors with the message that God would provide, Jakes made a choice. He could have instructed them that they had not only a right, but also a duty, to influence and contest the officials who, if left to their own devices, would determine the survivors' fate. He could have told the survivors that it was up to them to do their part, to organize themselves and demand accountability. But he did not.

The IAF minister who told the survivors that God's way of providing for human needs is through the work of human hands was describing the situation in a way that allowed its political dimension to come into view. His point was to get people to think of themselves as potential doers, with powers, rights, and responsibilities of their own. To imagine that God alone would provide is to render invisible the agency of two groups of human beings: the governmental, corporate, and philanthropic officials who were already in the process of deciding the survivors' fate; and the survivors themselves, who had been reduced by oppressive social circumstances and natural catastrophe to the status of *patients* acted on by others. To render human agency invisible in this way is to convey a view of the situation that is both false and debilitating.

Both Bishop Jakes and the IAF minister sought to *influence* the evacuees by conveying to them an understanding of the circumstances in which they found themselves, the agents operating in those circumstances, the rights and duties those agents had, the goods that were at stake, and the options that were open. All pastors exercise similar sorts of influence on a daily basis. Pastoral work is essentially a way of exercising influence. That is its point. To influence people is to have effects on them, including political effects. It is therefore fitting to reflect on what those effects, positive and negative, might be. If a pastor induces false and politically debilitating views in a congregation, the best that can be said of the resulting ministry is that it is negligent. If the effect is intentional, something harsher should be said.

For Jakes, God has promised abundance to those of us who accept Jesus. The forms of human agency Jakes highlights are acceptance of the divine blessing, charitable sharing of the fruits of that blessing, and preaching of the Good News. One question worth asking of Jakes's ministry as a whole is whether there are ethically important forms of human agency—and thus rights, responsibilities, and practical options—that he tends to push out of view. Another is whether his interpretation of divinely promised abundance focuses too narrowly, perhaps even idolatrously, on the enjoyment and possession of material goods at the expense of the common good of living in a community dedicated to mutual recognition of human worth. Yet another question is whether Jakes's conception of charitable works tends to undermine political activities that are essential to achieving and enjoying the common good. All three of these questions are commonplace in critiques of Jakes's ministry. Similar questions need to be addressed to every pastor's ministry.

When Daniel May first asked Father David Velasquez to get involved in organizing his parish, the priest was not opposed in principle to doing so. He just felt that he had his hands full. Father David changed his mind when police harassment in Maywood worsened and two priests from neighboring cities paid him a visit to talk things through. When I asked Father David why he had changed his mind, he said that he came to understand his obligation to help his brothers who are suffering. He now saw that his task as a pastor goes beyond celebrating the sacraments of the church, ministering to the personal needs of his parishioners, and administering St. Rose's charitable, educational, and ecclesial programs. He is also charged with attending to the spiritual formation of his flock. At a minimum, that means teaching his parishioners the full scope of their responsibilities, including their responsibilities as citizens. The decision to bring St. Rose of Lima into a citizens' organization was a *pastoral* decision with *political* consequences. To fulfill his responsibilities as a pastor was necessarily to address the political responsibilities of his parishioners.

Church members are also members of families, clubs, schools, corporations, cities, states, nations, and many other social units.

Each membership one has entails a corresponding responsibility for existing arrangements within a particular form of human communal life. Members of the church, by virtue of their multiple memberships, are also *in* the world and *responsible for* worldly arrangements. The church does not itself administer any arrangements other than its own, and it does not have any business endorsing candidates or parties, according to Father David, but it is obliged to impress on all of its members the responsibilities entailed by their memberships in bodies distinct from the church. Beyond this, the pastor also has the prophetic task of declaring to the peoples of the world, including the people of Maywood, that they are responsible for the arrangements they have made for themselves and thus for whatever injustices those arrangements entail. The church must hold the people and their rulers responsible for the injustices they have perpetrated and permitted. At times, it is a pastor's responsibility to speak prophetically on the church's behalf.

Father David's understanding of the pastor's role is widely shared by other Roman Catholics associated with IAF groups. Moreover, Reverend Jesse Pate and many of the other Protestant clergy who are active in such groups speak of their role in similar terms, though with the term *preacher* or *minister* taking the place of the term *priest* and with the terms *congregation* and *congregant* taking the place of the terms *parish* and *parishioner*. These terminological differences express different conceptions of internal organization within different churches, which in turn affect the roles of particular churches and clergy in citizens' organizations.[101] But many clergy involved in IAF speak roughly as Father David does about the political dimensions of a pastor's responsibilities. They take themselves to be pastors, not politicians. They are not tempted to run for public office. They strictly avoid endorsing parties or candidates. Yet they consider it their business as pastors to make clear that the ethical commitments of their traditions have political implications.

Many clergy consider themselves religiously obliged to undertake pastoral and prophetic tasks that have political consequences. As they see it, they cannot perform their *religious functions* with integrity unless they side with Father David against Bishop Jakes. Pastors like Father David are not, however, trying to establish their own faiths as the official religion of the state. They are not theocrats. They are not looking to disenfranchise people of other faiths or nonbelievers. But they do insist that freedom of religious expression is partly a matter of protecting the right of all citizens to bring their deepest concerns with them when they enter public debate. Moreover, the citizens' organizations these pastors participate in are strictly nonpartisan. The policy of "no permanent enemies, no permanent allies" permits such organizations to maintain a critical distance from candidates and political parties without withdrawing from the domain of political responsibility altogether. In this respect, IAF pastors differ significantly from pastors like Jerry Falwell. IAF provides them with a way of being politically engaged that does not entail becoming *identified with* a party.

Whatever position we end up adopting on the proper relation of religion and politics, it needs to make sense when applied to places like Maywood and New Orleans. The issue of church and state tends to be debated in the abstract or in terms of a highly limited collection of court cases and examples drawn from presidential politics. In my travels through the Southwest, I was able to see what the issue looks like from below, in communities currently under assault and struggling to make their voices heard. In many such communities, an overly restrictive interpretation of church-state separation would have disastrous consequences. While I do not share the religious convictions of Father David and Reverend Pate—and would also probably disagree with them on a number of important moral and cultural questions—I do feel certain that their cities would be worse off if their churches had not joined citizens' groups. Had these pastors not chosen to become involved with One LA and the Jeremiah Group, respectively, many things would be different. The consequences of omitted acts are rarely obvious, but they are no less important for that.

In Maywood, we have a case where one pastor's decision carried more weight than any other single factor in invigorating a local democratic culture. What would Maywood be like today if Father David had decided against involving his church in the political life of his community by joining One LA? It would probably be a place where the misery of poverty was compounded by the oppression of police harassment, where the interests of local businesses trumped the concerns of needy families, and where councilmen ruled without fear of being held accountable by the people. Turning the organizer away would have had consequences.

In New Orleans the situation is much more complicated, but it seems clear that whether ordinary citizens have an effective say in the future of their city depends on how many pastors bring their churches into the Jeremiah Group. It is hard to know what level of pastoral involvement would tip the balance in favor of ordinary citizens in New Orleans, but the chances improve with each pastor who behaves as Reverend Pate has done. If New Orleans someday deserves to be called a democratic city, it will be in part because religious organizations come to provide a balancing counterweight to big corporations in the local political culture. And that will happen only if there are many more pastors like Reverend Pate in the picture. The probable effect of eliminating pastoral leaders from that role would be to leave corporate bosses with unchecked power.

Democratic political power derives from being organized. Developers are already well organized. Corporate bosses in general derive power from organizations that use market incentives to induce cooperative behavior. For there to be a balancing counterpower of a sort that would foster democratic accountability, organizations of other kinds, including religious institutions, will have to provide it. Pastors, no less than CEOs, occupy leadership roles in politically significant organizations. There is no getting around this.

In my meeting with leaders of the Jeremiah Group in New Orleans, Reverend Pate explained that there is a lot of politics going on "amongst the churches themselves." The church isn't immune from political conflict, he said, but it can't duck its responsibilities, either. "The mindset of a lot of the churches around here is that if it's not our grandchild or if it's costing any money, then we're not really that interested. It's not our baby. That's not to say that every church does that, but some of the churches that we have approached, when we knocked on the door of that pastor, it was cordial, but you got a sense that he was thinking 'What's in this for me?' Not what's in it for my congregation, but what's in it for me?"

"Is the pastor the absolute key?" I asked. "Or are there churches that get involved without the pastor being the main person making it all happen?"

"Our faith," said Reverend Pate, "is reflected in action. When we have a lot of people of faith get together, that's politics. If there's a particular pastor that we wanted to approach, you're still talking to members of their congregation. In their congregation they have respected leaders that people look up to, the elders of the church. They may be keen on what the Jeremiah Group was doing and really think they need to be a part of that. So we aren't the only ones approaching the pastors at a peer level. Members of their congregation should be coming at them, and saying: 'There are some issues that are impacting our church and our neighborhood right here on Second Street, and we don't have the power to do it on our own.'"

Angela St. Hill considers what her church needs "to get involved with" and then brings issues to her pastor's attention. "The pastor may or may not be up on the current issues," she said. Some pastors take the lead, while others give lay leaders room to play that role. "You'll hardly see my pastor at a meeting or even a public action. But I represent him at everything. He gives me that authority or that freedom to be involved at whatever level I need to be involved."

"We're always recruiting," Reverend Jaime Oviedo said. "I remember with the Projects, that one pastor got it a little too late. But when all those people were forced out of their homes, gone, out of the churches and everything, now he sees, 'Hey, I should have been in a group like Jeremiah.' But now it's too late. They're gone. They're forced out, for whatever reason. So we're always proactive in the recruiting mode."

"Part of it," Brod Bagert explained, "goes to the craft of the individual meeting and what happens in those conversations. I've just started here in New Orleans, and my first priority is trying to meet with five hundred key institutional leaders in the city, some of whom I have connections with. So David Warren can set me up with his pastor, Elder Pierre. And Elder Pierre and I start to develop a relationship. And he's now going after another pastor in the neighborhood, and saying, 'Hey, this is somebody you need to talk to.' You need to do that power analysis internally just to get the conversation."

David Warren's relationship with Elder Pierre is like Angela's with her priest. In both cases, the pastor treats a lay member of the church as a reliable judge of people and of the issues that are attracting concern in the broader community. David and Angela defer to their pastors on some things, but their pastors defer to them on others. Authority in such relationships is more complicated than it initially appears to be, even where the tradition in question is doctrinally committed to hierarchy, as Angela's is. The pastor's flock does not consist of sheep.

"But then another side of it," Brod continued, "is whether I can find out enough about this pastor's interests. They're interested in their own institutions. Are they losing members? Do they have money? What can I do to agitate them, stir them up, and create a picture of how organizing could be directly related to their interests, so that they're not just doing it out of some abstract concern for goodness and kindness and justice? I think a lot of the craft of individual meetings is figuring out how to get a sense of somebody's interests and challenge them."

Reverend Pate said that the training he had received in Jeremiah had "changed the way I minister, period." He referred to pieces he had read in an IAF seminar on empowering the poor, one by Robert Linthicum on New Testament perspectives, the other by Walter Brueggemann on Old Testament perspectives. "When you put the two together, it's like a divine call. For me it's almost a sin to not be involved in a group such as Jeremiah, or any group like it. But the same thing does not have the same effect on some other pastors. In the end, they just haven't caught on. And yet, we still need them. The group still needs those to come aboard as well. We need to be as powerful and broad as we can get."

"Pastors are keys to the organizations," Jackie Jones said, "because pastors give you the okay to give you that power you're looking for in terms of the dues." Jeremiah's budget comes entirely from within the community, and most of its constituent institutions are churches. No commitment from pastors, no dues. No dues, no Jeremiah.

"Here's how it makes sense to me," said Reverend Pate, "the good Samaritan story. Basically, he picks this guy up, and gets him taken care of. Well, that's social ministry. Most churches do social ministry on some degree. But we're also called to do some social action. We can't really do that effectively by ourselves as an individual in a local congregation. But we can do it as a group. Had the good Samaritan gone to where the man got jumped and beat and robbed and wounded and saw there was a breach in that fence there and fixed that fence so that it wouldn't happen to the next person, I mean, that's social action. Now, for us to do that, I'm going to need to organize particular churches and get them involved. And then collectively we have that voice. I think that's what the other pastors don't really see. It's hard to get them to see that unity gives you power and a voice."

"Some of them have other concerns," I said, "or other political views."

"In the end," Brod said, "it's the issues that connect regardless of what our religious backgrounds are. We've had member churches that are pretty wealthy institutions from really wealthy areas, and you could sense there was some friction just in terms of direction. What you do is go back there and say fine, but there are issues that affect all aspects of the community." Brod counsels pastors against putting "all of your eggs in one basket. If you focus only on abortion, there are still quality-of-life issues that affect your congregation." If church members are "losing their jobs, or they're going to have to move, or they're having problems with their children because of crime, that has to speak to the pastor in some way."

"Well, I can tell you this," Jackie added. "Post-Katrina, I have never received so many messages from institutions who once said that politics had no place in the church. But they see it a little different now." Disastrous circumstances can make the antipolitical conception of pastoral responsibility seem foolish. Brod remarked that in New Orleans after the storm indifference was no longer the most prominent sin. In Houston the influx of Katrina survivors had had a similar impact on pastors. One pastor there who was starting up a new congregation admitted: "We were wrong about something. We were wrong to think that the church didn't have a role in politics. And it's clear to us now how politics affects the life of the congregation and the mission of the congregation and we are going to remedy that."

Reverend Samuel Chu was born and raised in Hong Kong, where his Southern Baptist parents were heavily involved in the democracy movement. He is now a pastor at Immanuel Presbyterian Church, a multiethnic congregation in Koreatown in Los Angeles, and was recently named interim executive director of California Faith for Equality. Many members of the Immanuel congregation are Latino immigrants from a Roman Catholic background. Others are Asians from a Protestant background. Sam wanted to be "at a place where multiculturalism didn't just mean multiple skin colors in some worship services. When I say 'Immanuel,' I don't just mean those who worship here. We mean all of those we're related to."

"Organizing kept me in the ministry," Sam told me. "It gave me hope that the church has value beyond what I had learned. I showed up at an action five years ago. Any group that could pack an auditorium that big must have its act together. The leaders were angry, but not in a yelling way." Sam decided to learn more, and eventually found his way to a ten-day IAF training session in Philadelphia. "It was better than three years at seminary and transformative for me personally. I got my first look at the overall picture and the unique role the church plays as a mediating institution versus just being oriented toward nurturing a person's spiritual life. So many people there were really impressive." This was during the period when One LA was being built. "It took us two years to learn the housing issue. Now the Housing Department calls us."

What can seminaries do better? "Above all they can help people think about investing in their own development and in accountability. Mainline Protestantism is like herding cats. Everybody is nice. Ordination is just a hazing process. There's no encouragement to challenge or disagree or say something that's not easy to hear. Internships didn't help at all. Nobody gets very good at anything in particular. Seminary didn't engage curiosity and creativity. It was deenergizing.

"I've been exposed to much more since seminary," Sam continued. "Now I have some idea of how to exegete institutions and communities. Pastoral care can't work in a community like Koreatown without engaging social structures and oppressive experiences as a group. We need to learn to listen to each other. Trust is a huge issue in the church."

Reverend Julie Fronk and her husband Reverend Michael Fronk are the pastors of the First Christian Church of Pomona, California, a Disciples of Christ congregation that I visited one Sunday with IAF organizer Anna Eng. Julie described American politics-as-usual as "fast-food democracy." Real democracy requires patience and gives sustenance. She said that her congregation's participation in One LA "has been transforming for me. The training I received from IAF taught me more than the coursework I did at Claremont. The whole thing has been very hopeful for me. Now I feel I have the ability to do something." Mike added that before First Christian joined One LA three years ago, it was "functionally invisible" in the community. Involvement in One LA is "changing the culture of the congregation."

John Whitney, a lay leader of First Presbyterian Church of Pomona, explained how easy it is to get sidetracked by things more mundane than Jesus and justice. His sanctuary has a copper roof that leaks in the winter, when the rain comes. "Do we pay our dues to One LA or fix the roof?" John then reflected on the Bible classes he taught for six years, before he became a leader in the citizens' organization. "I probably taught forty or fifty kids, and had very few relationships with adults. I kept confronting problems that I couldn't touch. Most of those kids are now in jail or dead."

Not everyone in the congregation is happy about having joined One LA, John reported. "Some people think that church is just about preaching the Gospel, evangelizing, and Bible study. But the Bible talks about injustice, too. IAF gets you talking about power. It teaches you how to be powerful. The term *power* has a negative ring. So the question you sometimes get is, 'What does the church have to do with power?' They ask, 'Why can't we talk about Jesus?'"

On hearing this, Anna, who in her role as organizer had kept her mouth shut since introducing me, couldn't resist jumping in: "But we can talk about Jesus!"

✻ CHAPTER SEVENTEEN ✻

The Contested Sacred

VOTES EXPRESS PREFERENCES. When I cast my vote, I am saying that I prefer one candidate to the others in the running. I might have a strong preference, but still have misgivings about the roster of choices and how it was determined. Perhaps I find all of the candidates mediocre or worse. If I play little role in determining the roster of choices, the candidates are apt to be serving powerful interests more than they are serving mine. So my role in the process becomes perfunctory. The candidates want me to prefer them to their rivals and to express that preference on the day of decision.

In this style of politics, the focus group and the survey are the main devices, apart from elections, for channeling influence upward. What travels upward is primarily information about preferences and the associated desires. The channeling does not depend on anyone in a leadership position having emotional contact with ordinary people. On occasion, there will be a town meeting in which individuals, often carefully selected for the staged event, are given an opportunity to tell a tale of woe so that the candidate can demonstrate a capacity to feel our pain. Woe is a topic of great political importance, but this is hardly a satisfactory way of having a discussion about its varieties, causes, and possible cures.

In the old-fashioned big-city machine, the negative effects of corruption were to some extent softened by the fact that the ward captain was in daily contact with the people he represented and spent a great deal of time listening to their stories about the various forms of misery they were experiencing. The ward captain knew what people on the block were concerned about, because he often met with them face to face. Nowadays, however, the connective tissue that sometimes made the old machines tolerable has largely gone missing.

Preferences do not necessarily correlate with concerns. The scale of my preferences from A to Z doesn't indicate much about what I care about. Suppose my niece has been run over by a car in my neighborhood. Yes, I would have preferred her being alive to her being dead. Yes, I would now prefer to have a traffic light installed at the dangerous intersection. And yes, other things being equal, I prefer candidates who favor the traffic light proposal to candidates who do not. What I am conveying to the organizer or the ward captain, however, is that I am grieving over the loss of my niece and angry over the bureaucracy's failure to respond to my phone calls. These are not essentially matters of preference, nor even of desire. They pertain to what I care about so deeply that I count its violation or destruction as horrendous.

It is no accident that "horrific" was the word that came to Angela St. Hill's mind in connection with the killing that had preceded my visit to Marrero. The horrendous does not fall on a scale. It keeps close company with our deepest concerns and passions. It is what happens when the people or things we care most deeply about—the people or things that are *sacred* to us—are violated, destroyed, or profaned.[102] Our responses to horrendous evils are passionate. The reasoning that surrounds these responses is, for the most part, neither comparative nor instrumental. It has to do with the special value, the sacred value, that some actions or events attack, demean, or crush. It has to do with what we treasure for its own sake, above and beyond any use it has for us. In Angela's mind, what she called "horrific" was related to what she called "the sanctity of life."

Evils are horrendous only if they violate, profane, or destroy something sacred. To be sacred is to be worthy of reverence. It is appropriate to respond to sacred things by celebrating their existence and excellences. It is also appropriate to express horror at the prospect of losing them, to mourn when they are lost, to commemorate them when our mourning is completed, to be angered by assaults on them, and to take offense when they are profaned. Yet another appropriate response is to protect them from violation, destruction, and profanation, for example, by instituting prohibitions of certain kinds.

None of these responses can be wholly excluded from political life so long as some people attribute sacred value to some things. They express their attitudes toward the sacred in claims about what deserves reverent celebration, commemoration, and protection. The sacred can be a source of social solidarity for any group that largely agrees on such matters. But a society like the United States encompasses many visions of the sacred, many conceptions of what, if anything, has intrinsic value and importance of a kind that warrants reverential responses.

The controversy at Harmony Elementary when I visited South Central had to do with the principal's decision to hold a memorial ceremony for the Latinos who had recently been gunned down outside the school. African Americans recalled many occasions on which blacks had been murdered and no such ceremony had been held. They suspected that the relatively new Latino principal would not be disposed to commemorate all loss of life in the community equally. This is a local example of the politics of commemoration. A national example is the decision to make Martin Luther King's birthday a national holiday. To commemorate King's life is, in part, to celebrate the overcoming of legally enforced racial segregation as a great national achievement. Doing so celebrates the dignity of racial minorities formerly excluded from the rights of citizenship, and symbolically incorporates them into the citizenry. Unless we stop celebrating national heroes and their accomplishments, we are bound to have disputes over which heroes, and thus which accomplishments, to celebrate.

A live issue involving the politics of celebration is the controversy over whether gay couples should be counted as married. Applying the concept of *marriage* to a couple implies that one holds the couple's bond sacred. The dispute might appear to be merely verbal, but it is not. When it is resolved, as it eventually will be, society will have given blessing, through public recognition of a status conferred in a ritual, to a kind of coupling that had long been abominated. This is not something that can be decided in abstraction from commitments concerning sacred value. It is *about* sacred value.

Our deepest divisions have less to do with celebration and commemoration than with which actions and practices are so horrendous as to warrant being outlawed. It took a civil war to settle whether slavery should be banned absolutely. Slavery now serves as a paradigm of domination, a kind of horrendous evil that we are implicitly committed to extirpating from our common life. But we repeatedly face heated controversies over what relationships qualify as sufficiently like the master-slave relationship in their arbitrariness to be formally ruled out.

Defenders of American slavery argued that far from being arbitrary, the master-slave relationship was rooted in essential differences between the races. These differences were said to be determined either by nature or God, and to be of a kind that justifies placing white slaveholders in something like parental authority over black slaves. The opponents of slavery had to attack these claims, and did so in part by unmasking their self-serving character, their weak empirical basis, and the ideological function performed in them by appeals to divine will. The debates over patriarchy, at first pertaining to the right of women to vote and later pertaining to equal pay and the structure of the family, went along the same lines. One side argued that a particular relationship exemplified domination because it placed some people in a position to exercise power arbitrarily over others. The other side responded with empirical and theological arguments intended to show that the relationship at issue is less like that of masters to slaves than it is like that of parents to children. The empirical arguments were then criticized as flawed, while the theological arguments were said to be self-serving and ideological.

Both sides agreed that relationships involving domination are not only horrendous for the dominated, but also, for this very reason, unjustifiable. The debates were over what should be counted as horrendous in this sense. Religious considerations entered the debates in two ways: through the conceptual connection between the horrendous and the sacred and through the invocation of God's will. In all such cases, religious communities generated the debates. Critics of the disputed relationships were fired up by concerns over the violation of sacred value, over something they considered horrendous. Defenders of the same relationships appealed to scripture and theology, hoping to show that those relationships, far from being so horrendously arbitrary as to warrant being banned, are in fact divinely sanctioned. The debates were in large measure about sacred value and divine authority, and they were carried out largely in religious terms in a society most members of which professed allegiance to some form of theistic religion. For the debates to be resolved in favor of major reform, many theists had to be persuaded that their theological convictions and scriptural interpretations could be adjusted to accommodate a reclassification of some relationships as forms of domination.

The debates over slavery, patriarchy, and Jim Crow, then, all had roughly the same structure. They were about domination. They involved questions about how to differentiate relationships of domination from relationships in which something like paternal authority is justified. The participants in these debates have trafficked heavily in appeals to God's will, but in each case the proponents of reform have managed to shift the burden of proof. One thing that helped shift the burden was the difficulty of justifying an interpretation of God's will, against those who saw things differently, without arguing in a circle. If defense of the interpretation itself has to appeal to premises that are themselves in dispute, the defender begs the question, which makes the argument arbitrary. The other thing that helped shift the burden was the force of the cui bono question: *Who benefits* from acceptance of the proposed interpretation? The slaveholder's God permits slavery, whereas the slave's God does not. The patriarch's God commands patriarchy.

The recent culture wars revolve around the questions of whether sodomy, early abortions, and all instances of euthanasia are actually horrendous. Some people are sincerely horrified by sodomy, while others aren't bothered by it at all. Some people find early abortion and consensual euthanasia horrendous, while others find them merely sad. The debates over torture and war are also about the linkage between the sacred and the horrendous. Which ways of treating prisoners of war and suspected terrorists shall we classify as horrendous, as violations of sacred value, and thus as worthy of being banned absolutely? Must we be pacifists, as the Mennonites say, or should we count some conceivable wars as required by justice? And if the latter, then which actions in war, if any, are to be ruled out absolutely? It is no accident that religious communities weigh in heavily in all of these disputes. So long as many of our fellow citizens are concerned with the sacred and the horrendous, and interpret these aspects of life in theistic terms, our political disputes are bound to have something to do with theology.

Democratic republics rule out some acts absolutely and institute severe penalties for committing those acts. The penalties not only seek to deter people from perpetrating horrors, but also express the public's outrage when deterrence fails. The strongest reason for maintaining a standing army is to protect citizens from the horrors of conquest, genocide, and terrorism. By the same token, one of the main purposes of government is to mitigate the impact of horrendous evils when they cannot be prevented, including the horrors of natural catastrophe, as in Hurricane Katrina.

Because the sacred and the horrendous are conceptually linked to what we deem highly important, our differences over these matters can threaten our ability to have a polity at all. If I consider something worthy of reverent protection, and you do not, our debate over whether lethal attacks on it must be outlawed might be hard to settle through compromise. My passion is likely to keep the issue alive.

Centrist party politics prefers the language of preferences and interests to the language of concerns and passions. Just as a passion such as grief or anger can be said to express an underlying concern for something important to us, a preference can be said to express an underlying interest. Political parties are often described these days as coalitions of interest groups. The term *interest*, which I used in chapter 3 as a rough synonym for "concern," tends, in party politics, to be used more narrowly, to mark an implicit contrast with the sort of concern Angela was expressing in her grief.

This contrast between interests and passions goes back to the early modern period, when some people, including some of the founders, became suspicious of passions in general, and religious passions in particular, as sources of political faction. Interests, in this more restricted sense of the term, are thought to be milder than passions and therefore less likely to cause social strife. Interests can also be used to tame passions if set against them in the right way. A paradigmatic instance of an interest, according to this way of thinking, is the desire for financial gain. A paradigmatic instance of a passion is religious enthusiasm. Albert Hirschman, in his historical study of this distinction, demonstrates that the concept of an interest gradually narrowed in a way that left "interests" referring to something essentially economic.[103]

Setting our concepts up in this way made it difficult for societies with burgeoning capitalist economies to rein in the economic interests that now dominate our politics. There were good reasons for early modern Europeans to view commerce as civilizing. It gave people an incentive to have peaceable relations with trading partners. Increasing productivity appeared to enhance the wealth of nations. Urban blight, industrial pollution, robber barons, and hedge fund managers were yet to arrive on the scene. There were also good reasons for early modern Europeans to view religious enthusiasm with suspicion, given the role it played in the state-founding wars that followed the Protestant Reformation. Interests, paradigmatically financial self-interest, appeared socially beneficial, whereas passions, paradigmatically religious passion, appeared socially corrosive. The twin results of thinking in this way were: first, that the unruly passion of greed for the most part went unnamed and, second, that the continuing relevance of sacred causes to our politics takes us by surprise or even leaves us aghast.

I noted in chapter 3 that organizers encourage citizens to reflect candidly on interests in the narrow sense, not least of all because many agents in a given political arena are in fact motivated by interests in this sense. It can take a lot of hard work to cultivate a broader sense of what interests are and how they can converge in the common good of the community as a whole. But grassroots democracy in all of its forms—in the Alinsky tradition, as well as in the great democratic reform movements—has self-consciously made room for reference to sacred value in the public square. The grassroots democratic organizer, from Garrison to Burns to Baker to Cortés, resists the reduction of politics to the negotiation of preferences and the coordination of interest groups in the narrow sense of "interest." The concerns elicited in one-on-one conversations and small-group meetings include passions of considerable vehemence. That is why democracy, according to this strand of the political tradition, is often said to have a spirit.

The organizer is looking for leaders. We have seen that one mark of leaders, according to Alinsky, is a capacity for anger; another is the capacity for empathetic uptake of other people's deepest concerns. It is a democratic leader's task to open up the political process to concerns that are deeper and broader than a preference for a slightly higher wage or a slightly lower tax rate. Grassroots democracy insists that a republic can be democratic only if its citizens infuse a democratic spirit into their shared political life. A democratic republic cannot do without expression of passions such as grief at catastrophic loss and anger at particular instances of domination, injustice, and indifference. Grassroots democratic activism is therefore fundamentally at odds with the view that interests *rather than* passions, and financial interests above all, are all that ought to get adjudicated in politics.

Citizens and legislators cast votes. Presidents and governors sign bills into law or veto them. Judges issue verdicts. All of these acts express preferences for one possible candidate, policy, judgment, or outcome over another. There are, however, other features of the political culture that open up channels for the expression of passions, despite the founders' worries about possible sources of faction. Judges write supporting and dissenting opinions, and in many cases, especially the most important ones, reveal much more than their preferences. The right to petition for the redress of grievances has a function quite different from voting. The etymological connection between "grievance" and "grief" points in the direction of passionate expression. Freedom of speech and religious expression open the channels up in another way. The most profound presidential speeches—such as Lincoln's Second Inaugural and Carter's so-called "malaise" address—are sometimes about our deepest concerns and bear on the difference between sacred value and utility. The point of assembling peaceably, or not so peaceably, in public is often to make clear that as far as we are concerned, some things being done are simply beyond the pale. At those moments, we aren't just saying that we don't prefer those things. When we demonstrate, the passion being demonstrated is often our anger.

Like the practice of voting, the activity of buying commodities on the market tends to reduce the results of our practical reasoning to an expression of preferences. In the end, we purchase this, but not that, and we are prepared to pay this much, but no more. The money we are willing to spend to acquire a certain product, rent someone's services, or produce a certain outcome assigns a quantifiable public value to it, which can then be compared on a single, graduated scale to all other things assigned value in the same currency. There is much talk these days among grassroots democratic organizers about the dangers of *commodification*. To commodify something, in the primary sense, is to treat it as something to be bought and sold and then perhaps discarded when it no longer has much usefulness. In the extended sense, I commodify something if I treat its value to me (or to others) as quantifiable in terms of how much I (or others) would be willing to spend for it.

The worry being expressed about commodification has to do with a perceived tendency for the culture surrounding a capitalist market to be corrupted by the attitudes and forms of reasoning appropriate to monetary transactions. The worry is that the capitalist market is encroaching on practices in which our deepest concerns are expressed and cultivated. To attribute sacred value to something is to imply that its value can neither be measured exhaustively in quantitative terms, nor reduced to utility, nor subjected at someone's whim to trade-offs of the sorts that markets are designed to facilitate.[104] So here we have another area in which attitudes toward the sacred impinge on politics.

There are many political controversies that have to do with where the limits of commodification should be set. Chattel slavery commodifies human beings by treating them as mere property to be bought and sold. Prostitution commodifies sexual activity by exchanging it directly for money. Pornography adds to this the element of spectatorship. Bribery commodifies political decision making. Treating the natural environment merely as a standing reserve of industrial resources commodifies such goods as a forest or a prairie. The distribution of orphans for a fee commodifies adoption. We need to decide which of these things take the mentality of cost-benefit calculation, of instrumental reason, too far. Our sense of what the limits should be is intertwined with what strikes us as horrendous, profane, or unjust—the destruction of a redwood grove being an instance of the horrendous, the placement of a sexually provocative billboard next to an elementary school being an instance of the profane, and bribery being an instance of the unjust.

When Bishop Fitzpatrick used diocesan funds to bring National Public Radio to the Rio Grande Valley, he was combating the commodification of news delivery. He was concerned to prevent the press, as a vehicle for the self-education of citizens, from becoming a vehicle merely for their diversion. When the citizens of New Orleans tried to keep their children from being exposed to prostitutes, they were trying in part to prevent the profanation of the setting in which those children are being raised. Both of these issues pertain to commodification. But the broader concern with commodification among grassroots democrats is not focused on any particular issue. It pertains to the general tendency of cost-benefit reasoning to dominate the culture as a whole.

An example of this tendency in the sphere of religion is Bishop Jakes's implicit conception of spiritual worth as something measurable in terms of financial prosperity. In the political sphere, the tendency can be seen wherever human beings who come to seem inferior to others in instrumental value—the displaced New Orleans underclass, the inmates of Angola Prison, the colonia residents of southern Texas, or the African-American isolates of South Central L.A.—are written off as waste products of the economic system. Attempts to honor their intrinsic worth by integrating them into the economic, social, and civic practices of the community meet resistance from some economists and executives, who say that liberty consists in freedom from interference and rationality consists in maximization of expected utility.

Many of the people who describe themselves as "spiritual, but not religious" appear to affirm a distinction between the sacred and the useful. Some liberal environmentalists attribute sacred value to nature, to particular ecosystems, or to endangered species, but without interpreting this in terms of formal religious doctrine. There are philosophers who employ the term ***human dignity*** as a secular marker for a kind of sacred value. They hold that human beings should never be treated merely as means—as mere objects of use.

The most common cultural manifestation of these "nonreligious" affirmations of sacred value is identification with a shared lifestyle rather than with a shared institutional base. Lifestyle liberals, as I shall call them, are weakly grouped. The symbolic medium of their shared spirit is not ritual so much as it is taste,[105] which expresses itself primarily in consumer choices expressive of identity: the Prius, T-shirts as message boards, backpacks, hiking boots, bands, and so on. These choices implicitly construct a distinctive profile for oneself while permitting potential friends, mates, and professional associates in the same social class to find one another. There is no danger here of absorption into an undifferentiated mass but also little cultural basis for cultivating and exercising power that could be used to restrain the multinational corporations at the center of a capitalist economy. Just as these folks are squeamish about formal ritual, they are also skittish about building institutions capable of articulating and enforcing absolute prohibitions. The sacred they affirm is fuzzy around the edges, like an environmentalist's beard or cut-off jeans.

Lifestyle liberals might be disposed to approve of broad-based organizing in principle, but relatively few of them are involved in it. They prefer to donate online to the Sierra Club and to candidates who make fuzzy calls for change. The prayers, liturgical celebrations, and doctrinal commitments that someone like Father Alfonso brings with him into the public square would give many liberals pause. In any event, to participate in a citizens' organization like

Valley Interfaith, one needs to be involved in a dues-paying institution—if not a church or a synagogue, then a PTA or a union. There are no lifestyle enclaves paying dues to participate in Valley Interfaith. Lifestyle liberalism and grassroots democracy share an antipathy for unrestricted commodification, but they have very different relationships to power. The former evaporates into subjectivity, while the latter builds organized strength.

I do not mean to disparage people who use the financial and symbolic means at their disposal to promote ethically admirable political objectives. I drive a Prius, and many of my other consumer choices express my ethical-political commitments—to environmentalism, fair trade, and so forth. During the Vietnam War, my bushy beard did political work, just as Malcolm X hats, spiky hair, and cross-dressing have done political work in other contexts. What worries me about lifestyle liberalism (as a temptation to which all members of my social class are prone) is its tendency to rest content with symbolic gestures and loose connections when other forms of action and gathering might do more good.[106]

The churches involved in broad-based citizens' organizations are committed to hammering out a relatively determinate conception of sacred value for their own members and to using their institutional power, in light of that conception, to fight the commodification and subsequent discarding of human beings. We have seen that the Roman Catholic churches are internally conflicted over just what their applications of the concept of sacred value should be taken to imply politically. Angela St. Hill, like the Opus Dei priest mentioned by Daniel May, considers "the sanctity of life" inviolable, but she used this concept while making a case for regarding prisoners and drug addicts as something more than discards. The narrowing of Catholic social teaching in some parishes appears to treat the fetus as a symbol of the purity of a society under threat and the resident alien and the terrorist as symbols of unwelcome permeation of the societal boundary. The difference between

Angela's view of sanctity and the religious right's is of considerable political importance for the broader community.

Similar divisions run through many American denominations. The sacred is contested not only across the boundaries of religious groups and lifestyle enclaves in the broader political culture, but also within most religious traditions. The contestation bears, as one would expect, on both the positive and negative faces of sacred concern: on what is deemed worthy of being celebrated or commemorated; on the symbolic register in which the rituals should be conducted; on what, if anything, should be absolutely prohibited; and on how, and by whom, the agreed-on prohibitions should be enforced.

We are bound to misrepresent the relation of religion to politics if we ignore either the presence of sacred concerns outside of organized religions or the contestation over sacred concerns within particular organized religions. There is no single thing worth calling "religion" to be at issue here. People who claim that religion as such is bad for politics, and should be minimized to the extent possible, have not had an easy time defining what they want to minimize, or explaining how the elimination of religion from politics is to be carried out by means that are both realistic and democratic.

It is clear why theocracy is incompatible with democracy, because theocracy is rule by people who consider themselves anointed by God to be in charge, and democracy is the attempt to combine an inclusive conception of citizenship with security from domination. Theocracy was the paradigmatic example of arbitrary rule on the world stage at the time when the modern struggle against domination got started. That struggle was defined over against it. In practice, theocracy puts one religious group in a position of political dominance over others. It is arbitrary because no noncircular answer is ever given to the question, Why are you to be considered God's authorized representatives? So the project of nondomination must reject it. Most of the people who first rejected it were themselves strongly committed theists of one sort or another. Theocratic domination is what the founders were trying to rule out when they prohibited Congress from establishing a national religion. They understood that there are many nontheocratic forms of religion, and that many of these are politically benign, if not beneficial.

If a polity counts as secularized only if the people participating in its deliberations are no longer concerned with sacred value, then our polity is not secularized. It is, however, secularized in the sense that the people participating in it cannot reasonably take for granted a single conception of sacred value, or even a broadly theistic conception of sacred value, when conversing or debating with one another.[107] The discussion does not proceed from a consensus on sacred value, but it does give expression to multiple, contestable, contested conceptions of sacred value. These conceptions matter enormously, but none of them functions as a canopy under which we all take shelter. One citizen's political behavior expresses a more or less well defined conception of sacred value. Another citizen's behavior expresses a rejection of sacred value. In a religiously diverse democratic republic, these differences are going to matter, and they do not seem to be going away.[108] Such is the cultural result of combining the two religion clauses in the First Amendment, the prohibition of an officially established religion and the freedom of religious expression.

Some people explicitly reject the sacred and argue that the polity would be better off if all reference to sacred value were eliminated from public discussion. All absolute prohibitions are declared superstitious. Cost-benefit reasoning, according to one influential version of this view, is the only appropriate basis for public discussion.[109] What the separation of church and state ultimately points toward, according to this view, is a day in which all citizens will substitute calculation of utility for the conception of sacred value they now accept.

This sort of utilitarianism hopes to modify the unfortunate effects of a market-centered culture not by attributing a qualitatively distinct kind of value to human beings, ecosystems, great works of art, and so forth, but rather by insisting that citizens should adopt the disinterested perspective of someone concerned with the greatest good for the greatest number, rather than one centered on personal profit, when engaging in cost-benefit calculation. This is not the place to pursue a discussion of the utilitarian critique of sacred value. I mention it here in order to contrast it with the appeals to sacred value that I have found in the reasoning of grassroots democrats. Those appeals are designed to place limits on cost-benefit calculation as such.

From the vantage of grassroots democracy, one might say that utilitarianism and egoism are the two forms that commodity fetishism takes in public philosophy. The two forms differ on what perspective one should adopt when calculating costs and benefits. But both are focused strictly on maximizing the ***utility*** of *consequences*, rather than on other forms and bearers of value—utility for everybody, in the one case, and utility for the calculator, in the other. Both reflect the current prestige of economic practices that reduce practical reasoning to cost-benefit calculation, rather than providing a radical critique of them. Grassroots democrats, in contrast, speak as if there are kinds of value that are distinct from utility and as if there are bearers of intrinsic value (such as persons and some acts and things) that are distinct from consequences (resulting states of affairs).

The deepest cultural division present in modern democracies might well be between people who take cost-benefit calculation to be definitive of practical rationality as such and people who use the concepts of sacred value and human dignity to defend some aspects of culture from commodification. On one side of this line, there is a debate between utilitarian moralists and unabashed defenders of the profit motive over whether an impersonal or an egoistic perspective should be adopted when calculating the costs and benefits of one's actions. On the other side of the same line, there are myriad disputes over *how* to restrict the scope of cost-benefit calculation and *why*. It is very important to see that the line between the champions of instrumental reason and its critics does not coincide with the line between the people who are committed to organized religion and the people who aren't. The politics of sacred value is a complicated affair, as well as one fraught with much conflict.

Grassroots democracy is neither theocratic in spirit, nor unwelcoming to religious communities committed to nondomination. What grassroots democracy proposes is an open-ended discussion among citizens who hold differing conceptions of the sacred, the excellent, the good, the mediocre, the bad, and the horrendous, as well as somewhat differing conceptions of the constraints that ought to be placed on our means and ends. Obviously, there are moments in which an exchange of this sort feels like a friendly conversation and others in which it feels like a civil war. The debate over slavery degenerated into actual warfare. Our deepest concerns can be politically explosive. But why suppose that we could ever succeed in filtering them out? If people care enough about something that has evident political relevance, they are going to express their concern publicly. What they care about most is bound to motivate them.

Grassroots democracy responds to the dangers of passionate excess in several ways, none of which involves invoking a distinction between passions and interests. People of different kinds are drawn into settings where they are expected to say what they care about and listen respectfully while others say what they care about. Because some of the settings are sacred spaces, and prayer is permitted, religious identifications are made evident, but the boundaries separating religious communities are also crossed. Small-group meetings transform initially inchoate concerns, expressed in the first-person language of desire and passion, into evaluative claims, expressed in the second-person language of reasons. The broader the coalition's base, the clearer it becomes that no single religious outlook can be taken for granted as a framework for discussion.

Moreover, one of the group's primary tasks is developmental. Leaders are trying not only to identify potential leaders, but also to cultivate them. The ethical transformation of citizens includes the transformation of grief and rage into tempered anger and courageous practical wisdom. Finally, leaders discuss the need for self-discipline. To earn the trust of the broader community, the group must place constraints on its own ends and means. If the members of a citizens' organization can make clear that they seek neither to dominate the polity, nor to mistreat their opponents, they can contribute to building up an atmosphere of trust and mutual recognition in the community as a whole. This gives others reason to conclude that it is not necessary, in this community, to choose between dominating and being dominated.

By choosing to act in a certain way, the members of a citizens' organization can demonstrate their commitment to the common good. There is a way of sharing the benefits and burdens of common life from which everyone seeking not to be dominated would benefit. Citizens of good will are trying to find that way. By trying to find it, they are already bringing it into being. Religious domination is one of the most important forms of domination we wish to avoid. Love of religious liberty is the flipside of the realization that it is horrible to live under an arbitrarily imposed conception of sacred value. To be self-consistent, we must offer the same liberty to all citizens, and do so in a way they can recognize as well motivated. Tolerating others who are evidently committed to the common good is widely recognized as a central democratic virtue.[110] Equally important, I would say, is the virtue of appropriate yielding, of visibly pulling back at those moments when others could reasonably take us to be imposing our concerns on them.

Both of these virtues appear to be missing in people who cannot resist making public their wish that the rest of us did not exist. Theocrats look forward with too much relish to the arrival of a kingdom in which everyone but the true believers burns in hell. The content of this hope is every bit as clear as the prideful self-assurance. Theocrats think they know who will be among the elect. Similarly, in utopian fantasies of secularization, religion miraculously disappears, or at least recedes into private life, as the light of reason dawns. In real life, the religious characters stubbornly refuse to exit the stage at the end of Act Three. Marxist-Leninism taught us how that drama plays out when force is used to make them leave. It looks a lot like the Spanish Inquisition, but with a revolutionary avant-garde in the roles of priests and the Gulag in place of the rack. Understood as a strategy, the attempt to eliminate religion from politics oscillates between merely wishing religion away and trying to crush it. The former version is ineffectual, the latter vicious. But even merely wishing religion away has an important short-term negative consequence, because it splits up people who might otherwise collaborate in an attempt to tame large-scale corporate and governmental power. Why cooperate with people who wish that your deepest concerns are either going to die off or get excluded from the discussion?

The problem is not that the culture warriors in our midst have made a mistake on the relation of the right to the good, or have failed to exercise sufficient care in policing the reasons they express in the public forum. The problem is that their behavior reveals what they are hoping for, which is to dominate, if not eliminate, the rest of us if given the chance. If our mirror neurons are functioning properly, we can tell at a glance who *intends* to dominate whom. As the saying goes, even a dog knows the difference between a trip and a kick. Canine society is a regime of domination, the only questions being who will grovel and who will stand tall. We have not lost our mammalian ability to intuit the intentions of beta males on the rise. Democratic republics are supposed to inaugurate another, more humane, possibility for coordinating our common life.

It would be unfair, however, to describe the religious right as essentially theocratic. Many people associated with the religious right claim, after all, to be defending *democracy* from forces that threaten to undermine it. Their claim is that the core values of democracy, including respect for human dignity, are likely to survive only in a culture committed to preserving the traditional family and to prohibiting abortion, euthanasia, and same-sex coupling absolutely. Democratic culture, according to this view, needs to defend itself against secularization, cultural decadence, and moral laxity if it is going to secure its own transmission from one generation to the next.

There is some analogy between this view and IAF's concern about the importance of reweaving the social fabric. The religious right also resembles broad-based organizing in its affirmation of the relevance of sacred value to some political questions and its commitment to organizing religious communities for political purposes. Pastors obviously play prominent roles in both of these forms of political practice. How, then, do broad-based grassroots organizing and the religious right differ? The short answer is that the religious right is a top-down social movement with strong ties to a particular political party, whereas broad-based organizing is neither top-down, nor a social movement, and deliberately distances itself from political parties.[111]

A longer answer, which I cannot develop here, would require looking closely at how issues and policy proposals are formulated and put into circulation by the religious right. This process is what makes the religious right in large part a top-down movement and thus something distinct from grassroots democracy in structure. One intended effect of the top-down process, when the opinion-making elite succeeds in controlling it, is a remarkably effective use of television, radio, and think tanks to frame issues, promote proposals, and win elections. The religious right has worked hard, and quite effectively, to find leaders, cultivate them, and move them into positions of responsibility commensurate with their gifts. That it has done less well in avoiding scandal and abuse of authority must have something to do with its paucity of structural means for holding leaders accountable from below.

Like other social movements, the religious right is oriented toward a single cluster of issues, which form the basis for mobilization of congregations and parishes. The national leadership has touted a small handful of cultural issues as of paramount importance to "religious" people, while downplaying the significance of issues such as fraudulent lending, exploitation of the workforce, and pollution. IAF insists that a fully democratic approach to organizing needs to focus principally on concerns that ordinary people express in face-to-face meetings. As we have seen, many people involved in IAF agree that abortion, euthanasia, and same-sex coupling should be rejected. They often complain, however, that acceptance of the religious right's agenda has made some religious communities increasingly complicit in the corporate elite's indifference to the suffering of exploited workers and the underclass. What the "traditionalists" have actually set in motion is a hollowing out of their own traditions.

Some of the issues that have been of central concern to the religious right over the last three decades have more recently been taken over by the considerably more volatile Tea Party movement. Insofar as the latter movement is a creation of media elites, it too qualifies as an example of top-down politics. The volatility of the movement derives, however, from the spontaneity of its populist spirit. The movement's distrust of elites and antipathy for gays, resident aliens, and "socialists" could rapidly morph into outright fascism if there were a further deepening of the economic crisis or a series of additional terrorist attacks on the scale of 9/11. In any event, it is easy to imagine the movement's bottom-up populism becoming a more prominent force in American politics in the coming years. In assessing this possibility and the dangers it poses, one needs to keep in mind a distinction between populist and genuinely democratic forms of sociality.

Both populism and grassroots democracy place power in the hands of ordinary people and encourage the flow of influence from the bottom of the social hierarchy upward. But *populism*, as I am using the term, treats "the people" as a relatively undifferentiated mass. It does without precisely defined constraints on ends and means; invests little time and energy in the ethical formation of participants; relies heavily on the scapegoating of alleged enemies; and attributes authority mainly, if not exclusively, to charismatic leaders. In all of these respects, it differs from grassroots democracy as practiced in the great reform movements of the past or in contemporary broad-based organizing. "Going rogue," to use Sarah Palin's expression, is very different from hammering out a disciplined, differentiated, bottom-up structure of authority. It is what happens when an undifferentiated, populist mass rigidifies its external boundary while abandoning its internal structures of normative constraint and democratically earned authority.

We are now ready to make the final stop in our journey from New Orleans to northern California. Our destination is Congregation Kol Shofar, a synagogue in Tiburon, just north of San Francisco. Sixty delegates representing citizens' organizations from San Francisco County, Napa and Sonoma counties, and Marin County are gathering for the first time to develop a regional strategy. They hope eventually to have an impact on the state level by joining forces with some of the people we have met during our stops in Maywood, Pomona, Koreatown, and South Central.

The delegates are gathering in the synagogue's main prayer hall. As I enter, I notice a stack of brochures printed on yellow paper. "Spirituality for Soccer Moms (and others too)," the announcement says. *Havdalah* is the ceremony that Jews use to end the Sabbath. The brochures describe it as a "cool service," and invite people to learn how to do it. "You'll gradually learn how to create *Shabbat* as your own work of art." Congregation Kol Shofar appears to be working hard at drawing in Jews who might otherwise be tempted to describe themselves as "spiritual, not religious." At the same time, the Congregation's commitment to broad-based organizing is an attempt to give its ethical idealism some substance.

Only a handful of the delegates present this evening are Jews, but all of the men are wearing yarmulkes out of respect for the setting. Kol Shofar's senior rabbi, Lavey Derby, opens the assembly with a prayer. The Lord, says Rabbi Derby, gave the tribe of Levi the task of carrying the sacred ark and furniture on their shoulders. Some burdens in life are to be carried on the shoulders. To carry these sacred things, as was their calling, the Levites had to lift them up. To lift something up is to hold it sacred. "I want to lift this burden up," he says. And to do this, we must "expand our conception of the divine and of what God might ask us."

Michael Saxe-Taller, now an organizer with the Bay Area IAF, was then the director of programming for Kol Shofar. He and Rosaura Segura of St. Helena Roman Catholic Church in Sonoma County were chairing the assembly. Michael and Rosaura give a warm welcome to the delegates. Michael says that he feels "a sense of expansion" in his chest on this occasion. Rosaura remarks that her parish is in the heart of wine country. "There are two worlds living there," she says. "They could be two beautiful worlds. There are the people who harvest the grapes. And there are the others. Two worlds that use each other." The people who harvest the grapes make meager wages. The police harass them. "That's why I'm here."

The next stage of the meeting consists of "who we are" stories. Someone speaks for each cluster of delegates, explaining to the others who they are and what the issues are in their communities. Velma Gaines-Miller is among the most impressive. She is a nurse.

Her church is St. Boniface in San Francisco. She describes the period during which her family had no health insurance. There is a story to be told about her husband's illness and death. Her IAF citizens' organization helped craft and pass San Francisco's universal health care legislation. She imagines what might be possible if many IAF groups united across the counties. "Are you willing to unite?" she asks the other delegates. "We need to grow and to build power. By uniting we will have power."

These different groups are feeling each other out. Some of the Christians have never been in a synagogue before, worn a yarmulke, or been led in prayer by a rabbi. The various clusters are seeing what this strange interfaith relationship means in practice. When the "who we are" stories conclude, the group breaks up into house meetings, during which the delegates swap stories about the details of their local efforts. They have all been in house meetings before, but never for this broader purpose. Over time, they will settle on some issues that transcend their local communities and work out a strategy for moving forward.

When the house meetings are finished, the delegates assemble again in the prayer hall, this time for a keynote address. The speaker discusses the importance of one-on-one meetings, of listening to stories as a way of developing trust and perspective. But creative politics is also a matter of agitation. He quotes Rabbi Jonathan Sacks on the importance of taking God seriously, not just ourselves. Democracy is about people who care, who have a sense of humor, but are capable of grieving and feeling anger. By the time he gets to his point about anger, he is quite agitated himself, and his yarmulke comes flying off. He gathers himself. The group's task is to build a strategy, he says, but that will also take building a common culture out of shared practices and habits.

The man with the flying yarmulke is Ernesto Cortés. His address is almost finished. To show respect for his hosts at Kol Shofar, he wants to conclude by touching on an explicitly Jewish theme. *Zimzum*, he says, is a term from the Kabbalah. It refers to the moment immediately preceding creation, when God withdrew enough from a particular space to make room for the world. The most creative act, Ernie says, is one that makes room for others. The sparks of divine energy that remain trapped in the broken vessels of creation must now be gathered. It is our task to gather them, to repair the world—*tikkun olam*.

The session ends with some brief remarks by Sister Judy Donovan, the lead organizer responsible for this gathering and the strategic initiative to which it belongs. When most of the people have filed out, I notice organizers meeting one-on-one with the various speakers, reviewing what went well and what didn't. Ernie approaches me, hoping that I will do the same for him.

✻ CHAPTER EIGHTEEN ✻

Across Great Scars of Wrong

THE DELEGATES' ASSEMBLY of the Bay Area IAF organizations is a good example of how broad-based citizens' organizations go about building coalitions. They neither exclude conceptions of sacred value from the discussion, nor require everyone to convert to a single conception of sacred value. Instead, they encourage citizens to speak openly about what matters most to them and to do so in the language most familiar to them, which is often the language of a religious tradition. Equally important, they go into each other's sacred spaces and listen, while people say who they are. And then they break into small groups that try to find lines of concern that might converge in a common good.

The Marin meeting is also, however, a good example of the rapidly expanding scope of "cellular" grassroots networks. If Appadurai is right, then there is a shift underway, globally, in how ordinary people behave politically. It is a shift much less remarked on than economic globalization, but no less important. The extent to which these networks succeed in gathering strength and sharing information might well determine what sort of impact economic globalization has, in the decades to come, on the lives of most people.

As early as the 1946 edition of *Reveille for Radicals*, Alinsky had written of the need for "uniting, through a common interest which far transcends individual differences, all the institutions and agencies representative of the people" (202). In the Afterword to the Vintage edition in 1969, he added: "A political idiot knows that most major issues are national, and in some areas international, in scope. They cannot be coped with on the local community level"

(225). He warned, however, against leaping directly to a "national organization," while skipping "the organization of the parts" (226).

It is a warning that Ernie Cortés often repeats. The danger of moving too quickly is that the people claiming to represent "the people" at the national or international level of decision making will not in fact speak for anyone but themselves. For reasons that we have already examined, the power of a grassroots democratic citizens' organization rests on the authority of its leaders to speak for others, authority as an earned entitlement. To claim to speak for others without having listened to them and without being held accountable to them is either to pretend to have power one does not in fact have, or to stand in a relation of dominance over one's followers. Neither of these outcomes would constitute genuinely democratic power.

The meeting in Marin is evidence that a patient approach to democratic organizing might be on the verge of adding up to something that transcends the local level. It is too soon to know what the globalization of grassroots networking will come to. Some people assume, however, that there is no way for the outcome to be genuinely democratic. Grassroots democracy, in their view, is subject to what Robert Michels called *the iron law of oligarchy*.[112] In this, it is no different from any other form of human association. If the iron law of oligarchy holds, then *no* form of human organization can slip between the horns of the dilemma I have just mentioned. Either grassroots organizations will fail to accumulate enough power to tame the economic-political-military establishment, or they will succeed. If they fail, then we will already be living in an oligarchy of the rich and the lucky, and realism demands that we come to terms with this. But if grassroots organizations do accumulate enough power to make a difference, they will inevitably stop behaving democratically.

One problem with the iron law of oligarchy is that it is hard to square with history. Large-scale reforms have been achieved by democratic means in the past, so history can't be quite as closed as Michels claims. If we neglect to keep this in mind, our current situation will immediately appear hopeless. Still, it does make sense to be vigilant for signs that a given citizens' organization is becoming oligarchical in substance. There are at least five ways in which such an organization can go bad by democratic standards—and thus five dangers that participants and leaders should anticipate and guard against.

In the first, which we have already encountered in the Back of the Yards organization in Chicago, as soon as the group acquires enough power to have a place at the bargaining table, it stops being concerned with the project of inclusive nondomination and begins using its power to conserve its own position against the aspirations of emergent groups. This is clearly what corrupted many of the big unions representing labor in the 1960s. The self-conscious shift from community organizing and race-based organizing to broad-based organizing is meant to address the first danger—and to do so without taking the concerns of either particular communities or particular minority groups off of the table.

A second danger is for a group to demonize opponents or otherwise treat them unjustly. Contemporary organizers anticipate this danger by cautioning against thinking that there are permanent opponents and by initiating depolarization after big fights, regardless of whether they end in victory.

A third danger is for organizers or core leaders to dominate the rank-and-file. This can happen either in consequence of a deliberate choice—as in Lenin's call for restricting leadership of the Bolsheviks to a centralized cadre of professional revolutionaries—or as the result of an unnoticed breakdown in an organization's internal practices of accountability. By emphasizing leadership development, listening, reflexivity, and internal accountability, IAF aims to guard against this danger.

A fourth danger is for a citizens' organization to become incorporated by the economic-political establishment, rather than maintaining enough independence to hold that establishment accountable. As a teenager, I saw this process occurring on the local level in the waning years of the civil rights movement, as movement leaders were enticed to drop their oppositional stance and accept appointments to administer government programs. Since the early years of COPS in San Antonio, Ernesto Cortés has wisely separated IAF from administration of the public programs it has successfully campaigned for.

A fifth danger is a simpler form of co-optation, in which a charismatic grassroots democratic leader, perhaps unwittingly, becomes a front for people and groups with antidemocratic agendas. This is the scenario depicted with cartoonlike simplicity in Frank Capra's 1941 film *Meet John Doe*, in which a protagonist who gathers a massive following by mouthing democratic ideals is actually being manipulated by his hypocritical speech writer and a media mogul with fascist leanings.[113] We have seen that IAF is unrelenting in its insistence on the foolishness of relying heavily on charismatic leaders. Here again an organization's attention to leadership development and internal accountability come into play. In the next chapter, I will consider whether the Obama presidency is to be understood as an example of *Meet John Doe* syndrome.

Suppose the best networks of citizens' organizations manage to avoid all five of the dangers just outlined. It could still be that those networks will never amass enough power to cure what ails our politics. So in the remainder of the present chapter, I want to stand back for a moment and contemplate the gap between what citizens' organizations have accomplished so far and the sorts of problems that can be adequately addressed only by action that transcends the local level. Many problems, including global warming and militarism, could serve as illustrations of this gap, but I want to focus on an issue more closely related to a theme that has emerged repeatedly in the previous chapters, the increasing dominance of the new business elite over the rest of the citizenry.

Despite the accomplishments of grassroots democrats over the decades, some old forms of domination have persisted or resurfaced, and new forms, made possible by unprecedented technological and economic change, have arisen. So despite the victories that have been won against chattel slavery, the exploitation of children as laborers, the abuse of farm and factory workers, the exclusion of women and blacks from the franchise, and so forth, the impression remains strong that when Americans take pride in having achieved a *democratic* republic, they are paying themselves a compliment they do not deserve.

Grassroots democrats offer what appears to be a devastating critique of politics-as-usual. It claims that party politics is incapable, by itself, of preventing dominant classes from having their way with the rest of us. *Unless enough ordinary citizens organize themselves, educate themselves, and hold the powers that be accountable*, interest groups, big money, and manipulation of the public are bound to keep the most important forms of domination in place. One wonders, though, whether the italicized part of the previous sentence should simply be deleted. Perhaps the powers that be are too large and unruly and skillful at manipulation to be tamed by anyone. In that case, there will never be enough organized and well-informed citizens to perform the task grassroots democracy assigns to them. The critique of politics-as-usual appears to prove more than it was intended to prove. The system seems so corrupt, so tilted in favor of the rich and the lucky, that no realistic program for increasing citizen participation could make the outcome genuinely democratic.

In New Orleans we saw how easy it was for developers to exploit a catastrophe to achieve a position of dominance over the dispersed citizens of the Ninth Ward and New Orleans East. The Jeremiah Group is doing its best to take back the city on behalf of its ordinary citizens, past and present. It has had some successes since the time of my visit, most notably a decision by the Louisiana Recovery Authority in the summer of 2008 to award $75 million for "soft" second mortgages, with more than $52 million of that slated to go to New Orleans. This is an example of what organizing can accomplish when citizens' networks transcend the local level. But victories of this sort have hardly shifted the overall balance of power.

In my meeting with Jeremiah leaders, Karl Weber made an instructive presentation on the culture and economics of Louisiana. The state is near the bottom in income, education, and health, he said, but also near the top in oil production and natural gas processing. "In transportation, we've got the Mississippi. Everything in this part of the country comes through the river. Louisiana is ranked fourth worldwide when it comes to port activity. Of the seven major railroads, six hub in Louisiana. In sugar cane production, we're ranked second among the states. In cotton, we're ranked fifth. In seafood, we're first in the lower 48 and second overall. In GDP we're like twenty-seventh for all the states. So something isn't gelling here." Karl was saying that Jeremiah would eventually have to address the question of where the money that enters the state ends up going. How does a state that is in the middle of the pack in GDP end up being at the bottom of the pack in income, education, and health? Somebody is making off with a lot of money. It isn't just the developers. There's a bigger picture that needs to be clarified and made known.

If we pull back, and bring the entire country into view, we can pose Karl's question of where the money is going at a higher level of generality. One way of doing so is to ask what happened to the money generated by the massive increase in productivity in the U.S. economy since the mid-1960s. Economists Ian Dew-Becker and Robert J. Gordon have looked closely at the data.[114] Here are some of their most important findings:

In the end, we find that only the top 10 percent of taxpayers had gains in real labor income per hour or in total income per hour that kept pace with productivity growth over either the 1966–2001 or 1997–2001 periods. (6)

Of the total increase in real labor income of over 2.8 billion dollars, less than 12 percent went to the bottom half of the income distribution. More income accrued to the top 1 percent than the entire lower 50 percent. (55)

Even the 90th percentile has . . . outpaced average productivity growth by only 0.20 percentage points. The 99th and 99.9th percentiles, in contrast, have done fantastically well, a true "Golden Age" for the top earners worthy of the Robber Barons of the 1890s. (58)

Nearly as much of the 1966–2001 real income change went to the top 0.1 percent as went to the bottom 50 percent. (62)

CEOs together with sports and entertainment stars explain what is going on in the top 1 percent of the income distribution. (74)

Still another and perhaps even more stunning way to describe our results is that the top one-tenth of one percent of the income distribution earned as much of the real 1997–2001 gain in wage and salary income, excluding nonlabor income, *as the bottom 50 percent*. (76, italics in original)

When one combines these findings with the more widely known recent increase in the number of U.S. residents falling below the poverty line, it is quite clear where the money is and isn't going.

Some degree of stratification can occur without necessarily entailing domination. In this case, however, it seems clear that the top earners, in particular the CEOs in 99.9th percentile, not only increased their wage and salary income by something like 500 percent during a period when many other people were losing ground, but also benefited from lower tax burdens and several decades of deregulation. In other words, their economic windfall was linked to, and largely depended on, their success in getting their way politically. They have clearly used their economic advantages to secure political advantages, which in turn drastically strengthened their economic advantages. Are they not now in a position to exercise their power arbitrarily over others? And if they are, what reasonable hope is there for ordinary citizens to make a difference?

Some readers might suspect that I am blowing things out of proportion. Most people assume that society, if represented graphically, would look like a pyramid. In the standard mental picture, the horizontal line running along the base represents numbers of households and the vertical dimension represents income in dollars. The working class is the broad base on which society rests. Above this are the middle class, the upper middle class, and finally the big shots, narrowing to the point representing the person with the highest income. The assumption is that if we pictured our society as having the shape of the pyramid on a dollar bill, the top earners would occupy the position of the crazy-looking eye at the pyramid's apex.

Now, if we exclude families with incomes below $20,000 a year and families with incomes above $200,000, the graph does look roughly like that, except for being taller and skinnier than the pyramid on a dollar bill. This ignores the poor, however, on whom the social system actually rests. Adding them to the picture makes the pyramid look less steady, because they aren't as numerous at any given moment as the working class. But the simplified pyramid also ignores the well-to-do people we were discussing a moment ago. If we include them, the top of the graph already starts looking more like a piano wire when it goes from $200,000 to around $250,000, which in 2005 constituted the ninety-eighth percentile. Above that level, a graphic representation no longer helps much at all, because the wire becomes nearly invisible and it just keeps going and going.

For this reason, the most widely used graph of American social stratification, a wonderful teaching device created by Stephen J. Rose, stops at the $150,000 mark.[115]

Imagine a rather tall and skinny pyramid, then, with a base a little more than a foot wide and the $150,000 mark a little more than two feet above the base—a good size for a blackboard sketch in a seminar room. How high would the graph have to go to include the executives who declared more than $10 million dollars in family income on their tax returns? Rose's answer is: twenty stories high. The graph isn't really a pyramid at all. It's more like a very shaky golf club that only a mythic giant could use, or, more accurately, a very long, very thin wire with a very heavy pyramid hanging on the end of it.

That's what social stratification would actually come to if represented graphically in terms of yearly income. The figures would be staggering even if they referred to lifetime income. The dominant members of society are many stories up on the extremely narrow but very long wire. The top-four-hundred taxpaying households in 2005 averaged $213.9 million in income each, up $40 million from the previous year and more than double the figure from 2002. "Even after adjusting for inflation," according to the *Wall Street Journal*, "the minimum amount of income required to make the top-400 list has nearly tripled since 1992." These figures do not include tax-exempt income from government bonds.[116]

The executives up at the top of our imaginary twenty-story graph not only have enormous incomes but are also running the megacorporations that in recent decades reshaped the world economy and then brought the whole thing to the verge of ruin. Top CEOs possess the power that comes from accumulating a vastly disproportionate amount of the economy's total wealth. They also possess the power that comes from administering the incentive and command structures of modern businesses, many of which are capable of achieving effects, for good or for ill, the world over.[117] Yet in the decades leading up to the financial crisis of 2008, the rise to dominance of the new executive class was barely so much as mentioned by the major political parties or by the newspapers and television news departments that belong to the same establishment.

Not long before Barack Obama began campaigning for the presidency, I was talking politics with my son Livy who was then in his early twenties and happened to be home for the holidays. After we went over some of the statistics I have just been laying out, he confessed to being puzzled about what keeps electoral politics from addressing the increasing stratification of the population. The top-four-hundred households don't amount to many votes, and it takes being in the top 10 percent of earners to have benefited significantly from U.S. productivity growth. Why hasn't the bottom 90 percent rebelled? Is the problem that lower-income religious voters have been distracted by issues such as abortion and gay marriage into voting against their economic interests? I pointed out that the facts just don't support this widely circulated explanation.[118]

What factors are involved, then? Labor unions and urban political machines are much weaker than they used to be, with the consequence that a smaller fraction of the citizenry is organized on a face-to-face basis. This means that concerns about the economic situation of ordinary people do not rise through the ranks and congeal into clearly defined issues. Independent citizens' organizations have grown significantly during this period, but not yet to an extent that would compensate for these losses. Because political campaigns at the state and national levels are now conducted through mass media, they are very expensive, which means that successful candidates depend heavily on fundraising. Campaign organizations are top-down operations, run by professional experts. Campaign managers package their candidates and strive to redefine opposing candidates in order to manipulate undecided voters. Candidates sincerely dedicated to changing things from the bottom up have reason to think that they must choose between selling out and being ripped to shreds. The system produces more of the same.

Equally important, but much less widely recognized, is the fact that far more poor people are now either resident aliens or incarcerated—and therefore ineligible to vote—than was the case when the civil rights movement's voter registration drives reached their peak in the 1960s.[119] The new American underclass is largely disenfranchised. Jim and Jane Crow are no longer sharecroppers praying they won't be lynched. They are browns praying that they won't be asked for their papers and blacks either doing time on drug charges or barred from voting as ex-cons. One of the penalties for being thrust into underground economies is exclusion from participation in the decision making that distributes benefits and burdens.[120]

The economic establishment's rise to dominance appears, then, to depend on at least three factors: first, an overall decline in the organizational strength of ordinary citizens; second, the elite's increased ability in the age of mass media to translate economic power into political power; and third, the political exclusion of two large segments of the underclass. My son confessed to finding this picture depressing: "Maybe your book should be called 'We're fucked!'" he said.

This was not, of course, the reaction I was trying to elicit. Concluding that we're screwed is an excuse for doing nothing, a recipe for paralysis. I was thinking that each of the three factors I mentioned is something that can be worked on. But Livy was thinking that the three factors are conjoined in a way that leads to a darker realization. We cannot fix the third problem until we fix the other two, and it is not clear that fixing the first alone would suffice. How many citizens in the tenth through ninetieth percentiles would have to get organized and come to their senses to compensate for the power of the rich and the disenfranchisement of the poor?

A couple of months later, I had a similar conversation with one of my colleagues, a gifted public intellectual in his thirties who cares as much about democratic ideals as I do. He needed no instruction from me concerning the facts of social stratification and the emergence of the new economic-political establishment. He put my son's thought a little differently. Referring to the political system as a whole, he said: "It's broke! It's just broke!"

"We're fucked!" "It's broke!" The reasons for thinking that democracy is endangered, and needs the active engagement of many ordinary people to be kept alive, are also reasons for suspecting that it is already dead. They can even become reasons for thinking that democracy has *never existed* in the modern world: democracy isn't dead, but only because it was never really alive. Our ancestors claimed to have a democratic republic, but what they really had was a system for exploiting slaves, women, and other disadvantaged groups while setting up equally effective mechanisms for dominating the peoples of Asia, the Middle East, Africa, and South America. Stare long enough at the many types of domination perpetrated by Europe and the United States since the founding of so-called democratic republics, and you are apt to experience a Gestalt-shift that makes democracy seem completely unreal.

Domination is such a pervasive feature of human existence that, once we pay serious attention to its protean forms, it can easily make all efforts to fight it seem hopeless. Because democracy is now widely thought to be a good thing, the term *democracy* is often used to legitimize relationships of domination. Some of the people using the term in this way might be aware of the discrepancy, but most are no doubt sincere. Either way, the term comes to perform an ideological function; it masks and legitimizes actual domination by labeling it positively.

The nature of the deception comes to light once we recall how Lincoln applied the concept and then notice how differently the ideologues of capital and empire apply it. As we saw in chapter 11, Lincoln differed from the founders in giving "democracy" a positive connotation, but he was able to do so by using it as shorthand for "democratic republic" and by taking a republic to be genuinely democratic only if it satisfies a stringent standard of providing security against all forms of domination, with the master-slave relationship as the paradigmatic instance. What the ideologues of capital and empire do is to retain the positive connotation that the term *democracy* acquired in the middle decades of the nineteenth century, while drastically relaxing the criteria for applying the term. The term comes to stand for any system of government that holds regular elections and has certain other formal features analogous to the U.S. Bill of Rights.

The point can be made more precisely by distinguishing, for each of several different conceptions of democracy, between what *counts as* a democracy and what is *supposed to follow* from classifying something as a democracy—that to which the concept is applied versus the consequences of applying the concept.

- What James Madison counted as a democracy was direct rule by the common folk. What followed from rightly classifying something as a democracy, for him, was a negative judgment with respect to it, at least as a way of conducting public life for a large society.
- What Lincoln counted as a democracy was a republic capable of satisfying stringent criteria of inclusion and security against domination. What followed from rightly classifying something as a democracy, for him, was a positive judgment with respect to it.
- What the ideologues of capital and empire count as a democracy is a regime that satisfies minimal criteria concerning elections and citizens' rights, where the criteria are not spelled out in stringent requirements of inclusivity and security against domination. What follows from rightly classifying something as a democracy, for these ideologues, is a positive judgment with respect to it.

What we have, then, are three distinct conceptions of democracy. I have argued that the tradition of grassroots democracy is committed to the second of these conceptions. I am now suggesting that the contemporary debate over democracy is confusing in part because all three conceptions appear in it. Which of them is at issue is often hard to determine. Verbal disagreements are rife in this debate, but so are merely apparent agreements.

The ideologues of capital and empire are the main beneficiaries of the resulting mystification. As far as their purposes are concerned, the less closely we look at the concept of democracy, the better. The reason for this is that the positive connotation of "democracy" derives primarily from struggles against domination—and thus from people like Abraham Lincoln, Ralph Waldo Emerson, Susan B. Anthony, Martin Luther King Jr., and Ernesto Cortés, who have invoked the second of our three conceptions of democracy. It is not immediately clear, in the third conception, what is supposed to license the transition from classifying a regime as a democracy to judging it legitimate. When the reasons are made explicit, however, they often have something to do with a conception of freedom as noninterference, a notion that elicited my doubts in chapter 11.

The upshot of all this for the present chapter is that many of the people now making dark pronouncements about democracy—by declaring it dead, or saying that it has never existed, or granting that it does exist but is a very bad thing—are caught up in these same terminological confusions. It can be very hard to know what they think democracy is and what they think we should do now that democracy is understood to be nonexistent, dead, or despicable.

The most familiar way of reaching the conclusion that democracy is a bad thing is to embrace the first conception's criterion for applying the term. If democracy is rule by the common folk, and the common folk in a large society are essentially a herd, then democracy is a leveler of all the distinctions on which any sort of excellence, including political excellence, depends. My analysis of democratic sociality in chapter 11 and the evidence I have provided throughout this book of the cultivation of excellences in grassroots democratic organizations respond to this type of antidemocratic stance. It is true that *when* common folk remain in the condition of an ignorant herd they are injustice waiting to happen. That is precisely why the populism of the Tea Party movement is worrisome. But this criticism does not apply to broad-based organizing or to the great democratic reform movements of the last two centuries, so I shall now leave it aside.

In the academic left, an increasingly popular way of reaching antidemocratic conclusions begins with the third conception of what democracy is and then breaks with the assumption that democracy is a good thing. Capital and empire will go on using the term *democracy* to distract attention from the realities of domination, regardless of what social critics say. Let them have the term, says the radical antidemocrat, and then let social critics demonstrate the extent to which democracy as the establishment thinks of it and domination as radicals think of it are intertwined. All existing nation-states, not least of all the wealthy "democracies," are implicated in oppression of the underclass, exploitation of workers, and the latter-day forms of imperialism. Democracy (in this sense) has, from the beginning, been so implicated in such horrors as to deserve our wholehearted condemnation. Such, for example, is the view of Alain Badiou, who considers Lenin the theorist with the best grasp on what democracy is.[121] It is the form of the state that capital and empire use to stabilize and justify the bad things they do to people and to the natural world. It is therefore one of the things that all decent people who are conscious of what is actually going on must resist. Democracy, so the argument goes, is the political face of the most globally far-reaching system of domination there has been.

It should be clear from the analysis I have been offering that what radical antidemocrats call democracy and then denounce is not the same thing that grassroots democrats practice and praise. Radical antidemocrats and grassroots democrats share an antipathy for domination. They differ enormously in rhetorical strategy. They apply the concept of democracy differently *and* draw different implications from what they take to be its proper application. Do their different rhetorical strategies then amount to a merely verbal difference? Not really, because the reasons that they have for speaking in their respective ways are in conflict, and so are the practical programs they enact.

When the radical antidemocrat declares modern democracy a bad thing, the intended effect is to deprive capital and empire of whatever legitimacy they might seem to derive from the pride still associated with the historic movements of reform. The antidemocrat is inclined to explain those movements away, either by debunking their apparent achievements as accidental effects of nonmoral causes, or by absorbing them into a broader context that includes overwhelmingly negative developments (such as the Holocaust and the emergence of the prison-industrial complex). From the vantage point of grassroots democracy, the Leninist rhetorical move and the debunking of democratic reform that goes along with it are equally unwise. The rhetorical move is unwise because it leaves the masters of capital and empire in charge of what counts as democracy, at a time when most people still think of democracy as a good thing. The debunking of historic reform movements is unwise because it leaves the present struggle against domination without an inspiring past to learn from and inherit.

Grassroots democrats hold that the *application* of the concept of democracy remains worth fighting over. The term has positive associations for a reason, namely because the great reform movements embodied the ideal of inclusive nondomination in political practices that achieved things of considerable importance. It is no small matter to outlaw slavery, enfranchise women, or get blacks to the front of the bus. We ought to be able to celebrate such accomplishments and gather their wind in our sails without being tricked into thinking that the current financial system and the military-industrial complex uphold liberty and justice for all.

"It is across great scars of wrong" that grassroots democrats identify with a *tradition* of struggle against domination.[122] Many of those scars have come into view in this book. But we need to keep in mind the counsel to avoid the cant of "Ain't it awful?" and take note of what it means to numerous ordinary people, including undocumented aliens, to do the work of a citizen. The point of speaking favorably of a grassroots democratic tradition is to call attention to continuities, over time, in the ideals being hammered out and in the practices of organizing and accountability in which those ideals have been embodied. To employ the expression *grassroots democracy* as a name for that *tradition of thought and action* is not the same thing as paying any existing *nation-state* the compliment of actually living up to the standards embodied in that tradition.[123]

Grassroots democrats do wager that we are better off employing such concepts as *citizen* and *liberty* in the senses defined here than we would be otherwise. It is easier to rectify these concepts, by adjusting their criteria of application, than it is to relinquish them. Antidemocratic leftism, especially in the academy, prefers to sidestep the question of what institutional forms are going to provide *security* against domination by elites after modern democracy supposedly collapses. Grassroots democracy is reluctant to let go of such political innovations as the ballot box, the free press, and the separation of powers, given that these innovations have been essential to achieving what the great reform movements achieved. It is possible to believe that some constitutional provisions have lasting value and still think that the established power relations in society are riddled with domination. The imperial nation-state and globalized capitalism are not, on the whole, democratic in any sense that warrants a positive judgment on them. But there is no need to discard the baby with the bathwater, especially at a moment when the foes of civil liberty and the friends of torture are urging us to throw out the baby and keep the bathwater.

As I pointed out in chapter 11, an understandable yearning for a complete break with existing conditions tends to be embodied these days in weakly structured groups that are ill equipped to create change and have only a vague conception of what to hope for. The coming community being projected on the horizon has little substance, and the groups trying to bring that community about are themselves ill defined. Why assume that groups with little internal structure and vaguely articulated norms can take us where we need to go? Why suppose that power relations after the imagined collapse of capital and empire will be any better than before? Why suppose that they won't be an Orwellian nightmare? Why think that they will fulfill the hopes of the people yearning for them?

There are two possible ways for the antidemocratic left to take on a more determinate shape and internal structure and for its conception of nondomination to acquire more substance. In the first, antidemocracy will come to resemble grassroots democracy in its mode of sociality and its ethical substance, but without the same nomenclature. In the second, the leadership will become an avant-garde, and adopt a relationship of superiority to rank-and-file members unlike the one of mutual recognition personified in the organizing of Ernie Cortés and Ella Baker. Either way, it seems to me, the grassroots democratic tradition proves preferable. The first way sacrifices a useful and illuminating vocabulary without evident gain. The second way reintroduces arbitrary rule, albeit in the style of Lenin, rather than in the style of Dick Cheney.

Let us now consider another somewhat amorphous option, known as *fugitive democracy*. Fugitive democrats retain the stringent criteria for applying the term *democracy* associated with the second conception, and are also committed to using the term to express a positive judgment. But they deny that the term can any longer be used truthfully, in this sense, to refer either to nation-states or to a realistic project for the fundamental reform of nation-states by democratic means. Authentic democracy, according to this view, is an essentially fugitive, marginal affair, an episodic upsurge of idealism around the edges of institutions and practices that masquerade as democratic.

Sheldon Wolin is a leading theorist of "the evisceration of democracy" in our day, and the expanded edition of his landmark volume, *Politics and Vision*, is the canonical account of fugitive democracy.[124] He is read with great seriousness in the Southwest IAF network, but appropriated selectively. The problem we are facing, as he presents it, has a cultural and an institutional dimension. Culturally, at least in the United States, political participation is in long-term decline. In most recent elections citizens have voted in low numbers. As Wolin makes clear, many of them do not think of themselves as having a share of responsibility for the political order they inhabit (590–94). Given that they work mainly in corporate and governmental bureaucracies, they are in the habit of deferring to superiors and then expressing their resentment privately. They have learned the habits of the economic culture they inhabit.

The condition of our political culture reflects the condition of our basic institutions. According to Wolin, we now live in a world dominated militarily by the American superpower and economically by corporate conglomerates, the same world we found being played out in microcosm in the Astrodome after Katrina. The procedures of accountability characteristic of "democratic" republics now appear incapable of constraining the mutually reinforcing powers of empire and capital. Organizationally speaking, Wolin concludes, we have entered a postdemocratic era, an era in which the cultural and institutional conditions for democracy are no longer present.

Democracy survives under such circumstances, according to Wolin, only by splitting in half. On the institutional level, as the mere semblance of an accountable form of government, the democratic republic is a structure of electoral and other procedures in fact controlled by empire and capital; it is the means of disguise by which empire and capital legitimize their control of government. On the cultural level, as a set of social practices dedicated to demanding real accountability, democracy becomes fugitive. It becomes a perpetual but necessarily ephemeral struggle to contest powerful organizations of all kinds, if only for a moment and symbolically. Fugitive democracy depends on "the ingenuity of ordinary people in inventing temporary forms to meet their needs" (603). It does not aspire to govern, he says, because that would involve accommodating itself to hierarchical institutions. It aspires instead simply to "nurture the civic conscience of society" (606).

I share Wolin's concerns about the evisceration of democracy, and I am more than happy to join him in an attempt to nurture the civic conscience of society. Better fugitive democracy than no democracy at all. Yet I am suspicious, for the reasons given in chapter 11, of the overly simple contrast between hierarchical and democratic forms of sociality that Wolin is drawing here.[125] The fugitive democrat's distaste for assuming the responsibilities of governance spills over into distaste for earned representative authority within democratic organizations. No wonder democracy strikes the fugitive democrat as ephemeral. It is hard to imagine groups formed on this basis accomplishing anything but Romantic expressivity.

I also worry that fugitive democracy is self-defeating. Its picture of our situation is too bleak to sustain the hope for a measure of security against domination by elites but also too bleak to be entirely accurate. Like its close cousin, fugitive Christianity, it threatens to become a mere "ought" that has lost both its roots in the soil of social life and any hope of effecting change in the institutions it criticizes. It is the spirit of spiritless conditions, the sigh of creatures who take themselves to be powerless against the major agents of their oppressed condition.

The fugitive democrat sees *grounds* for democratic hope only at the local level. It is true that local arrangements are inherently easier for citizens to hold accountable than national and global arrangements are. The managerial elite now holds by far the greatest concentration of power, operates freely at the national and global levels, and transforms most political officials at both of these levels into its tools. But the arrangements required to keep power concentrated in this way—deregulation of corporations, imperial control of oil-rich countries, a shift of societal burdens from rich to poor, and an electoral system that allows big money to dominate public discussion—depend for their survival on the deference and torpor of ordinary people.

To abandon the hope that we who are not in the top percentile of wealth or income might, by changing our own behavior, be able to use governmental structures to exercise a greater degree of control on the economy than we now do is also to resign ourselves to ever-increasing domination by corporate elites. While it is foolish to think that the election of decent candidates to political office would transform government into something other than a sprawling hierarchical bureaucracy, it is too early or too despairing simply to concede essentially unconstrained global power to the wealthiest CEOs. It is also premature to cede control of the legislative and electoral processes to big money or control of the judiciary to people who believe that the U.S. Constitution's Bill of Rights, the Universal Declaration of Human Rights, and the Geneva Accords became obsolete on 9/11.

Even from the perspective of a strictly fugitive democracy, the question of who holds office in the three branches of government in the United States remains an issue of great consequence. Fugitive democracy in the United States is parasitic on judicial respect for the First Amendment, understood as a set of provisions intended for protecting human beings from domination, rather than for protecting corporations from interference. If we lose freedom of speech, freedom of religion, and the right of assembly, democracy will not be fugitive; it will be subterranean. If the legal system is to survive as a significant institutional repository of practical wisdom, it needs judges who are prepared to nourish the spirit of democracy and protect the Bill of Rights. Who will appoint those judges if the friends of democracy abandon the mechanisms of government to the interests of empire and capital? I conclude that a strictly fugitive democracy, as a politics that has lost all hope in the representative function of government as a means for holding rulers accountable, is self-defeating in practice.

If fugitive democracy is self-defeating, is that because Wolin's picture is too bleak or because it is not bleak enough? The completely bleak conclusion would be that democracy can survive in the decades ahead, if at all, only by going underground, by abandoning its hopes of holding any institution accountable and becoming instead a subterranean affair of clandestine meetings and occasional imprisonment and martyrdom. It is not obvious to me, however, that citizens will prove incapable of taking collective responsibility for their institutional arrangements. There are citizens already engaged in this effort, and no one knows either how far the existing networks of citizens' organizations *can* be extended, or how far those networks would *need* to be extended in order to bring capital and empire under sufficient control.

The Jeremiah Group, Valley Interfaith, and the other groups considered here demonstrate that it is still essential to promote face-to-face democratic involvement of a sort that bridges racial, ethnic, class, religious and other divisions. Without such involvement, there would be no publics with the capacity to hold local elites accountable. Wolin would grant this, I believe. His question is whether such involvement is sufficient to create publics of accountability capable of addressing issues that are national and international in scope.

In a globalized political economy, the power of the people will still find its organizational basis, if it does so at all, in local, face-to-face contact in institutions where citizens are already gathering. Even if that basis were fully in place, however, a massive amount of networking among local groups would be required to bring adequate pressure to bear on the elites running national bureaucracies and multinational corporations. The good news, as I reported in chapters 8 and 17, is that such networking is beginning to happen. It is far too early to know what will come of it.

Many of the accomplishments of IAF's Southwest network have resulted from successful attempts to combine the efforts of citizens' organizations in multiple locales within a single state. This was true even in the colonias struggle in Texas in the 1980s. It is not hard to imagine how an extension of the networking now being constructed in places like Louisiana and California could create a public of accountability at the level of national politics, nor how an expanded network along those lines might intersect with the global cellular patterns that Appadurai is discovering in his fieldwork. No theory can demonstrate, in advance of events, that such things are impossible.

The political program I am advocating, then, has multiple dimensions, indeed, one dimension for each level at which power is now being exercised by governmental and corporate elites: local, county, state, national, regional, and international. It is no accident that the terms *elite* and *accountability* have become key words in recent presidential campaigns. But such campaigns barely address the underlying problem, because they are vehicles that elites use to gain and enhance power, vehicles that function mostly to help those elites escape accountability. If democracy is to succeed in addressing the problems of our day, it will do so by reviving the practice of accountability at the local level, in roughly the way IAF does, and by networking in ways that create publics of accountability at the other levels. To be effective, those publics will have to be able to tame elites striving for dominance, including the people near the top of the thin wire from which the social pyramid hangs.

Someday, the nation-state will probably be less central to our political thinking than it is today. We would, however, be gravely mistaken to think that it no longer matters, that globalization has rendered presidential elections and the like irrelevant. Nation-states are likely to remain important for some time, not only because of the powers of regulation, taxation, horror prevention, horror mitigation, surveillance, punishment, and war-making they have at their disposal, but also because they will surely be the principal sites of contestation over how the powers currently held by nation-states will be distributed in the future. We withdraw from such contestation at our peril. Parody and protest around the fringes, in the style of fugitive democracy or contemporary anarchism, will not be enough to protect the vulnerable from horrors.

It is likely that the coming geopolitical era will be one in which at least some of the powers now lodged in nation-states will be pushed downward, toward states, counties, and local governments, whereas others will be pushed upward, toward regional and international agencies that have yet to be invented. Yet nation-states will be absolutely crucial during this transitional period, and it would be foolish to assume that all of their most important powers will simply be transferred, either upward or downward, over the next several decades.

Democratic thinking needs to adapt to the new situation. Assuming that the grassroots democratic project remains our best political hope, it can no longer be pursued *exclusively* with the modern nation-state in mind. The democratic challenge is to construct effective publics of accountability for every existing or emerging power holder, ranging from the sheriff of a small town to the CEO of a company with workers, stockholders, and effects all over the world. That includes local, state, and national governments, but is hardly limited to them.

Citizens convinced that democracy still matters need answers to a number of pressing questions: How have grassroots democratic movements, from abolitionism to civil rights, succeeded in the past? What forms of organizing currently being attempted might have the best chance of succeeding if attempted on a larger scale? How might citizens of all kinds, including intellectuals, clergy, and members of the press corps, best assist the work of democratic organizations on the ground? And, finally, how, if at all, can grassroots democracy gain a foothold above the local level in a country where the national discussion, being conducted under the aegis of the infotainment industry, tends to be dominated by big money, sound bites, and spin-doctors? In this book, I have tried to place such questions on our agenda and to contribute to the process of answering them.

The point, however, is not essentially theoretical. It is to encourage a kind of action that includes questioning but goes beyond it. The delicate task of the social critic is to adopt a perspective that makes the dangers of our situation visible without simultaneously disabling the hope of reforming it.

✻ CHAPTER NINETEEN ✻

The Organizer President

When classmates in college asked me just what it was that a community organizer did, I couldn't answer them directly. Instead, I'd pronounce on the need for change. . . . Change won't come from the top, I would say. Change will come from a mobilized grass roots.

—*Barack Obama*

WHILE I WAS COMPLETING the research for this book and beginning the process of writing it, Barack Obama emerged as a major figure in national politics. I couldn't help noticing how often he made reference, in his speeches and books, to the need for a revival of grassroots politics. His campaign aimed to give hope to people who had grown alienated from party politics and the culture wars—in particular, to young people like my son, who suspected that the political system was simply beyond repair.

The future president had entered public life as an organizer on the South Side of Chicago, the same city where Saul Alinsky had first worked. Obama spent three years as director of the Developing Communities Project (DCP) and also played a role in a network of citizens' organizations known as Gamaliel. Neither the DCP nor Gamaliel was officially affiliated with IAF, but both relied in part on Alinsky's vocabulary and tactics. Coincidentally, another candidate for the Democratic presidential nomination, Hillary Clinton, had written her honors thesis at Wellesley on Alinsky.[126] So here we had two major candidates for the most powerful political office in the world, both of whom had entered political life thinking seriously about the promise and limitations of grassroots democracy as Alinsky understood it.

There were many echoes of Alinsky's thinking in Obama's speeches: that without an organized and actively engaged citizenry, the public accountability of corporate and governmental office-holders tends to atrophy; that genuinely democratic change therefore has to come from the bottom up, not from the top down; and that the religious values of the people, far from being irrelevant to the proper conduct of democratic politics, inevitably and rightly find expression in it.[127]

As a candidate Obama sought to energize popular involvement in political life: to "change this country brick by brick, block by block, calloused hand by calloused hand."[128] The project needs to proceed block by block because it depends essentially on face-to-face engagement, as Alinsky had taught. It wasn't about the candidates, Obama said, but about us. He was not talking simply about the need to increase voter turnout. His message was that a form of political participation that goes well beyond the voting booth is required to restore the spirit of democracy to nominally democratic institutions.

Hillary Clinton must have understood where Obama's principal themes came from and why they were attractive to citizens who had grown disenchanted with electoral politics, for she herself, as a young adult, had found them sufficiently attractive to spend the better part of a year studying Alinsky's earlier formulation of them. But her immediate task as a candidate after Obama won the Iowa caucuses in early January 2008 was to neutralize her opponent's oratorical skills and appropriate his call for change. She began portraying him as mere rhetorician, ill equipped for a role that involves exercising enormous power, overseeing a vast bureaucracy, and shepherding legislation through Congress. His speeches might be uplifting, she suggested, but they are incapable by themselves of bringing about change. The theme of bottom-up change might sound inspiring, but the person who gets elected is going to be in charge. The job is not speech-giver in chief.

Obama, she said, had little experience as a wielder of power or as an administrator. Moreover, because his proposals were lacking in detail, his call for change was too vague to be meaningful. Voters needed to know exactly what changes they were voting for and how those changes were going to be made real. There are entrenched interests that have a stake in opposing reform. So the next president would have to fight to make change happen. It is easy to promise an end to the partisanship of recent decades, but in the real world, the people need a president who will fight the good fight on their behalf.

While campaigning in South Carolina, before the primary to be held there on January 26, Clinton said that grassroots activism had not been enough to get the Civil Rights Act of 1964 through Congress. The political savvy and experience of President Johnson were also necessary, and she was running for Johnson's job, not Martin Luther King's. This comment was both true and to the point, yet because charges of racism were already in the air, as a result of remarks made a few days earlier by former president Bill Clinton, Obama was able to spin his opponent's comment as an implied slap at King.[129] Hillary Clinton did not manage to disentangle her arguments against Obama from her husband's suspect remarks until after the primaries and caucuses of February 5–19, which involved thirty-four states and territories, and left Obama with a lead in the delegate count that he never relinquished. From that point on, however, Clinton's strategy of neutralizing his advantages and exposing his inexperience gave many voters pause.

It is hard to say how much the two candidates actually disagreed on the legacy of grassroots democracy. Although Alinsky himself had offered Clinton a job when she came out of college, she turned it down to enter law school. It is possible that doubts she had raised in her honors thesis, about the ability of local organizing to effect large-scale change, motivated this decision. Obama spent three years as an organizer, but he too eventually made his way to law school. In explaining that decision, he later wrote of his realization that there were things he needed to learn, "things that would help me bring about real change."[130] The implication seems to be that the local efforts of an organizer fail to get at the issues that affect everybody everywhere. His thought, when he set himself on the path that led him eventually to the presidential campaign trail, was probably not entirely unlike Senator Clinton's: Grassroots democracy is a good thing but finally too limited in scope to resolve the most pressing issues facing the republic. Better to be the next Lincoln, or failing that, the next Johnson, than to be the next Alinsky.

As Clinton's critique of Obama began to stick, he adjusted his rhetorical style by soaring less and dwelling more on policy. Having already established his ability to inspire, he now sought to prove his capacity to govern. He needed to say just enough about the details of his policy recommendations to rebut Clinton's portrait of him as a purveyor of vague ideals, without painting himself into a corner if he won the nomination. But the principal rhetorical theme of his campaign remained the same: "Real change comes from the bottom up, not the top down."[131]

Obama sees a causal connection between his capacity to inspire and his capacity to govern. The more actively engaged ordinary citizens become, the easier it will be for a president to achieve genuinely democratic reforms. By inspiring citizens to make their concerns known, and by providing them with an organizational framework for doing so, Obama seeks to strengthen his own ability to change the system. He wanted us to view his candidacy, and now wants us to view his presidency, as a vehicle for bottom-up change. His signature speeches are intended to perform something like the inspirational function of King's speeches during the civil rights movement. The greater the pressure that ordinary citizens exert on Congress to take their concerns seriously, the more far-reaching the resulting reforms can be.

Obama implicitly proposes to combine the roles of King and

Johnson, or Garrison and Lincoln, in his own person. As president, he will use the bully pulpit to inspire citizens to apply pressure on the government, but that very pressure will free him to achieve reform despite resistance from lobbyists and special interests. He will be both the stimulus of grassroots activism and the conduit of the democratic concerns he has aroused. His own political organization is meant to provide citizens with a way to exert pressure effectively. He views it as a bridge between grassroots democracy and partisan politics at the national level. By linking these two things together organizationally, he hopes to overcome both the limited scope of the former and the special-interest bias of the latter in a single stroke.

The organization that was called Obama for America during the presidential campaign has since been reconfigured as Organizing for America (OFA). Its chief architect is David Plouffe, who served as Obama's campaign manager. The Organizing for America website is awash in the rhetoric of grassroots democracy. At the top of the home page, just to the right of the logo, is a quotation from the president: "I am asking you to believe. Not just in my ability to bring about real change in Washington . . . I'm asking you to believe in yours." The website invites citizens "to join grassroots OFA campaigns to support the President's agenda." Elsewhere on the site is a list of links to Obama sites on Facebook, MySpace, Twitter, and various other Internet venues. There are also announcements of "listening tours," in which OFA representatives will go around the country, meeting with citizens to elicit their "thoughts on how best to organize in their communities."[132] Shortly after OFA was launched, my wife received an e-mail from Plouffe himself, inviting her to a "house meeting."

David Plouffe can invite you to a meeting that is held at someone's house, but he couldn't invite you to a house meeting even if he wanted to. No one whose job is to strengthen the hand of an officeholder can speak of his work as "grassroots organizing" and convene a "house meeting" without creating confusion about what grassroots democracy is and how it works. We have seen that house meetings, as conceived in broad-based organizing, belong to a process that permits the concerns of ordinary citizens to congeal into issues. The meetings function as they do because hundreds of one-on-ones precede them and because they give rise to a power analysis, a research committee, and a core team of indigenous leaders charged with formulating concrete proposals and a strategy for getting them enacted. When the proposals have been hammered out, the core team is in a position to identify allies and opponents in the upcoming fight. There will be public rites of commitment to clarify the difference and a phase of polarization in which allies are expected to stand forward. Opponents are held accountable for their opposition, and declared allies are held accountable if they fail to come through on their promises. Only when the fight concludes is it time for depolarization, at which point the process of taking soundings at the one-on-one level can begin again.

OFA's "house meetings" and "listening tours" do not belong to a process of this sort. OFA organizers work for a partisan political organization, under the auspices of the Democratic National Committee. One of their functions is to listen carefully while citizens express their concerns, but their main function is to mobilize support for proposals hammered out in deliberation at the highest levels of government and in negotiation among major power holders. The citizens being assembled have little or no role in the process of defining issues and formulating proposals. Their concerns remain amorphous until someone else gives them shape. The role of the OFA organizer is essentially that of a focus group leader. A focus group is not a house meeting. It is an occasion for a member of an elite to test tactical options in light of the immediate reactions of ordinary citizens. If citizens' groups do not maintain independence from the partisan politician's organization and define issues for themselves, it is misleading, if not intentionally deceptive, to represent the process as bottom-up change.

I see nothing wrong with having a president who inspires citizens to exert pressure on the government. But when the message of bottom-up change comes from on high and the organizational vehicle being proposed for such change is a retooled version of a politician's campaign apparatus, people are apt to be confused about what is actually going on. Perhaps Obama is confused about this himself. If not, he is a sly politician indeed. A man who used to be a community organizer now holds the most powerful office in the world. He holds the fate of our economy in his hands. He commands the most awesomely destructive military force there has ever been. The band plays "Hail to the Chief!" before he speaks. He now has his own war to fight and a gargantuan bailout of Wall Street to defend. If anyone needs to be held accountable, he does. Yet he has many people thinking that an organization of his own devising, created in part by his campaign manager, is an apt vehicle for bottom-up change.

In the Astrodome, we came across a good example of the good that can come when a partisan politician holding office at a moment of crisis recognizes the importance of grassroots organizing. The politician in that case was Mayor Bill White, who had the good sense to invite TMO organizer Renee Wizig-Barrios to the meetings in which he and other officials discussed how to respond to the crisis. He also gave Renee and her colleague Brod Bagert freedom to organize in the Astrodome. Mayor White saw the wisdom of doing this because TMO had, over the course of several years, established its representative authority and earned his trust. Renee and Brod—not the mayor's campaign manager, Mustafa Tameez—rounded up potential leaders, held house meetings, and initiated the process in which Katrina evacuees transformed their grief and anger into concrete proposals for action.

David Plouffe cannot perform both his role and a role like Renee's without compromising the latter. The example of OFA helps us see that the differentiation between a citizens' organization and a partisan political organization is not motivated solely by the desire, on the part of citizens' groups, to maintain their tax-exempt status. This differentiation is analogous in its rationale to the separation of executive and legislative powers within the government. The system of checks and balances is designed to minimize opportunities for domination and to maximize opportunities for ordinary citizens to influence and contest what officials do. The lesson to be learned from a comparison of TMO and OFA is that the ability of a citizens' group to *formulate issues* and to *hold politicians accountable* is seriously hampered when the independence of grassroots organizing is compromised. OFA is top-down partisan politics disguised as grassroots democracy. Whatever Obama and his campaign manager intend, the organization serves mainly to legitimize what the president decides to do and to conceal the nature of the decision making process he undertakes. In short, the effects of OFA are ideological.

Return for a moment to the example of Johnson and King. We forget that before King rose to prominence, Rosa Parks refused to go to the back of a bus, and before that, she had attended a citizenship school run by Myles Horton and Septima Clark. As Joanne Bland recently put it, every town that invited King in to speak had already been organized.[133] If this were not so, President Johnson wouldn't have had to confer with him. Many people, Clark among them, were ill at ease with King's role as spokesperson on those occasions. But when the time comes for pivotal negotiations, someone must play something like the role King played when he met with Johnson behind closed doors in the White House. Johnson's campaign manager would not have been suited to the task. Nor would his vice president, Hubert Humphrey, despite Humphrey's long record as an opponent of racial segregation. The spokesperson for reform, when negotiations are being conducted at the highest levels of government, needs to be someone whose representative authority rests on an extensive organizational basis.

At a fundraiser during his campaign for the presidency, Obama reportedly told the potential donors assembled there of a meeting between President Franklin D. Roosevelt and A. Philip Randolph, founder of the Brotherhood of Sleeping Car Porters. Roosevelt had asked Randolph for his views on racial segregation and listened patiently while Randolph replied. When Randolph had finished, Roosevelt encouraged him to go out and make him do what was necessary to bring racial segregation to an end. Roosevelt recognized that the organizational basis for putting an end to segregation was not yet in place. He was signaling to Randolph that if it were in place, reform would have a friend in the White House.

Candidate Obama told this story because he wanted his supporters to understand that he would not, if elected, be able to accomplish major reforms on his own. But Obama seems not to have grasped Roosevelt's reason for giving his signal to Randolph, an independent organizer, instead of to a partisan operative or to a group of campaign donors.[134] Unfortunately, on the principal questions facing his presidency Obama has no one to whom he can say, "Make me do it," and expect that enough organized pressure will be brought to bear on the base of his spine to permit him to resist the demands of organized corporate power. He has had little choice but to bow to Wall Street on the substance of responding to the financial crisis, to the insurance companies on the question of health care reform, and to the military establishment on the questions of the War in Afghanistan, the detention of suspected terrorists, and the maintenance of more than seven hundred U.S. bases overseas.

Obama's policies on all of these topics have come from the top down. They have resulted from compromises worked out among the president's appointed professional advisors, the key players in Congress, and representatives of the corporate executive class. In a given policy debate, Plouffe and others are called on to mobilize "grassroots" support through OFA only at the moment when the parameters of negotiation among the ruling elites have become relatively clear, and Obama seeks to strengthen his hand during the weeks preceding a major decision. Until this point in the negotiating process is reached, Obama is nearly always careful to keep his policy proposals indeterminate. His call for change is *essentially* vague.

By keeping the nature of the change he is calling for indeterminate, Obama taps into the vaguely defined concerns of ordinary citizens without needing to commit himself to very much in particular. This strategy gives him maximal room for maneuver during the negotiating process, and permits him, in most cases, to declare at least a modest victory when the negotiating ends. The constituency most likely to find this strategy acceptable—Obama's base—consists of lifestyle liberals, whose sociological disposition is, as we have seen, to gather loosely around vaguely defined ideals of freedom and equality, while confining their own participation in the political process to voting and to relatively inconsequential symbolic and philanthropic gestures. The primary value commitment expressed in these acts is that the world would be a better place if we were all nicer to one another.

This commitment makes a great deal of sense in the context of the culturally diverse neighborhoods, associations, and workplaces fostered by an economy increasingly centered on information, but Obama appears to have little sense of the limitations of niceness as a virtue. It doesn't help people identify the forms of domination in their midst, distinguish appropriately between their actual allies and opponents, or prepare for a fight against the extremely powerful individuals and groups now establishing dominance over our political economy. The lifestyle liberal's conception of niceness, as a virtue one is obliged to display until one is given no alternative but to fight back, determines Obama's character as a political leader. His instinct is to begin the negotiating process by offering seats at the table to representatives of all groups whose perceived self-interest might incline them not to be nice. He imagines himself as the representative of the people who genuinely want everyone to get along, who already identify their interests as converging in the common good. To them, he offers the hope that postpartisan amity, of the sort that his leadership style is designed to exemplify and to foster, will permit an inclusive, peaceable, and magnanimous society to emerge in the wake of the culture wars.

It should be clear that Obama's nice-guy pragmatism differs fundamentally from grassroots democracy as practiced by the citizens' organizations examined in this book. The process Obama uses to solicit the concerns of ordinary citizens is structured in a way that permits elites to define both the issues and the parameters of debate. By presenting his own political organization as a vehicle for grassroots democracy, he seeks to legitimize his own claim to be the people's representative at the negotiating table. In fact, however, he rarely does much at all, beyond symbolic expressions of his good will, to earn the entitlement to speak for ordinary citizens. His approach to policy negotiations begins with depolarization and builds, very late in the game, to polarization, but only when a debate among ruling elites has already settled what exactly needs to be decided.[135]

This approach reverses the pattern of grassroots citizens' organizations, which take care to exercise their own agency in defining the issue to be decided, proceed to a phase of polarization around the issue they have defined, and move to depolarization only when the fight is resolved. Both approaches rightly reject the permanent-polarization model of the culture warriors, but do so in quite different ways. The practical effect of Obama's approach, his rhetoric to the contrary notwithstanding, is to eliminate accountability from political life. A politics of accountability presents politicians with precisely articulated choices designed to distinguish allies from opponents. Opponents are held responsible for their opposition. Allies who fail to follow through on publicly expressed commitments are held responsible for their failure. Officeholders must answer for any grave injustices they have committed before the public can extend forgiveness to them and a process of reconciliation can be initiated. From the beginning, the new president demonstrated his reluctance even to name and renounce, let alone prosecute, the numerous high crimes and misdemeanors of the previous administration. For Obama, reconciliation comes first, before the reasons for being angry with tyrants and oligarchs have even been acknowledged. Accountability is thereby rendered a meaningless, ineffectual afterthought. Accountability isn't always nice.

When the pivotal stages of negotiations on any given issue are reached, Obama makes his own judgment concerning which of the policy options still on the table would be in the best interest of ordinary people. If he thinks he can strengthen his position as a negotiator, he then uses OFA to mobilize "grassroots" support for the policy he favors. In the health care debate of 2009 and 2010, he was prepared to leave the details of his policy recommendations unstated until late in the game, at which point the other major players in the debate had jointly narrowed the options. By approaching the process as he did, Obama tied his own hands. He did not permit himself, when initially framing the issue, to hold the insurance industry accountable for fattening itself at the public's expense. Instead, he permitted insurance executives to exclude a single-payer health care system and a public health insurance option from serious consideration.

To achieve a more progressive result, Obama would have had to frame the topic of health care reform as something that needed to be addressed first of all, over the course of many months, by independent citizens' organizations. Perhaps the citizens' organizations we now have are insufficiently developed to play this role, but it is revealing that President Obama has ignored them entirely, and treats OFA, by implication, as their technologically more advanced, but authentically "grassroots," successor. His approach to health care reform reinforced the ignorance of the public in a way that played into the hands of the insurance companies. When he called on his supporters for help in the summer of 2009, most of them didn't know much at all about the options on the table, let alone where he stood, so they were reluctant to give him much backing. Because the general public was in a state of disorganization, it was especially susceptible to the lies and half-truths put into circulation by the insurance lobby and its right-wing allies. As we have seen throughout this book, well-organized citizens are not so easily fooled.

In setting the new administration's course on foreign policy and economic affairs, ordinary citizens had even less of a role. That course was already determined in May and June 2008, when it became clear that Obama could not be prevented from winning the presidential nomination and he began negotiating with Senator Clinton's camp to unite the party for a campaign against the Republican nominee-to-be, Senator John McCain. Hillary Clinton's eventual appointment as secretary of state, together with the retention of Robert Gates as secretary of defense, tells us all we need to know about what transpired behind closed doors in June. The antiwar candidate essentially handed over the two most important foreign affairs seats in the cabinet to prominent figures in the war establishment. This meant that the most we could expect from his presidency in the area of foreign affairs was a shift from the right wing to the center-left of that establishment. Six months earlier, Senator Clinton and Senator John McCain had given surprisingly clear public indications that they would rather see each other as commander-in-chief than an unpredictable outsider such as Obama.[136] But now Obama felt compelled to signal his loyalty to the war establishment as the price of party unity. This was not a decision on which he chose to consult his many antiwar supporters. Obama for America did not hold focus groups, let alone house meetings, to discuss the issue.

Around the same time, Obama appointed the team of economic advisors who would guide him through the remaining stages of the campaign. The three most important of these were Robert Rubin and Lawrence Summers, both of whom had served as secretary of the treasury under Bill Clinton, and Rubin's close associate Jason Furman, whom Obama appointed in early June as his director of economic policy. Not included on the list was Joseph Stiglitz, a Nobel laureate who had served in the Clinton administration as Chairman of the Council of Economic Advisors in 1995–97 and subsequently as senior vice president and chief economist of the World Bank. During the Clinton presidency, Rubin and Summers were often sharply at odds with Stiglitz, especially over the policies designed by the Treasury Department and carried out by the International Monetary Fund for the purpose of helping poor countries. Stiglitz used his position at the World Bank to disclose the negative effects of IMF imposition of Rubin-Summers monetary policies on poor countries. The appointment of Furman as director, the inclusion of Rubin and Summers among the official advisors, and the exclusion of Stiglitz appeared to imply that Obama intended to resolve the Clinton administration's split over economic policy by coming down clearly on the side of Rubin and Summers.

The significance of this from the perspective of grassroots citizens' organizations is twofold. First, as we saw in chapter 8, the work for which Stiglitz won the Noble Prize has provided an opportunity for such organizations to argue that inequalities of access to information have in many cases skewed the operations of markets in the direction of inefficiency. If many markets suffer from information asymmetry, and ordinary citizens repeatedly find themselves on the wrong end of that asymmetry, there will often be good reasons to consider corrective governmental intervention in those markets. Second, perhaps for reasons that derive from his interest in access to information, Stiglitz has been a strong advocate for including all sorts of potentially affected groups, including ordinary citizens, in deliberations on major issues concerning economic policy. Unlike Summers in particular, Stiglitz favors a relatively open and inclusive deliberative process.[137]

When the financial crisis arrived only three months after Obama assembled his advisors, the impact of his appointments was magnified. Another Rubin associate, Timothy Geithner, eventually became Obama's treasury secretary, as Summers became Obama's director of National Economic Policy. This is not the place to detail the decision-making process undertaken by these men. For the purposes of this book, all that matters is that the process is as perfect an example of top-down management as any dystopian author could have dreamt up.

Change comes from the bottom up only if ordinary citizens initiate it, organizing on their own and holding elites, including the president and his associates, accountable. If change is to come in this way, if accountability is to be more than a quadrennial affair of too little, too late, then ordinary people cannot rely on the organizer president to do their work for them. They will need to form independent groups so powerful that no president or legislature could afford to ignore them—groups structured in a way that permits their own leaders, too, to be held accountable. This is what grassroots democracy claims to be both possible and necessary. Letters to the editor, static in the blogosphere, and an occasional public demonstration are not enough to rein in the rich and the lucky. But neither is participation in an organization the true purpose of which is to strengthen the hand of a particular politician. It is irrelevant that he regards himself as the permanent ally of the average citizen.

Obama seems to have forgotten the Alinsky maxim that eloquent speeches, big rallies, and major policy initiatives, if not preceded by sufficiently careful organizing, are apt to be counterproductive.

One of my purposes in this book is to underline the importance of keeping this maxim in mind at this particular juncture in our national life. There were always dangers in running for the presidency *on behalf of grassroots democracy* without first achieving the fundamental change in our political culture that Obama was rightly calling for. The dangers varied depending on whether he won or lost the election of 2008.

The risk of awakening the hope for large-scale change and then losing the election was obvious from the start. Alinsky advised citizens' organizations to begin gathering momentum by choosing fights that can be won. Winning generates hope, which generates more action. The corollary of this bit of practical wisdom is that losses, in particular when they come too early in the organizing process, can be dispiriting, and are sometimes fatally so. Hope needs to be nurtured into audacity. Early in the process of rebuilding democratic confidence, electoral defeat can turn hope into despair in the blink of an eye. Obama's victory did generate hope.

The risk of winning the election was somewhat less apparent, and it must now be faced squarely. Either Obama's presidency will achieve the fundamental change he was calling for in our political culture, or it will not. In this chapter, I have been explaining why I suspect that it will not. Suppose for the purposes of argument that my suspicions prove correct. Then the rhetoric of grassroots democracy will have become the mask of legitimacy worn by a federal government that remains beholden to the privileged and continues to reinforce relationships of domination at home and abroad. This outcome is much worse than the same situation without the mask. The mask has caused many of the people who could have been organizing more productively to think that they can achieve bottom-up change by funneling their money to David Plouffe.

Obama's claim was that the crisis of democracy is a matter of an imbalance of power between ordinary citizens and the ruling elites. The claim struck a chord because it is true. He argued that the crisis will turn in democracy's favor only if ordinary citizens take it upon themselves to resolve it. This argument was also correct. Alinsky taught that democracy is alive in the habits of the people only when they organize themselves effectively and hold corporate bosses and government officials responsible for the arrangements and policies that are in place. Electing a president who believes that Alinsky was right is hardly the same thing as building an effective culture of accountability by something like Alinsky's means.

The threats to civil liberties that emerged in the years after 9/11 created the best opportunity for discussing the meaning of the U.S. Constitution since Watergate. The deceptions perpetrated in the lead-up to the Iraq War created the best opportunity for discussing the principles of American foreign policy since Vietnam. The financial crisis of 2008 created the best opportunity for discussing the legal infrastructure of the megacorporation since the Great Depression. In each of these cases, powerful elites exploited a crisis as an opportunity for placing unprecedented powers in the hands of a few. There are many catastrophes on the horizon. Every age faces some. It seems likely that our catastrophes will be ferocious and that they will weaken our grip on liberty. Grassroots democracy needs to prepare itself to respond to catastrophes. But this means more than keeping an eye out for growing imbalances of power and the occasional usurpation of power. It also means treating crises as opportunities for transforming vague concerns into well-defined issues. Ordinary people need to be as prepared for crises as elites are.

I see no reason to think that Obama will be better at preparing us for the next crisis than he has been at helping us hold him and his associates accountable. The former professor of constitutional law chose not to use his campaign as an occasion to teach the public what a democratic republic is and what forces, at home and abroad, are currently endangering our liberty. As a critic of the Iraq War, he chose not to enunciate clear principles for deciding what future wars, if any, might be required by justice. And in the period leading up to the financial crisis, his speeches demonstrated little awareness that the economic disparities described in the previous chapter might pose a threat to democracy. He fancies himself an heir to the heritage of Lincoln, but he does not take it upon himself to explain what the ideal of liberty and justice for all means, concretely, when applied to the world we live in.[138]

Barack Obama is the spirit of the fog.[139] The more the politicians talk about change, the more things remain the same. They talk about change because they know we are unhappy with how things are going, but they don't want to commit themselves to anything substantive. The term *change* has done the trick because of its vagueness. We will know that significant change is coming when citizens too well organized to be tricked—and too powerful to be ignored—demand laws and institutions able to prevent corporate elites from exercising power arbitrarily over others at home and abroad. If there is someday a president whose opposition to fraud, torture, and empire actually means something, it will be ordinary citizens, organized in the right way, who made it happen. That, to say the least, is a very big "if."

✻ CHAPTER TWENTY ✻

Walking in Our Sleep

None of us knows what the future holds, of course, and I have no predictions to offer on the fate of grassroots democracy. The great reforms of the past were accomplished against what then seemed to be great odds. If there are still great reforms to come and if ordinary citizens are going to compensate for the emergence of new classes of masters, these things will be accomplished in the teeth of what will often appear to be insurmountable opposition.

Of some things, however, we can be certain. To maintain a position of dominance, even the most powerful people in the world rely on the inaction of others and the resignation that lies beneath it. The powerful became powerful by organizing others to work for them and creating incentives for profitably cooperative activity. It appears to be against the interests of the rich and the lucky for everyone else to be similarly well organized. The rich and the lucky *benefit* from making large-scale democratic reform *appear* hopeless. Paradoxically, they also benefit from making large-scale change seem *easily* achievable, for example, by casting a vote every four years for a candidate who promises something called "change."

Our roles, relationships, institutions, laws, and policies are not so fixed that we could not change them if we decided to do so. Each person or faction might seem powerless to effect large-scale change when viewed separately, but such change has happened before, and when it has, the dependence of ruling elites on the deference of ordinary people has become plain.

Thoreau was trying to reveal the nature of this dependence to the readers of *Walden* in the following passage in which the railroad, the third major form of economic organization (after the plantation and the mill) to impose domination on ordinary Americans, becomes a metaphor for American society itself:

> Men have an indistinct notion that if they keep up this activity of joint stocks and spades long enough all will at length ride somewhere, in next to no time, and for nothing; but though a crowd rushes to the depot, and the conductor shouts "All aboard!" when the smoke is blown away and the vapor condensed, it will be perceived that a few are riding, but the rest are run over, — and it will be called, and will be, "A melancholy accident."

Thoreau returns to the metaphor some pages later, where a pun on the term "sleeper" becomes the occasion for a meditation on the need to be awakened from the slumber of false consciousness:

> We do not ride upon the railroad; it rides upon us. Did you ever think what those sleepers are that underlie the railroad? Each one is a man . . . . The rails are laid down on them, and they are covered with sand, and the cars run smoothly over them. They are sound sleepers, I assure you. And every few years a new lot is laid down and run over; so that, if some have the pleasure of riding on a rail, others have the misfortune to be ridden upon. And when they run over a man that is walking in his sleep, a supernumerary sleeper in the wrong position, and wake him up, they suddenly stop the cars, and make a hue and cry about it, as if this were an exception. I am glad to know that it takes a gang of men for every five miles to keep the sleepers down and level in their beds as it is, for this is a sign that they may sometime get up again.[140]

The sleepers are those on whose backs the economy runs. It is their being asleep and remaining prone that permits the economy to take this form. If the sleepers rise one by one, they will immediately be struck down, either by the trains or by the gangs of men whose job it is to keep sleepers prone. To rise in this way is to be a sleepwalker, to be less than fully aware of the extent to which the whole system depends on sleepers remaining in the prone position.

Thoreau is suggesting that there is ground for social hope in the nature of the dependence. The system would have to change if the sleepers woke up and rose up together. The uprising can effect change only if it is organized, coordinated, and self-aware. And the uprising can be beneficial to the ones rising up only if the ideal of inclusive nondomination is actualized in it. What would this mean, concretely? Ultimately, it would mean changing some features of the legal infrastructure that permitted the mills and the railroad, and the large corporate hierarchies that followed them, to dominate the people they employ and purport to serve. The sleepers will ultimately need to decide, and will decide if they ever stop walking in their sleep, whether the limited liability, relatively unregulated megacorporation is compatible with democracy.[141] This is the same thing as deciding whether the upright posture of citizenship is compatible with accepting the prone position of a sleeper in the economy.

In 2004 I traveled to Knoxville, Tennessee, to give a lecture on the worrisome condition of American politics. My claim was that the current crisis of democracy is grave enough that concerted action on the part of many citizens would be required to overcome it. I was trying to awaken Thoreau's sleepers. Toward the end of the question-and-answer period, I called on a young man who identified himself as a freshman at the University of Tennessee. He found my diagnosis of democracy's ills persuasive, he said. But my prescription for those ills seemed both doomed to fail and unhelpfully vague. If I was right about the severity of the situation, how could ordinary citizens possibly revive the patient? And what, exactly, did I expect them to do?

The seriousness with which the student posed his questions impressed me. He was neither expressing cynicism nor trying to score points. He wanted a concrete, honest, informative answer. I recommended that he try to organize people who felt as alienated from the system as he did. It is hard to have an impact entirely on your own, but easier when you join forces with others.

This was Thoreau's point about what happens to people who are walking in their sleep instead of organizing one another to stand up. Ordinary citizens have brought about large-scale change before, and they can do so again. Each time they have done so, they have created organizations, infused them with ideals, and generated power. Thoreau was thinking of abolitionism in its post-1830 phase, and hoping that a form of economic domination less obvious than chattel slavery could be added to the list of things slated for change. Megacorporations are now all the more worrisome, and global in their reach. It is harder than ever to evade the sphere in which they dominate. There is, nonetheless, a tradition of democratic reform with which I can identify that is somewhat distinguishable from the relationships of domination I would like to transform. It is the tradition that Thoreau and other members of his generation were still in the process of founding when he published *Walden* in 1854.

My advice to the student from Tennessee was meant to be encouraging, but it was too abstract to do any good. I had not explained how people currently addicted to fast "food" and "reality" television might actually take back the country from the plutocrats, militarists, and culture warriors now dominating our politics. The truth is that I had only a vague idea, drawn from memories of the civil rights and antiwar movements I had participated in as a teenager and from sporadic involvement as an adult in the politics of my own community. I was not myself rooted in an extended social network capable of generating dependable leadership or fostering significant change. So my advice to the student from Tennessee was hollow.

Before long I was back on the road, traveling to many locations in the United States and to two provinces in Canada, lecturing on the dangers facing democracy and listening to people expressing their hopes and concerns. Between trips, back at my desk, I tried to pull my thoughts together in the form of a book. But my message, like that of my Knoxville lecture, was too abstract to serve my purposes. Everywhere I went, people told me that they were deeply worried about the future of democracy. They felt alienated from both the electoral process and the culture wars, and were groping about for plain language in which to express their discontent. They were relieved to hear all of this being talked about in public and were buoyed, as I was, by the realization that many people feel the same way. Barack Obama must have been having the same sort of experience with his audiences at roughly the same time.

At nearly every stop I made, someone asked me more or less the same questions that had been posed to me by the student from Tennessee. They were all asking why they should have hope and what a better way of conducting our political affairs might look like in concrete terms. To answer these questions, I knew that I would need to look closely at examples of democratic practice. The abolitionist movement in which Thoreau participated is a good example, but an old one. I discovered that young people who came to hear me had trouble identifying even with the civil rights movement. To address their doubts, I would need to offer them examples of *contemporary* democratic practice that might conceivably be a basis for addressing the issue of stratification that Thoreau had tried to highlight, more than a century and a half ago, in the passage on sleepers.

The present book is essentially my considered response to the student from Tennessee and to thousands of people like him, young and old, who want to know how the spirit of democracy might be actualized *concretely* under our circumstances, but who either suspect that the endeavor is now hopeless or expect the ills of democracy to be cured by putting a charismatic reformer in the White House.

Hope is not the same thing as thinking that what one ardently desires is *likely* to happen. It is the virtue one needs when grim facts might tempt one to give up on promoting or protecting important goods. In this case the goods are liberty and justice, and the temptation is to assume that they are now essentially out of reach. The temptation, in short, is despair. Democratic hope is a virtue that needs grounds, but not grounds capable of demonstrating that the goods in question will in fact be achieved, or are likely to be achieved, if we behave in a certain way. They are grounds for thinking that we have a chance of making a significant difference for the better.

When despair is the disease one hopes to remedy, anecdotes can be antidotes. That is why this book is full of stories and has such a high ratio of quotation to commentary. The ideals of grassroots democracy are embodied in a particular pattern of coordinated action, which the stories display. To understand grassroots democracy one needs to experience something like the face-to-face interactions in which its spirit takes shape and acquires organizational and evaluative substance. The stories I have been recounting and reflecting on are, I believe, enough like those interactions to make a reader experience the emotional component of the hope that the tellers of the stories embody in person. But the student from Tennessee wasn't merely looking for an infusion of hopeful passion. He also wanted a determinate idea of what to do, of what it is to collaborate with others democratically.

The various examples discussed in this book include highly successful campaigns, such as the fight over the colonias. The concrete evidence they provide that success is possible is another ground for hope. But while success stories are necessary for purposes of self-instruction, they are not sufficient. The stories about power failure, as in the cases of Arizona and southern California, when complacency set in among the organizers, help put democratic excellence in relief. The concept of excellent democratic practice comes into clearer focus when we determine, case by case, how to distinguish successes from near misses and complete failures.

We discover how to behave democratically by participating, by observing others participate, and by taking in the stories of people who have participated. The stories would be less instructive if they focused on famous people. Larger-than-life heroes tend to dwarf the rest of us. The stories of Lincoln and King are debilitating when they lead us to think that our task is to wait for the emergence of the next heroic figure and then donate a little money or spare time to the cause. At least some of the stories we contemplate need to be about people more like ourselves, behaving reasonably well.[142]

Needless to say, we are not all in the same situation. For readers who find themselves in communities already in the process of getting organized, this book offers various concrete models of involvement and perhaps some incentive for being receptive to the organizing effort. In the examples you now have before you, you should be able to find sufficient evidence of the value of organizational activity to justify taking the plunge. It is important to recognize that the local institutions discussed in this book fall at many points along a wide economic spectrum, from Maywood to Marin. An extremely poor parish can benefit greatly from getting involved, but so can a relatively wealthy congregation that senses the need to overcome the limitations of lifestyle liberalism. For institutions on the wealthier end of the spectrum, the broad-based citizens' organization is an alternative to paternalistic "good works." Solidarity with the poor is an institutional matter, not a matter of charitable giving or sentiments. The first step is the kind of internal organizational activity I have described in detail. Congregation Kol Shofar benefited as much from that as St. Rose of Lima did.

Readers who find themselves in communities not yet in the process of getting organized might feel somewhat disadvantaged, compared to most of the people described in these chapters. In fact, however, a reader disadvantaged in this way is in roughly the same situation Sister Christine Stephens was in when she served on the planning group that brought Ernie Cortés to San Antonio in the 1970s. Christine saw her situation as an opportunity. Looking back, she takes pride in having been "present at the creation" of COPS. Anyone reading about her work has advantages she lacked, including her example to emulate and the now rapidly developing networks of successful citizens' organizations that can be found here and there around the United States and in various other countries.

There is a way to begin. Do a preliminary power analysis. Talk to one institutional official in your community. Then talk to another. Search out potential leaders. Begin cultivating their skills and virtues, as well as your own. Keep talking until you can form a planning group. And reach out to professional organizers for help. This is what some of us are now doing in my own county in central New Jersey. How much we can accomplish remains to be seen.

It should now be clear why I have put this book together as I have, but my hard-won lesson about the value of examples also has curricular implications. An organizer in New Orleans complains about how democracy was treated in the university he attended. Pastors in Los Angeles County remark on the superiority of their IAF training to anything they learned in seminary. A principal in South Central says much the same thing about his college experience. It seems to me that the misgivings are justified. Most of our institutions of higher education do a poor job of conveying a concrete sense of what praiseworthy involvement in the public life of a community looks like, whether on the part of an individual citizen, a civic association, or a religious institution.

The examples taken up in this book do not show that democracy is in good health overall. Disaster capitalism in New Orleans, the condition of resident aliens in Maywood, and the ethnic strife of South Central L.A. are evidence that momentous forces are at work, reshaping the landscape within which concerned citizens are struggling to get a foothold. It is indeed possible that the most powerful people in the world already have the means to exercise their power arbitrarily over us for the foreseeable future. It is also possible, however, that ordinary people have a fighting chance of winning some significant victories for liberty and justice.

In this book I have simply tried to get some of our most promising practices and the forces currently arrayed against them into the same picture, one in which both grounds for hope and a realistic sense of the situation's gravity can be found. The picture should at least help us guard against resting our hopes in famous, powerful leaders. This is the world we have.

Are the practices I have described here literally the best that contemporary democracy has to offer? I don't know enough to claim that, but in any event it will take many kinds of groupings and forms of conduct to serve our needs as citizens. My purpose is not to argue that broad-based organizing should *replace* such activities as Internet fundraising, single-issue movements, or organizing for specific purposes along lines of class, race, gender, sexual orientation, vocation, or religious affiliation. To the contrary, I assume that, until proven otherwise in a given case, each of these things exists because it serves a real need.

I do want to claim, however, that the imbalance of power between ruling elites and ordinary citizens is the principal cause of democracy's current ills and that it can be set straight only if broad-based organizing is scaled up significantly, only if it extends its reach much more widely throughout American society than it has to date. We have seen that this will take patience, as well as effort, assuming that it can be done. Moreover, the danger of oligarchy within the emerging networks of citizens' groups is as real as the danger of settling for the excessively loose connections most citizens have now.

Scaling up the activities of broad-based organizing does ask a great deal of the citizenry, and there is no guarantee that it will succeed. All that can be said on the basis of available evidence is that there are promising signs of democratic life all around us, if we take care to look for them. The Southwest IAF network is only one of them. Its power continues to grow, and its effects have on several occasions reached the statewide and regional levels. Thus far, I see no signs that Cortés and his associates have succumbed to the internal temptations of oligarchy. The work of Metro IAF—which encompasses organizations in Chicago, New York, Boston, and London, among other places—strikes me as similarly encouraging. Whether such developments can be extended further without either losing power or being corrupted by oligarchy remains to be seen. The examples of broad-based organizing considered here are both of paramount importance and inherently limited in predictive value.

The imbalance of power between ordinary citizens and the new ruling class has, in my view, reached crisis proportions. The crisis will not be resolved happily *unless* many more institutions and communities commit themselves to getting democratically organized and *unless* effective publics of accountability are constructed at many levels of social complexity. Of this I have no doubt. Whether these conditions will be fulfilled is very doubtful indeed, in roughly the way that all collaborative undertakings of great social import are doubtful. It is impossible to know whether enough people will join forces to make a big difference. A question for each individual to answer is what he or she might do that would make some difference. For citizens in professions with a direct bearing on the health of democratic culture, this question acquires a distinctive meaning.

Consider the case of intellectuals. Citizens' organizations are short on expertise and information. In their capacity as "public universities," they need volunteer faculties and access to facts. An intellectual can contribute to grassroots democracy by sharing factual knowledge with people disposed to make democratic use of it, but also by clarifying and illustrating what domination and democracy are. Political concepts that have been turned to antidemocratic ends require rectification. New concepts await invention for the naming of new configurations of power and authority. The struggle for liberty and justice would benefit if the ideals implicit in it were made explicit and subjected to critical scrutiny. There is a need, too, for examples that crystallize domination and democracy, as they now exist, in concrete images. The democratic imagination wants replenishment on a daily basis.

The press can foster the growth of grassroots democracy not only by reporting facts relevant to domination and to its overcoming, but also by portraying ordinary citizens as empowered agents. One reason for having a free press is to help citizens gather, inform themselves, and give voice to their concerns. Inquiring minds ought to know that grassroots organizations exist and occasionally succeed. A press that earns its freedom serves democratic ends by democratic means.

Clergy are often said to have no role in politics. We have seen, however, that grassroots democracy would be a paltry thing, especially among the poor, if clergy did not lend a hand to organizers. Neither prophetic critique nor charitable assistance, by itself, alters the basic relationship of the dominant to the dominated. Organizing of the right kind, however, can make ordinary people less vulnerable to domination. It can also pump new life into the religious communities that engage in it.

There is a role for charismatic orators to play in reviving democratic culture, as well. The scaling-up process has need of leaders with rhetorical gifts to speak on behalf of people who have done the hard work of face-to-face organizing. Many kinds of gift can be turned to democratic purposes. When organizers search for potential leaders, they are looking for people with gifts—with charisms—to be cultivated or perfected. Some of those gifts are rhetorical, the trust-generating gifts of public persuasion.

The grassroots critique of charisma, in the restricted sense of the term, expresses a justified worry about excessive reliance on a particular kind of gifted individual. The reliance need not be excessive, however, if the gifts are cultivated properly and the audience is encouraged to keep its senses. Let everyone make their gifts manifest. But let them also be mindful of the need to empower others when speaking for others or to them. Genuinely democratic oratory is an exercise in empowerment. It fosters self-reliance, as well as solidarity, in its audience and holds itself accountable to the people being spoken for.

Despite the hopeful signs I have noted, much remains to be done and many important roles in the struggle go unfilled. Too many citizens complain about injustice, violence, and corruption without ever getting around to doing anything that makes much of a difference. Their ideals are neither precisely articulated, nor transformed into effective practical power. Their concern remains inert,[143] goes fugitive, or else recoils from the whole mess and transmutes into antidemocratic or postdemocratic despair.

While demonstrators create a little mayhem, the G8 summit carries on with its business unperturbed. Radical social critics preach to the choir, while the choir says Amen, but the ritual exchange of sentiment serves only to persuade the participants that their own dispositions are righteous. Meantime, centrist politics masquerades as grassroots democracy. The only things that move easily from the bottom up in the current political-economic system are wealth and deference. Mainstream candidates offer something indeterminate to hope for and an equally indeterminate way of bringing change about. The presidential rhetoric of change puts the idealistic cart before the organizational horse, and then neglects to feed the horse.

When we expect liberty and justice to appear miraculously, like fast food, without more rigorous forms of participation, definition, and sacrifice, we are like farmers who curse the dirt and pray for rain, but "want crops without plowing the ground."[144] Yet some people are already plowing.

> I see always the under side turning,
> fumes that injure the tender landscape.
> From which up break
> lilac blossoms of courage in daily act
> striving to meet a natural measure.[145]

⁕ *Acknowledgments* ⁕

A few small fragments of this work appeared in: "Comments on Six Responses to *Democracy and Tradition*," *The Journal of Religious Ethics* (published by Wiley-Blackwell) 33, no. 4 (December 2005): 737; "The Spirit of Democracy and the Rhetoric of Excess," *The Journal of Religious Ethics* 35, no. 1 (March 2007): 4, 16–18; and "A Prophetic Church in a Post-Constantinian Age," *Contemporary Pragmatism* (published by Editions Rodopi) 4, no. 1 (June 2007): 42–43. I am grateful to the respective editors and publishers for permission to reprint.

Early versions of my thoughts on the dangers threatening contemporary democracy were delivered at a conference at the University of Tennessee in October 2004; in October and November 2005 as the John Albert Hall Lectures at the University of Victoria in British Columbia; as the Priestley Lectures at University College of the University of Toronto in February 2006; and as the Jellema Lectures at Calvin College in March 2006. I delivered other lectures related to the issues covered in this book at Arizona State University, Brown University, Central Michigan University, Duke University, Georgia State University, LaSalle University, Lehigh University, New College (Sarasota, Florida), the University of North Carolina (Greensboro), the University of Notre Dame, Vassar College, Yale University, and meetings of the American Academy of Religion.

I wish to thank those who hosted me on these occasions and those whose questions and criticisms have influenced the finished product, especially David Bromwich, Conrad Brunk, Linnell Cady, Mark Cladis, Rom Coles, Beth Eddy, Bob Gibbs, Stan Hauerwas, Jonathon Kahn, Cathy Kaveny, Derek Krueger, Henry Levinson, Doug Langston, Tal Lewis, Mike Michalson, Tim Renick, Charlie Reynolds, Gene Rogers, Lou Ruprecht, Emilie Townes, and Nick Wolterstorff.

This book owes much to my colleagues and students. I will not attempt to name all of them, but should single out Leora Batnitzky, John Bowlin, Eddie Glaude, Eric Gregory, and Cornel West as my closest faculty collaborators. Philip Pettit is another Princeton colleague whose influence on this book is considerable. A number of points made in this book are influenced by the work of my friend Harry Frankfurt on what it is to care about something and on the role of caring in practical reasoning. I want to thank John Gager and Lorraine Fuhrmann for many years of friendship and for doing much to make my department a congenial place.

The need to follow up *Democracy and Tradition* with a more accessible book that says more about power was first impressed on me by the members of a local democratic book club and then by various critics, students, and friends. Of these, the one who pushed hardest and most productively for the inclusion of more examples was Elliot Ratzman. Vince Vitale commented helpfully on a very early draft. Conversations with him on sacred value, with Ian Ward on the role of religion in politics, and with Joe Winters on mourning contributed to my thinking on those topics.

A number of people were kind enough to comment on some or all of the penultimate draft: David Bromwich, Steve Bush, Joseph Clair, Josh Dubler, Beth Eddy, Molly Farneth, Eddie Glaude, Clifton Granby, Leah Hunt-Hendrix, Timothy Jackson, Stan Katz, Henry Levinson, Philip Pettit, Lou Ruprecht, Eli Sacks, Livy Stout, Ezra Tzfadya, Cornel West, Terrance Wiley, Kevin Wolfe, Bob Wuthnow, and an anonymous reader for the Press. Danielle Allen and John Bowlin gave me especially detailed and insightful comments that led to extensive revisions. Peter J. Dougherty, Fred Appel, Dimitri Karetnikov, and Debbie Tegarden of Princeton University Press assisted me in various ways during the writing and production of this book. Jack Rummel did an excellent job with the copyediting.

My sons Noah and Livy spent many hours typing up transcripts of recordings I brought home from New Orleans and Texas. I am very grateful to them. A paper that my daughter Suzannah wrote before she entered medical school planted the thought that I ought to study IAF more closely. Her service to the poor in Camden and San Francisco has been an inspiration to me. I am more than grateful to my wife, mother, brother, and sister for supporting me in countless ways.

It is a pleasure to acknowledge my debt to the many IAF organizers and leaders who graciously contributed their voices to this book. I want to give special thanks to Broderick Bagert for driving me all over New Orleans; Elizabeth Valdez for driving me throughout the Rio Grande Valley; Sister Christine Stephens, Sister Pearl Ceasar, and Sister Judy Donovan for sharing their wisdom with me on multiple occasions; and Anna Eng and Daniel May for showing me the ropes in Los Angeles. Daniel also gave me an especially detailed written account of his organizing experience in Maywood, from which I have quoted extensively and for which I am most thankful. Carlota García kindly collected remarks and corrections from various organizers on the penultimate draft.

"If Ernie Cortés invites you down to discuss your stuff with his organizers," Stan Hauerwas warned me, "they'll kick the shit out of you." Stan took delight in the thought and laughed hard. I am grateful to him for encouraging Ernie and me to get together. When we did, Ernie immediately struck me as a man of remarkable perseverance, hope, and practical wisdom. Everything I have learned from and about him since has confirmed that first impression. I am immensely thankful to him and his associates, not only for the work they do, but also for making this volume, in its current form, possible.

The book is dedicated to the memory of three dear friends who passed away while I was working on it. It is, in no small part, an extension of my conversations with them over the course of three decades and more.

✻ Notes ✻

THE MAIN TEXT of this work is meant to be accessible to the general reader. A few of the endnotes are addressed to scholarly readers who might want to know how the positions taken in this book relate to the academic literature on such topics as democracy, power, domination, authority, and sacred value. Biblical references in the text are to *The New Oxford Annotated Bible with the Apocrypha* (New York: Oxford University Press, 1991).

The Anaya epigraph at the beginning of the volume is from Geoff Rips, *Changing the Political Culture of the Texas Border: The Industrial Areas Foundation and Texas Colonias,* a report to the Ford Foundation for the Texas Center for Policy Studies (September 2000). The epigraph by Joanne Bland is from her remarks at a conference on religion in the civil rights movement, Princeton University, April 3, 2009.

Preface

1. In addition to Tocqueville and Whitman, I would cite the lesser-known Harriet Martineau as one of my nineteenth-century models in itinerant public philosophy. All three merged their observations as travelers with reflections on the nature and prospects of democratic life. Behind this modern tradition of political thought stands an ancient etymological connection in Greek between *travel* and *theory,* which Tocqueville in particular had very much in mind. See Sheldon S. Wolin, *Tocqueville between Two Worlds: The Making of a Political and Theoretical Life* (Princeton: Princeton University Press, 2001), 34–36. For further reflections on the importance of traveling for political theory, see Romand Coles, "Moving Democracy: The Political Arts of Listening, Traveling, and Tabling," in *Beyond Gated Politics: Reflections for the Possibility of Democracy* (Minneapolis: University of Minnesota Press, 2005), 213–37.

2. Readers are free to concentrate on the stories and skip the extended re-

flections. The former are easy to find, because of the prevalence of quotation in them. But I would caution scholarly readers against skipping the stories. The journey undertaken here is not only a movement through actual American terrain but also a cyclical movement from the concrete to the reflective and back again.

3. See candidate Obama's address at the "Take the Country Back" conference in June 2007. The "Yes we can!" chant was first used, I believe, by the United Farm Workers. Many of Obama's campaign speeches made reference to the need to restore accountability. The Obama postelection transition team created something called the "Government Accountability Project." The president's Inaugural Address promised that "those of us who manage the public's dollars will be held to account."

4. All quotations in the text that are not accompanied by citations in the notes will be from conversations I have had with organizers and leaders involved in the Southwest network of the Industrial Areas Foundation. Most of those conversations took place in the summer of 2006 and the winter of 2007.

5. I have benefited greatly from reading the existing empirical literature on contemporary broad-based organizing. See especially: Stephen Hart, *Cultural Dilemmas of Progressive Politics: Styles of Engagement among Grassroots Activists* (Chicago: University of Chicago Press, 2001); Paul Osterman, *Gathering Power: The Future of Progressive Politics in America* (Boston: Beacon Press, 2002); Robert D. Putnam and Lewis M. Feldstein, *Better Together: Restoring the American Community* (New York: Simon and Schuster, 2003), chapter 1; Mark R. Warren, *Dry Bones Rattling: Community Building to Revitalize American Democracy* (Princeton: Princeton University Press, 2001); and Richard L. Wood, *Faith in Action: Religion, Race, and Democratic Organizing in America* (Chicago: University of Chicago Press, 2002).

Chapter One. The Responsibilities of a Citizen

The epigraph comes from Thomas More, *Utopia*, in *The Complete Works of St. Thomas More*, volume 4, edited by Edward Surtz and J. H. Hexter (New Haven: Yale University Press, 1965), book I, 53. Quoted in Wolin, *Tocqueville*, 36.

6. Saul D. Alinsky, *Reveille for Radicals* (New York: Vintage Books, 1989; originally published 1946); *Rules for Radicals: A Pragmatic Primer for Realistic Radicals* (New York: Vintage Books, 1971). For a biography of Alinsky, see Sanford D. Horwitt, *Let Them Call Me Rebel: Saul Alinsky—His Life and*

Legacy (New York: Vintage Books, 1989). For the reflections of latter-day organizers in the Alinsky tradition, see Edward T. Chambers (with Michael A. Cowan), *Roots for Radicals* (New York: Continuum, 2004); and Michael Gecan, *Going Public: An Organizer's Guide to Citizen Action* (New York: Anchor Books, 2002). For relevant social scientific studies of IAF, see the works by Osterman, Warren, and Putnam and Feldstein cited above, which focus on the same IAF groups in Texas that I treat in chapters 7 and 8. That my findings essentially cohere with those of Osterman and Warren has given me confidence in the descriptive component of my account of those and similarly structured groups.

Other works that include illuminating treatments of IAF groups are Harry C. Boyte, *Community Is Possible: Repairing America's Roots* (New York: Harper, 1984); Romand Coles, *Beyond Gated Politics*, chapter 7; Samuel G. Freeman, *Upon This Rock: The Miracles of a Black Church* (New York: HarperCollins, 1993); William Greider, *Who Will Tell the People? The Betrayal of American Democracy* (New York: Touchstone, 1993), chapter 10; David Harvey, *Spaces of Hope* (Berkeley: University of California Press, 2000), 121–30; Alexander von Hoffman, *House by House, Block by Block: The Rebirth of America's Urban Neighborhoods* (New York: Oxford University Press, 2003).

Luke Bretherton, *Christianity and Contemporary Politics* (West Sussex, UK: Wiley-Blackwell, 2010), chapters 1 and 2, offers a theological perspective on Alinsky and IAF, but appeared too late to be taken up in any detail here.

7. Richard L. Wood gives a detailed comparative account of the advantages and disadvantages of faith-based and race-based organizing in *Faith in Action*. His example of faith-based organizing is a group located in California that is affiliated with the Pacific Institute for Community Organization, a network with many affinities to IAF. Mark R. Warren discusses IAF attempts to bridge racial boundaries in *Dry Bones Rattling*, chapters 4 and 5.

8. As this book goes to press, the codirectors of IAF are Ernesto Cortés and Michael Gecan. The plan is for them to alternate, year by year, with Sister Christine Stephens and Arnold Graf.

9. Walt Whitman, "Democratic Vistas," in *Whitman: Poetry and Prose*, edited by Justin Kaplan (New York: Library of America, 1982), 929–94. The reference to the question of character comes on p. 936. The reference to robbery on the part of the business class comes on p. 937. The references to justice and the experiences of the fight come on p. 952. I discuss Whitman's way of framing the question of character in *Democracy and Tradition* (Princeton: Princeton University Press, 2004), chapter 1.

10. I am grateful to Eli Sacks for pressing me to clarify how, as I see it, grassroots democracy differs from other forms of democracy.

11. For a sampling of the sociological literature on social movements, see *The Social Movements Reader: Cases and Concepts,* 2d edition, edited by Jeff Goodwin and James M. Jasper (West Sussex, UK: Wiley-Blackwell, 2009). See also David S. Meyer, *The Politics of Protest: Social Movements in America* (New York: Oxford University Press, 2007); and Charles Tilly and Lesley J. Wood, *Social Movements, 1768–2008,* 2d edition (Boulder, CO: Paradigm, 2009).

12. Philip Pettit, *Republicanism: A Theory of Freedom and Government* (Oxford: Oxford University Press, 1997), chapters 2 and 3.

13. Ibid., chapter 6.

14. See David Bacon, *Illegal People: How Globalization Creates Migration and Criminalizes Immigrants* (Boston: Beacon Press, 2008). Similar arguments arise concerning the political effects of disproportionate incarceration of the African-American population. See James Samuel Logan, *Good Punishment? Christian Moral Practice and U.S. Imprisonment* (Grand Rapids, MI: Eerdmans, 2008), chapters 1 and 2.

15. Harry Frankfurt, *The Reasons of Love* (Princeton: Princeton University Press, 2004).

16. See Walter Lippmann, *Public Opinion* (New York: Harcourt, Brace, 1922); and John Dewey, *The Public and Its Problems* (New York: Holt, 1927). Richard Rorty, despite his firm allegiance to Dewey on most other questions, affirms Lippmann's position on the appropriate relationship between elites and the masses in *Achieving Our Country: Leftist Thought in the Twentieth Century* (Cambridge: Harvard University Press, 1998). In the present book, I am offering what amounts to an updated defense of Dewey's position.

17. The task, as A. R. Ammons has put it in a masterful book-length poem, is "to go below and check the ballast: how it is that what was / enough for both sides has become too much for one side and not / enough for the other: you gather a force and go down to make / a correction." *Sphere: The Form of a Motion* (New York: W. W. Norton, 1974), 76.

Chapter Two. A Power Analysis

18. An excellent interactive map of New Orleans prepared by Dan Swenson for the *Times Picayune* details how the storm waters engulfed many of the city's neighborhoods on August 28, 2005: http://www.nola.com/katrina/graphics/flashflood.swf.

19. The complete text of Jeremiah 29:7 reads: "But seek the welfare of the city where I have sent you into exile, and pray to the Lord on its behalf, for in its welfare you will find your welfare."

20. For a more favorable perspective on neighborhood associations, see Ken Thomson, *From Neighborhood to Nation: The Democratic Foundations of Civil Society* (Hanover, NH: Tufts University, 2001). While I find Thomson's book valuable, I do not accept the contrasts he draws between neighborhood associations and what he calls "Alinsky-style organizations" on pp. 82–83.

21. Charles M. Payne, *I've Got the Light of Freedom: The Organizing Tradition and the Mississippi Freedom Struggle* (Berkeley: University of California Press, 1995).

Chapter Three. Organizing for the Common Good

22. In *The Shock Doctrine: The Rise of Disaster Capitalism* (New York: Metropolitan Books, 2007), Naomi Klein defines disaster capitalism as a pattern of "orchestrated raids on the public sphere in the wake of catastrophic events, combined with a treatment of disasters as exciting market opportunities" (6). I do not place as much emphasis on the element of orchestration in the definition of this phenomenon as Klein does. The degree of self-conscious collaboration among elites in responding to catastrophe differs considerably from case to case.

23. Alinsky, *Reveille for Radicals*, 184.

24. Given the extent and duration of his professional experience, Cortés is in a good position to know whether local institutional life is changing for the worse in this respect, at least in the relatively disadvantaged communities where most of his organizers have worked over the years. For works by influential social scientists who make related claims about a weakening of civil society, see Robert N. Bellah, Richard Madsen, William M. Sullivan, Ann Swidler, and Steven M. Tipton, *Habits of the Heart: Individualism and Community in American Life* (New York: Harper and Row, 1985) and *The Good Society* (New York: Knopf, 1991); Robert Putnam, *Making Democracy Work* (Princeton: Princeton University Press, 1993) and *Bowling Alone: The Collapse and Revival of American Community* (New York: Simon and Schuster, 2000).

See also Brian O'Connell, *Civil Society: The Underpinnings of American Democracy* (Hanover, NH: Tufts University, 1999), especially chapter 6, "Limitations of Civil Society, Threats to It, and the General State of It"; Jean Cohen, "Trust, Voluntary Associations, and Workable Democracy," in *Democ-*

racy and Trust, edited by Mark E. Warren (Cambridge: Cambridge University Press, 1999), 208–48; Thomson, *From Neighborhood to Nation,* 2; Henry Milner, *Civic Literacy: How Informed Citizens Make Democracy Work* (Hanover, NH: Tufts University, 2002), especially 15–20. In note 44 below, I raise doubts about Putnam's central analytical category of *social capital* and cite some of the relevant critical literature on that category.

25. Ernesto Cortés Jr., "Reweaving the Social Fabric," in *The Southwest IAF Network: 25 Years of Organizing* (Austin, TX: Interfaith Education Fund, 1999), 58–61.

26. Ian Shapiro refers to a similar definition of the common good as a "stripped-down" conception and traces it to Machiavelli's *Discourses.* See *The State of Democratic Theory* (Princeton: Princeton University Press, 2003), 35. A full-fledged democratic conception of the common good would need to fill out what virtues, practices, institutions, and forms of recognition would actually be held in common by citizens whose basic relationships were both secure against domination and in other respects just. A stripped-down conception provides a starting point for a discussion that should eventually lead to something much more substantial.

27. On "power" and "self-interest" as terms that wear "the black shroud of negativism and suspicion," see *Rules for Radicals,* 48–62. The quoted phrase comes on p. 53.

28. I owe this way of putting the point to Molly Farneth.

Chapter Four. Rites of Solidarity, Commitment, and Mourning

29. David I. Kertzer, *Ritual, Politics, and Power* (New Haven: Yale University Press, 1988), 18.

30. Molly Farneth has pointed out to me in personal correspondence that "in some states (Maine and Vermont), individuals who have been convicted and are currently incarcerated can also vote—making prisons an even more important site for voter registration and organizing work in those places."

Chapter Five. Domination, Anger, and Grief

The epigraph is from Abraham Lincoln, "On Slavery and Democracy," *Speeches and Writings 1832–1858*, edited by Don E. Fehrenbacher (New York: Library of America, 1989), 484.

31. For an analysis of post-Katrina zoning decisions in New Orleans as a

resegregation of the city, see Lizzy Ratner, "New Orleans Redraws Its Color Line," *The Nation* (September 15, 2008): 21–25.

32. Harriet Martineau recounts a conversation she had with a southern white woman before the emancipation of slaves. The woman was puzzled as to why a particular slave, who had a *benevolent* master, had run away three times, thereby placing himself at great risk. The third time, the slave "was found in the woods, with both legs frost-bitten above the knees, so as to render amputation necessary." The woman thought the slave deserved this fate—and much worse—for having tried to escape a good master. Martineau explained that the slave wanted to be *free*: "From any master." *Society in America*, abridged edition (New Brunswick, NJ: Transaction, 2005), 158. The story illustrates something important about antipathy for domination. The animus is not merely against actual cruelty, harm, or interference, but against any arrangement or relationship that leaves one party *in a position* to inflict such things arbitrarily on someone. This is why I take Thomas E. Wartenberg's definition of "domination" to be inadequate for my purposes. See n. 35 below and Pettit, *Republicanism,* 31–35, 63–64.

33. The effects in question can be good or bad, but they must be significant—in the sense that someone cares about them, or would care about them if they occurred, or should care about them. A power analysis takes no interest in the capacity to produce politically indifferent effects. The effects in which it takes an interest can, however, be intentional or unintentional. A power analysis of a community would obviously need to attend to the capacity of the police to oppress a racial group on purpose, an effect that is both intended and counted as bad by the analyst. But attention would also need to be given to the capacity of the police to produce disproportionately *bad unintended* effects when using firearms and to achieve *beneficial intended* effects, such as the protection of law-abiding citizens from criminals.

In defining power as the capacity to produce socially significant effects, I am leaving open whether the capacity is exercised. Unexercised power will often require attention whether our concern is with good or bad potential effects (or both). Consider first the case of a church that, by joining together with other civic institutions and holding a public meeting of some kind, could contest unjust decisions recently made by a governmental official. An organizer might want to disclose this capacity to church leaders, precisely because it is not currently being exercised and would increase democratic accountability in the community if it were exercised. Here the potential effects of the as-yet-unexercised capacity are good.

But now consider a community in which whites are in a position for the most part to impose their will on blacks. To have the capacity to impose one's will on others is to dominate them. To be dominated is to lack security against someone's arbitrary exercise of power, even if that power is never in fact exercised. So for this reason, too, unexercised capacities, as well as exercised capacities, require attention in a power analysis. The conceptions of power and domination I am developing for my purposes are somewhat more inclusive than the ones Philip Pettit develops, but I have found his schema illuminating. See his book, *Republicanism*, 51–79.

If power is the capacity to produce socially significant effects, alert readers will want to know whether the agents of power highlighted in IAF power analyses—namely, individuals, groups, and institutions—are the only sources of socially significant effects actually worthy of consideration, or even the most important ones. A recent trend in power theory, associated with the work of Michel Foucault, involves shifting attention to what might be called anonymous sources of power.

Consider two especially important kinds of social effect. The first is the array of propositions that people living in a given place at a given time are in a position to entertain, accept, or reject. The second is the array of possible social identities that people living in a given place at a given time can acquire, adopt, or attribute. Foucault argued that individuals, groups, and institutions typically do not, in any straightforward way, produce either of these two kinds of effects. Much of his work was designed to illustrate the extent to which effects of these kinds and the forms of domination correlated with them must be accounted for without reference to the usual *human* suspects. The most significant social effects, according to Foucault, are often to be accounted for simply as unintended by-products of earlier similar configurations of effects, interacting with historical contingencies without necessarily needing much direct help from intentional human agency.

If we disentangle Foucault's analyses of anonymous sources of "power-over" from some of his obscure methodological pronouncements, the former can be viewed as supplementing, rather than conflicting with, the agency-oriented power analyses conducted in IAF and similar groups. Agents need not be disempowered by learning how they have been shaped by the vocabularies and identities lodged in their discursive and formative social practices. To the contrary, such knowledge can and should inform deliberate choices concerning which social practices to support, how to embed them in institutions, and how the norms and identities embodied in them should be revised.

Foucault does not himself offer much help with these questions. We shall see that IAF leaders and organizers pay a good deal of attention to them. But in doing so, IAF employs what strikes me as a much richer reflective vocabulary than Foucault uses when he speaks of power and domination. On this point, practitioners on the ground have something to teach the theorists.

The questions I have just listed cannot be framed properly unless power is understood in relation to the normative notions of authority and responsibility and unless domination is understood normatively. Domination is not merely any form of power-over people, but rather the defining trait of relationships in which one person or group is in a position to exercise power *arbitrarily* over others. So it, too, is a normative notion. Foucault was uneasy about treating it as such, I suspect, because he was backing away from a quite different normative conception of domination as oppression of the true inner self or essential subject. I think he was right to reject that notion, but wrong to reduce domination to "power-over." Exercising power over someone is not necessarily a bad thing, but domination is.

By setting power and domination in relation to other terms that are essential for social critique and by taking responsibility for the normative commitments we adopt as users of those terms, we can avoid the disempowering reductionism that many readers have seen lurking in some of Foucault's formulations. I am basically agreeing with Ian Shapiro, *The State of Political Theory* (Princeton: Princeton University Press, 2003), 36–39; and Nancy Fraser, "Foucault on Modern Power: Empirical Insights and Normative Confusions," in *Unruly Practices: Power, Discourse, and Gender in Contemporary Social Theory* (Minneapolis: University of Minnesota Press, 1989), 17–34. Readers unfamiliar with Foucault's methodological writings can take the following works as points of entry: *The Archeology of Knowledge and the Discourse on Language,* translated by A. M. Sheridan Smith (New York: Tavistock, 1972), and *Power/Knowledge: Selected Interviews and Other Writings,* edited by Colin Gordon (New York: Harvester, 1980). Foucault's later writings on ethics and care for self complicate matters considerably, but this is not the place for me to take them up. Judith Butler treats some of the complications in *Giving an Account of Oneself* (New York: Fordham University Press, 2005).

34. Charles E. Lindblom, *The Market System: What It Is, How It Works, and What to Make of It* (New Haven: Yale University Press, 2001), chapters 2–7.

35. Thomas E. Wartenberg makes much of the contrast between having

power over someone and having power to do or achieve something. See his book, *The Forms of Power: From Domination to Transformation* (Philadelphia: Temple University Press, 1990), chapters 1 and 4. Wartenberg argues that "the most basic use of 'power' within social theory is . . . as a means of criticizing a social relationship" (4). It is not clear what he means by "most basic" here, because he grants that having power over someone *depends on* having the power to do various things (19). Perhaps he is thinking: (a) that domination and emancipatory power are the most important types of power for social theory, (b) that domination is a type of power-over, and (c) that emancipatory power, which is a type of power-to, can be exercised only in situations where domination is already present.

In any event, it seems to me that the power to emancipate someone from domination, the power to achieve a society of mutual recognition, and the power of ordinary citizens within such a society to influence and contest the decisions of elites are all forms of power-to that need to be highlighted by a critical theory of society. Contemporary critical theory tends to exacerbate alienation and foster impotence when it brings domination to light while leaving in the dark the power to overcome domination, the power to protect people from domination, and the power to hold elites accountable. When Wartenberg discusses "transformative power" in chapter 9 of his book, he restricts his attention to a kind of power-over and thus to a phenomenon that is distinct from the forms of power-to just mentioned. What he calls transformative power is only one of several beneficial forms of power that require analysis.

IAF power analyses do not restrict themselves in the ways that Wartenberg's theory of power does. They are designed to bring many forms of power-over and power-to into focus simultaneously. Performing a power analysis itself is an exercise of power-to. Its purpose is to enhance the power-to of those who are subject to domination or at risk of being dominated. "Domination," as I am using the term, leaves one person or group in a position to exercise power *arbitrarily* over another. Wartenberg (119) means something different by the term: a systematic use of power over a person or group *at the expense* of that person or group. My reasons for preferring my definition of domination to Wartenberg's will emerge below.

36. Ellen Meiksins Wood, *Empire of Capital* (New York: Verso, 2005), 2–3, 10–14.

37. Presumably, an employer would qualify as just if he or she (a) avoided taking advantage of the available opportunities for exploitation of workers

and the underclass and (b) used his or her political power to help create economic arrangements free from domination. It is possible, then, for there to be just employers in an unjust economy. It is therefore ethically important for citizens who seek to create a just economy to distinguish between just and unjust employers and to treat them differently.

38. In the Introduction to the Vintage edition of *Reveille for Radicals,* Alinsky claimed that he had "learned to freeze my hot anger into cool anger" (ix). The title of Mary Beth Rogers's book on Ernesto Cortés and COPS appears to allude to this passage: *Cold Anger: A Story of Faith and Power Politics* (Denton: University of North Texas Press, 1990). Paul Osterman emphasizes the importance of "personal anger that can be translated into political action" (*Gathering Power,* 48). He quotes Sister Christine Stephens's claim that democratic action provides an opportunity to "own the anger, deal with it, use it" (49). In *Rules for Radicals* Alinsky wrote that while he once considered "a deep sense of anger against injustice" the basic quality of an organizer's character, he now placed even more importance on the imaginative capacity to project oneself into the plight of humankind (74).

39. Here and in the next several paragraphs, I am drawing on Plato's treatment of generous passion in the *Laws* (5.73Ib), Aristotle's discussion of anger and spiritedness in the *Politics* (book 7, section 3), and especially Philip Fisher's wonderful book, *The Vehement Passions* (Princeton: Princeton University Press, 2002), chapters 9–12.

40. Fisher, *Vehement Passions,* 190–98.

41. Ibid., 199–226.

42. I am grateful to John Bowlin for helping me clarify the role that courage plays in the moral psychology of justly focused and expressed anger.

Chapter Eight. The Authority to Lead

The Alinsky epigraph is from *Reveille for Radicals,* 67.

43. The most influential sociological theory of charismatic authority is that offered by Max Weber in *Economy and Society: An Outline of Interpretive Sociology,* volume 2, edited by Guenther Roth and Claus Wittich (Berkeley: University of California Press, 1978), 1111–57.

44. There are many forms of authority that are relevant to democratic politics. Most of them involve the entitlement of one person to receive a certain sort of response from one or more others. Each citizen in a democratic society is entitled to have his or her concerns taken into consideration by other

citizens deliberating on questions of public import. This entitlement can be classified as a sort of authority, but when I speak of an individual's ethical, moral, or intellectual authority, I have in mind something a bit more demanding. A person's life or conduct has ethical authority insofar as it deserves to be treated as exemplary by others. If I acknowledge the authority of someone's moral judgment, I grant that, other things being equal, I ought to defer to that person's judgment on such topics as moral obligation and character. If I acknowledge someone's intellectual authority or expertise, I grant that, other things being equal, I ought to defer to that person's judgments on at least some matters of fact. (The line between moral and intellectual authority is, of course, as fuzzy as the line between moral and factual judgments is.)

Officeholders possess political authority, as I use this expression, just in case they are entitled to exercise the powers of their office. In some cases, such powers include the issuing of verdicts, rulings, commands, or orders; when that is so, the presumption is that the official's action ought to be accepted or obeyed. Representative authority is the entitlement to speak for, or on behalf of, one or more persons or institutions. There are also forms of authority in which a nonpersonal entity such as a law, text, or tradition merits deference. Rather than regimenting my discussion of these various types of authority in this chapter by repeatedly calling attention to these distinctions, I will rely on context to clarify which sort of authority I have in mind at any given point in what follows.

Many academics—and some organizers influenced by them—now speak of what I am calling the authority of a leader as a form of social or cultural "capital." I have several reasons for not following their lead. The economic metaphor underlying this way of speaking disposes people to underestimate the differences among various kinds of goods. An economic good like capital is something rightly valued only instrumentally, and its distribution is often, if not typically, a zero-sum affair: more capital for me means less for others. Goods like learnedness, trust, and democratic authority are not like that. We rightly value them for their own sakes, as well as for their utility to us. And in a well functioning democratic culture, it is not the case that an increase of these goods for one person implies a decrease of these goods for someone else. Moreover, to possess economic capital is not to possess a normative status, whereas to possess the authority to lead is to have a normative status.

As I am using the concept, attributing authority to someone involves a normative judgment—indeed, a kind of normative judgment that is intrinsically resistant to quantification (though not always to ranking). It is to take a stand on who is actually entitled to something. In my analysis of what has happened in the Rio Grande Valley, for example, I am prepared to assert, as part of an explanation of certain organizational and political *successes*, that Carmen Anaya *earned an entitlement* to deference and trust from other people participating in Valley Interfaith. The notion of authority as an earned entitlement is normative. Employing it in an explanation requires me to make a normative commitment concerning who actually deserves to be treated in certain ways by others. If I felt compelled to eliminate normative concepts from my explanations, I would have trouble accounting for the differences between Valley Interfaith under Anaya's leadership and other citizens' organizations in which leaders have not earned an entitlement to deference and trust by listening well, keeping their word, demonstrating courage, making wise decisions, and so on. Among the types of cases to be accounted for are: (a) those, like the Anaya case, in which an earned entitlement helps explain a group's success; (b) those in which a group's failure to achieve its objectives can be traced in part to the leadership's failure to do what *would have* earned the deference and trust of group members had the leadership behaved better; and (c) those in which leaders acquire influence over group members not by earning it democratically, but by means of manipulative and deceptive speech or by arbitrary threats and rewards. In all three of these types, the explanation of outcomes requires us to make judgments concerning excellences and entitlements or the lack thereof. In cases of type (c), what often needs explanation is how a kind of misrecognition or mystification operates, that is, how group members come to make attributions of authority on the basis of *bad* reasons or reasons of the *wrong* kind.

Consider a couple of analogies. Some sports teams achieve their objectives, while others fail. The difference is often to be explained in part by how a coach or a captain behaves. We do not hesitate, in these contexts, to say that a team failed in part because a leader failed to earn the respect and confidence of the team. In saying such things, we are framing our explanations in normative terms. This should not be surprising, given that the point of the explanations is to guide future conduct.

By the same token, some marriages are successful, while others fail. Highly rewarding marriages are to be explained in part by reference to the excellences of the spouses. One such excellence is the discernment a husband and wife once exercised in rightly regarding one another as sufficiently kind and faithful to qualify as excellent prospective mates. Some failed marriages are obviously to be explained by the vices of one or both of the spouses. Perhaps the husband was abusive, and the wife was attracted to him not for good reasons, but because he unconsciously reminded her of her similarly vicious father. It makes perfect sense to say of such a case that the husband's cruelty destroyed the marriage and that the wife would have been wiser to shun his proposal in the first place. There are also marriages that last, but in a condition we are not disposed to view as genuinely happy for the people involved. Suppose a husband is cheating and lies to his wife repeatedly. She is both gullible and cowardly. The marriage lasts, but we recognize that the spouses are not in a genuinely happy relationship. Again, explanatory and normative issues are intertwined. Explanations of the differences between happy and unhappy marriages would not be improved if we somehow filtered the value-laden or normative concepts out of them. And so it is with our explanations of the differences among political groups or societies.

The concept of social capital is not only grounded in a questionable metaphor that invites a reductive approach to democratic theory, it also often functions as a rather blunt instrument on its own terms. On this point, my reservations are similar to the ones Paul Lichterman expresses in *Elusive Togetherness: Church Groups Trying to Bridge America's Divisions* (Princeton: Princeton University Press, 2005), 3–4, 26–28. Lichterman is responding critically to Putnam, *Making Democracy Work* and *Bowling Alone*. For another valuable critique of recent "Toquevillian" work on civil society, see Mark E. Warren, *Democracy and Association* (Princeton: Princeton University Press, 2001).

45. Carmen Anaya, quoted by Geoff Rips in *Changing the Political Culture of the Texas Border: The Industrial Areas Foundation and Texas Colonias*, a report to the Ford Foundation for the Texas Center for Policy Studies (September 2000), 8.

46. Annette C. Baier, "Claims, Rights, and Responsibilities," in *Moral Prejudices* (Cambridge: Harvard University Press, 1994), 225–26. See also my discussion of this passage in *Democracy and Tradition*, 204–9. Of course, there are strands of modern Christian social ethics that do not share the spirit of the Milton-Whitman-Anaya tradition. One of these is that of the Catholic Worker Movement, which self-consciously adopts the posture of the beggar. One of Peter Maurin's digests reads in part: "People who are in need / and not afraid to beg / give to people not in need / the occasion to do good / for goodness' sake." It is called "To the Bishops of the USA," and can be found in Dorothy Day (with Francis J. Sicius), *Peter Maurin: Apostle to the World* (Maryknoll, NY: Orbis Books, 2004), 147. For a sampling of Day's references to begging, see her book *Loaves and Fishes* (Maryknoll, NY: Orbis Books, 1997; originally published in 1963), 23, 51, 85, 89.

47. See Pettit, *Republicanism,* 61, 71.

48. Attributions of the former type of authority express what Stephen Darwall calls "appraisal respect." Attributions of the latter type of authority express what he calls "recognition respect." See Darwall, *The Second-Person Standpoint: Morality, Respect, and Accountability* (Cambridge: Harvard University Press, 2006), 122–26.

49. Alinsky, *Reveille for Radicals*, 72–73.

50. Ibid., 76, 153, 77.

51. For disturbing confirmation of Ninfa's view of McAllen's medical establishment, see Atul Gawande, "The Cost Conundrum," *The New Yorker* (June 1, 2009), available online at: http://www.newyorker.com/reporting/2009/06/01/090601fa_fact_gawande.

52. B. Greenwald and J. E. Stiglitz, "Externalities in Economies with Imperfect Information and Incomplete Markets," *Quarterly Journal of Economics* 101, no. 2 (May 1986): 229–64.

53. For an example of the sort of empirical work I am referring to here, with specific policy recommendations concerning the minimum wage, see Alan B. Krueger, "Inequality, Too Much of a Good Thing," in *Inequality in America: What Role for Human Capital Policies?* edited by James J. Heckman and Alan B. Krueger (Cambridge: MIT Press, 2003), 1–75.

54. Arjun Appadurai, "Grassroots Globalization and the Research Imagination," in *Globalization*, edited by Arjun Appadurai (Durham, NC: Duke University Press, 2001), 1–21, 3.

55. Arjun Appadurai, *Fear of Small Numbers: An Essay on the Geography of Anger* (Durham, NC: Duke University Press, 2001), 131–37.

56. Of course, this is not to say that vertebrate forms of authority and organization have atrophied to the point that they are no longer relevant. Nor is it to suggest that all cellular forms of organization currently taking shape around the world are democratic. Some of them, notoriously, are committed to imposing theocracy of one sort or another on any population they can while punishing the rest.

57. Jaroslav Pelikan, *The Vindication of Tradition* (New Haven: Yale University Press, 1984), 65.

Chapter Nine. On the Treatment of Opponents

58. Peter Applebome, "Changing Texas Politics at Its Roots," *New York Times*, May 31, 1988, consulted online at: http://query.nytimes.com/gst/full

page.html?res=940DEEDA1F3CF932A05756C0A96E948260&sec=&spon=&pagewanted=1.

59. Alinsky, *Rules for Radicals,* 24–47.

60. For a discussion of the etymologies of "terror" and "horror," see Adriana Cavarero, *Horrorism: Naming Contemporary Violence*, translated by William McCuaig (New York: Columbia University Press, 2009), chapters 1 and 2. I am applying the category of the horrendous somewhat more widely than Cavarero does in the context of introducing the neologism "horrorism" in her chapter 7.

61. I extend these remarks about the horrendous and the sacred in chapter 17.

62. Quoted in Dennis Shirley, *Valley Interfaith and School Reform: Organizing for Power in South Texas* (Austin: University of Texas Press, 2002), 16–17. Shirley's book is one of the best empirical studies of an IAF network's approach to a single issue. For another account of IAF work on the same issue, see Richard J. Murnane and Frank Levy, *Teaching the New Basic Skills: Principles for Educating Children to Thrive in a Changing Economy* (New York: Martin Kessler Books, The Free Press, 1996), esp. 85–101. Warren, *Dry Bones Rattling,* and Osterman, *Gathering Power,* are more general studies, but they shed a good deal of light on IAF efforts in the area of school reform.

63. *Rules for Radicals* begins with three epigraphs. The first is a lofty line from Rabbi Hillel. The second is a passage in which Thomas Paine declares that he would prefer to "suffer the misery of devils" over making a whore of his soul. The third is a sentence in which Alinsky himself, with characteristic naughtiness, refers to Lucifer as "the first radical known to man who rebelled against the establishment and did it so effectively that he at least won his own kingdom" (ix).

Chapter Ten. Organize, Reflect, and Reorganize

64. Paul Lichterman, *Elusive Togetherness*.

Chapter Eleven. The Compelling Force of the Ideal

The epigraph is from Ralph Ellison, "The Little Man at Chehaw Station," in *The Collected Essays of Ralph Ellison,* edited by John F. Callahan (New York: Modern Library, 1995), 489–519, quotation from 501.

65. Mary Douglas, *Natural Symbols: Explorations in Cosmology* (London: Routledge, 1996, originally published 1970), 153.

66. This is one of the important lessons of Barbara Ehrenreich, *Nickel and Dimed: On (Not) Getting by in America* (New York: Metropolitan Books, 2001).

67. Douglas, *Natural Symbols,* 154.

68. I am referring, of course, to the book by Putnam cited earlier, but also to the important corrective to it offered by my colleague Robert Wuthnow in *Loose Connections: Joining Together in America's Fragmented Communities* (Cambridge: Harvard University Press, 1998).

69. Lichterman, *Elusive Togetherness*, 47–49, 255–56.

70. I am saying that political debate in republics with democratic aspirations tends to be centered on *paradigms* of domination and tends often to proceed by analogical reasoning in relation to those paradigms. The first such paradigm to give ethical substance to modern republics was the relationship of a monarch, who claims to rule by divine right, to his or her subjects. The second was the relationship of an empire to a conquered or colonized people. The third, which marked the onset of the democratic era, was the relationship of master to slave as understood in the antislavery movement. For more on the concept of a paradigm and its role in the study of ethico-political and scientific history, see my essay "The Rhetoric of Revolution," in *Religion and Practical Reason,* edited by Frank E. Reynolds and David Tracy (Albany: State University of New York Press, 1994), 329–62.

71. My interpretations of *substantial freedom* and *ethical substance*, like much else in the present inquiry into the *spirit* of grassroots democracy, are indebted to the nineteenth-century German philosopher G.W.F. Hegel. Readers with enough scholarly curiosity to pursue the Hegel connection further might wish to consult Robert Brandom's forthcoming study of Hegel, *A Spirit of Trust,* and Gillian Rose's important book, *Hegel Contra Sociology* (London: Verso, 2009).

72. People who consider legal constraint a *necessary* evil, and thus something to be minimized to the extent possible, are sometimes called libertarians. People who consider legal constraint an *unnecessary* evil, at least at the level of a nation-state, are sometimes called anarchists. But the term *anarchism* is used these days to refer to various sorts of groups, some of which are more similar to broad-based citizens' organizations than others. The crucial variables for a comparative analysis of such groups would be whether they are aiming for *security* from domination or freedom from legal constraint as such;

what sort of polity, if any, they are striving for; and whether their members achieve solidarity by adopting relatively determinate roles and norms. For an account of contemporary anarchist groups, see Richard J. F. Day, *Gramsci Is Dead: Anarchist Currents in the Newest Social Movements* (London: Pluto Press, 2005).

73. Ralph Waldo Emerson, "Experience," in *Essays and Lectures*, edited by Joel Porte (New York: Library of America, 1983), 471–92, the quoted phrase coming in the final line. Emerson's most famous defense of the need to differentiate oneself from the mass is, of course, "Self-Reliance," 259–82, which, unfortunately, is often misread as a defense of freedom from constraint, interference, and influence.

Chapter Twelve. Face-to-Face Meetings

74. Richard S. Newman, *The Transformation of American Abolitionism: Fighting Slavery in the Early Republic* (Chapel Hill: University of North Carolina Press, 2002), 153, 155, and passim. For a vivid depiction of the role Emerson played in the culture of New England abolitionism, see Albert J. von Frank, *The Trials of Anthony Burns: Freedom and Slavery in Emerson's Boston* (Cambridge: Harvard University Press, 1998), especially 230: "Others thought the time *had* come for regular organizing, and the first and unlikeliest of these was Ralph Waldo Emerson" (italics in original).

75. Nancy F. Cott, *The Grounding of Modern Feminism* (New Haven: Yale University Press, 1987), especially chapters 2 and 3. The language of "parlor meetings" is quoted on p. 55. For perspectives on an earlier stage of feminist organizing, see Ellen Carol DuBois, *Feminism and Suffrage: The Emergence of an Independent Women's Movement in America, 1848–1869* (Ithaca, NY: Cornell University Press, 1978).

76. Charles M. Payne, *I've Got the Light of Freedom: The Organizing Tradition and the Mississippi Freedom Struggle* (Berkeley: University of California Press, 1995), especially chapter 8. For a sociological study of the organizational infrastructure of the civil rights movement, see Aldon D. Morris, *The Origins of the Civil Rights Movement: Black Communities Organizing for Change* (New York: Free Press, 1984).

77. See Payne, *I've Got the Light*, chapter 12, which is subtitled "The Demoralization of the Movement."

78. The movement had already lost much of its momentum by the time King, Carmichael (later known as Kwame Ture), and others attempted to broaden and further radicalize its agenda.

79. Ludwig Wittgenstein, *Remarks on the Philosophy of Psychology,* volume 2, translated by C. G. Luckhardt and M.A.E. Aue (Oxford: Blackwell, 1980), section 570.

80. Maurice Merleau-Ponty, *The Maurice Merleau-Ponty Reader,* edited by Ted Toadvine and Leonard Lawlor (Evanston, IL: Northwestern University Press, 2007), 174.

81. The distinction between mediation and immediacy that Wittgenstein employed in this context has to do with the presence or absence of inference in reaching a judgment about what someone else feels. Wittgenstein was not saying that the resulting judgment is something that someone who lacks training in the use of the relevant concepts could reach.

82. On the theme of the individual's exposure of her own particularity in face-to-face encounter—for example, in the feminist consciousness raising group—see Adriana Cavarero, *Relating Narratives: Storytelling and Selfhood,* translated by Paul A. Kottman (London: Routledge, 2000), especially, 36, 72–76.

83. This conversational development, which begins from particularity but moves in the direction of the universal, makes Cavarero anxious to defend particularity against the universal. She proposes "an altruistic ethics of relation," which "desires a *you* that is truly an other, in her uniqueness and distinction. No matter how much you are similar and consonant, says this ethic, your story is never my story. No matter how much the larger traits of our life-stories are similar, I still do not recognize myself *in* you and, even less, in the collective *we.* I do not dissolve both into a common identity, nor do I digest your tale in order to construct the meaning of mine." *Relating Narratives,* 92; italics in original. In the context of her discussion of feminism, Cavarero objects to a process in which particular women are subsumed under the universal, *woman,* which for Cavarero merely repeats, albeit in a different register, the patriarchal dialectic in which particular men are subsumed under the universal, *man.*

It seems to me that Cavarero oversimplifies the possibilities. In a genuinely democratic form of sociality, it is true that your story is never my story and that I am not absorbed into an undifferentiated *we.* Yet it is possible for me to identify myself as a differentiated member of the broader group and to view my story as both unique in some respects and representative of broader social patterns in other respects. I need not choose between an utterly unmediated particularity and a complete absorption of my identity into the group. Our stories already employ concepts. They are not a parade of proper names and demonstratives. Noticing similarities and differences among our stories involves a further use of concepts, but it need not be a heavy-handed one, in which the universal, so to speak, dominates the particular. It would leave us mindless if, in an attempt to avoid such heavy-handedness, we made our intuition of the particular dominant. There can be no politics oriented toward the protection of vulnerable individuals and the cultivation of their agency without achievement of an appropriate balance (and tension) between concrete example and that which the example is taken to exemplify. See Judith Butler's discussion of Cavarero in *Giving an Account of Oneself* (New York: Fordham University Press, 2005), 30–35. On the relationship between examples and what they exemplify, see Jeffrey Stout, *Democracy and Tradition,* chapter 7.

84. This, Brod tells me, is the truth in Hauerwas's ambiguous claim that "justice is a bad idea." See Stanley Hauerwas, *After Christendom? How the Church Is to Behave if Freedom, Justice, and a Christian Nation Are Bad Ideas* (Nashville: Abingdon Press, 1991). For my response to Hauerwas, which Brod also had in mind, see my *Democracy and Tradition*, chapter 6. Hauerwas first publicly withdrew the claim that justice is a bad idea in a symposium on *Democracy and Tradition* at the annual meeting of the American Academy of Religion in 2003. A more recent (and to my mind, a more promising) turn in Hauerwas's work is evident in Stanley Hauerwas and Romand Coles, *Christianity, Democracy, and the Radical Ordinary: Conversations between a Radical Democrat and a Christian* (Eugene, OR: Cascade Books, 2008).

85. I have treated the theme of public reasoning at some length in *Democracy and Tradition,* chapters 3 and 8–12. The discussion there responds to two accounts of public reasoning—one liberal, the other traditionalist—both of which assume that public reasoning can be a rational affair only if widespread agreement is reached at a high level of abstraction: in the one case, on a conception of justice, in the other case, on a conception of the good. While my response was for the most part equally abstract, given that I was practicing immanent criticism, my aim was to promote a turn away from excessive abstraction toward the examination of concrete practices and their embodiment in institutions. On the "abstract rejection of abstraction" as "a way to induce abstract consciousness to begin to think non-abstractly," see Rose, *Hegel Contra Sociology,* 160. The present work picks up where its predecessor left off. I begin with concrete practices, but rather than observing a principled resistance to abstraction as such, as Cavarero claims to do, I am trying to show that democratic practices, insofar as they involve mutual accountability, themselves give rise to concepts and claims. My account of this

process is influenced by Robert B. Brandom's *Making It Explicit: Reasoning, Representing, and Discursive Commitment* (Cambridge: Harvard University Press, 1994), chapter 3, and by Stephen Darwall's *The Second-Person Standpoint*.

86. Cavarero describes the consciousness-raising group as "a *separatist* scene," which permits those participating in it to deconstruct a masculinist point of view without being dominated, in the course of the discussion, by the defenders of that point of view (*Relating Narratives*, 60). Judith Butler, in *Gender Trouble* (New York: Routledge, 1990), 45, 138, and 168, refers to the forms of linguistic innovation developed in such contexts as "resignification." One way to resignify is by inventing new concepts and establishing expectations, at first within the small group, concerning their use. The other way is by taking over old concepts and adjusting either their circumstances of application or their consequences of application—that to which they apply or what follows from properly applying them—or both. The Lincoln-Emerson resignification of "democracy" adjusted both the circumstances and consequences of application.

In "Feminism and Pragmatism," Richard Rorty listed many examples of groups that, in their separatist phase, gathered "their moral strength by achieving increasing semantic authority over their members, thereby increasing the ability of those members to find their moral identities in their membership in such groups." The examples include "the early Christians meeting in the catacombs" and the "workingmen gathering to discuss Tom Paine's pamphlets." *Truth and Progress: Philosophical Papers* (Cambridge: Cambridge University Press, 1998), 202–27, quotations from p. 223. For an important critical response to Rorty, see Nancy Fraser, *Unruly Practices: Power, Discourse, and Gender in Contemporary Social Theory* (Minneapolis: University of Minnesota Press, 1989), 93–110.

87. Alinsky, *Rules for Radicals,* 74.

88. Marco Iacoboni, *Mirroring People: The New Science of How We Connect with Others* (New York: Farrar, Straus and Giroux, 2008), 115. What I am saying about recent developments in neuroscience draws heavily on Iacoboni's book, as well as on Giacomo Rizzolatti and Corrado Singaglia, *Mirrors in the Brain: How Our Minds Share Actions and Emotions,* translated by Frances Anderson (Oxford: Oxford University Press, 2006). I am indebted to Eleonore Stump for drawing my attention to the significance of mirror neurons.

89. Iacoboni, *Mirroring People,* 157–83.

Chapter Thirteen. The Passion of St. Rose

90. Mary Rourke, "Her Calling: To Help Others Find a Voice," *Los Angeles Times*, August 12, 2002, consulted online at: http://articles.latimes.com/2002/aug/12/news/lv-sister12.

91. Frank Del Olmo, "Maywood's Mean Money Machine," *Los Angeles Times*, August 3, 2003, consulted online at: http://articles.latimes.com/2003/aug/03/opinion/oe-delolmo3.

92. Doug Smith and Jean Guccione, "Study Reveals Vast Scope of Priest Abuse," *Los Angeles Times*, October 13, 2005; consulted online at: http://articles.latimes.com/2005/oct/13/local/me-priestdata13.

93. For a reference to "political jujitsu," see Alinsky, *Rules for Radicals*, 152. On p. 129 Alinsky writes that the significance of "the action is in the reaction." He refers to "corporate jujitsu" on p. 176. Two aphorisms from p. 136 are also worth noting: "The real action is in the enemy's reaction." And: "The enemy properly goaded and guided in his reaction will be your major strength." Alinsky's use of the term *enemy* in these contexts needs to be interpreted in light of the IAF dictum that there are no permanent enemies. The term is not meant to imply, then, that one's opponent of the moment is an unfitting candidate for reconciliation.

94. Thucydides, *History of the Peloponnesian War*, book V.

Chapter Fourteen. Blood and Harmony

95. The report aired on KNBC in Los Angeles on August 16, 2008. I consulted an online version at: http://www.knbc.com/news/17208825/detail.html?rss=la&psp=news.

Chapter Fifteen. Fathers and Sisters for Life

96. Pope John Paul II, *The Gospel of Life* (New York: Random House, 1995), 140.

97. *The Gospel of Life* does sternly warn against the temptation of defining democracy in purely procedural terms, thus emptying it of its ethical content. When this happens, according to John Paul, democracy drifts in the direction of an unacceptable relativism, according to which whatever the majority currently thinks qualifies automatically as right (35–37, 126–29). Joseph Cardinal Ratzinger, shortly before being named Pope Benedict XVI, underlined

this warning in a homily that declared the morally empty form of democracy "a dictatorship of relativism." The official translation of the homily, *Pro Eligendo Romano Pontiface*, is printed in *Common Knowledge* 13, no. 2–3 (spring–fall 2007): 451–55. For a detailed analysis of these papal claims, see my essay, "A House Founded on the Sea: Is Democracy a Dictatorship of Relativism?" in the same double issue of *Common Knowledge*, 385–403.

98. I have conversed with Southwest IAF organizers about works by intellectuals such as Romand Coles, Mary Douglas, Terry Eagleton, Jean Bethke Elshtain, Stanley Hauerwas, Adam Hochschild, Nicholas Lash, Alasdair MacIntyre, Charles Payne, Pope Benedict XVI, Richard Rorty, David Tracy, Michael Walzer, Cornel West, and Sheldon Wolin.

99. Quoted in Paul Osterman, *Gathering Power*, 95.

Chapter Sixteen. Pastors and Flocks

100. Libby Copeland, "With Gifts from God: Bishop T. D. Jakes Has Made Millions by Reaching Millions, Not That There's Anything Wrong with That," *Washington Post*, March 25, 2001; consulted online at: http://www.trinityfi.org/press/tdjakes01.html.

101. Catholic priests belong to a male hierarchy headed by the pope, whereas some Protestant ministers are female and answer directly to their congregants. A Catholic parish is organized geographically, and its boundaries often coincide with the boundaries of a secular political unit, most obviously so in New Orleans, where the Catholic term has been taken over by the secular polity. If you are a Catholic, and live within the geographical boundaries of a given parish, you are a member of that parish. Many Protestant congregations, in contrast, count as members only those people who voluntarily affiliate themselves, regardless of where they live. Some African-American Protestant congregations in South Central L.A. are no longer made up mainly of South Central residents, a fact which gives them a role in the community very different from that of the Catholic parishes there. The differences multiply further, of course, when we take into account Jewish, Muslim, Buddhist, and other religious institutions in Los Angeles County and elsewhere.

Chapter Seventeen. The Contested Sacred

102. I agree with Ronald Dworkin's *Life's Dominion: An Argument about Abortion, Euthanasia, and Individual Freedom* (New York: Alfred Knopf,

1993) that commitments concerning sacred value are central to our politics. But my thinking on the nature of sacred value and its relation to horrendous evil has been more deeply influenced by Robert Merrihew Adams, *Finite and Infinite Goods: A Framework for Ethics* (Oxford: Oxford University Press, 1999), chapter 4; Marilyn McCord Adams, *Horrendous Evils and the Goodness of God* (Ithaca, NY: Cornell University Press, 1999), and *Christ and Horrors: The Coherence of Christology* (Cambridge: Cambridge University Press, 2006); and conversations with Timothy Jackson and Vince Vitale. For another perspective on the language of horror, see Cavarero, *Horrorism*.

103. Albert O. Hirschman, *The Passions and the Interests: Political Arguments for Capitalism before Its Triumph* (Princeton: Princeton University Press, 1977).

104. Steven Lukes, "Comparing the Incomparable: Trade-offs and Sacrifices," in *Incommensurability, Incomparability, and Practical Reason,* edited by Ruth Chang (Cambridge: Harvard University Press, 1998), 184–95.

105. See Pierre Bourdieu, *Distinction: A Social Critique of the Judgment of Taste*, translated by Richard Nice (Cambridge: Harvard University Press, 1984).

106. I am grateful to Molly Farneth for helpful comments on this point.

107. I discuss these senses of secularization in *Democracy and Tradition,* chapters 3 and 4.

108. There is also the crucial case of Islam to consider, but I will need to take it up on another occasion. Unfortunately, my travels in the Southwest IAF network did not give me enough information about mosques to write responsibly about their emerging significance in citizens' organizations. Michael Gecan, who does for Metro IAF (Chicago, New York, Baltimore, Boston, and London) what Ernie Cortés does for Southwest IAF, told me in the summer of 2008 that a number of influential mosques had recently joined broad-based citizens' organizations in IAF networks. As an example, he cited a large mosque in Chicago that had already conducted hundreds of one-on-one meetings with mosque members and identified sixty leaders. More recently, Metro IAF has launched a campaign against excessive interest rates. The banner of the campaign is "10 percent is enough." Gecan and Luke Bretherton, who works with Metro IAF in London, have both told me that there is strong Muslim participation in this campaign. For information on the campaign and its use of the traditional category of usury, see: http://www.10percentisenough.org/sites/default/files/documents/10%20Percent%20Is%20Enough.pdf.

109. Peter Singer, *Rethinking Life and Death: The Collapse of Our Traditional Ethics* (New York: St. Martin's Press, 1994).

110. Every group needs to distinguish among the things it values, the things it tolerates, and the things it regards as intolerable. As democratic coalitions form, the participants in them are required to think about these distinctions and adjust them. Tolerance degenerates into a vice when it leads to toleration of the *intolerable*, in particular the horrendous. It also needs to guard against indifference toward, or acceptance of, what should be *regretfully* tolerated.

A healthy democratic coalition will often include citizens who regard one another as wrong or unjust in their attitudes toward something important. They regret these differences but are prepared to tolerate them in order to achieve something together. Achievement of a society in which benefits and burdens are shared without anyone dominating anyone else is impossible, under conditions of diversity, without mutual toleration of differences even on some of the most important questions, including what to hold sacred and what to count as horrendous. To qualify as democratic, a coalition aiming to create such a society needs to view some examples of dominance and injustice as intolerable, as worthy of being prevented. To qualify as a coalition, however, it needs to bring together people who disagree in various ways even on some things that matter deeply to them. Tolerating one another, in order to pursue the common good, does not require being indifferent toward such disagreements. I am guided in these thoughts by John Bowlin's forthcoming book on tolerance and forbearance, which is by far the best work I have read on the topic.

111. For defenses of the claim that both sides of the culture war are elite-driven, see Alan Wolfe, *One Nation, After All* (New York: Penguin, 1998), chapter 7; and Hart, *Cultural Dilemmas of Progressive Politics,* 223–25. Mark R. Warren compares IAF and the religious right in *Dry Bones Rattling,* 241–45. For a general account of the religious right, see Clyde Wilcox, *Onward Christian Soldiers? The Religious Right in American Politics,* 2d edition (Boulder, CO: Westview Press, 2000). I should add that when I refer to the religious right, I am thinking of the sort of organizing done by Ralph Reed, not of that done by someone like John Perkins (which more nearly resembles IAF organizing). See John Perkins, *A Quiet Revolution,* 2d edition (Pasadena, CA: Urban Family Publications, 1976); and Charles Marsh, *The Beloved Community: How Faith Shapes Social Justice, from the Civil Rights Movement to Today* (New York: Basic Books, 2005), 153–206.

Chapter Eighteen. Across Great Scars of Wrong

112. Robert Michels, *Political Parties: A Sociological Study of the Oligarchical Tendencies of Modern Democracy,* translated by Eden and Cedar Paul (New York: Free Press, 1962), especially 342–56.

113. I discussed Capra's movie at length in the second of my Stone Lectures at Princeton Theological Seminary (2007). I intend to develop those lectures into a book on religion, politics, and ethics in film.

114. Ian Dew-Becker and Robert J. Gordon, "Where Did the Productivity Growth Go? Inflation Dynamics and the Distribution of Income," paper presented at the 81st meeting of the Brookings Panel on Economic Activity (2005).

115. Stephen J. Rose, *Social Stratification in the United States* (New York: The New Press, 2007).

116. Tom Herman, "There's Rich, and There's the 'Fortunate 400,'" *Wall Street Journal,* March 5, 2008, consulted online: http://online.wsj.com/article/SB120468366051012473.html.

117. When assessing the power of top corporate executives, it is important to keep three things in mind. First, as Lindblom remarks, "the collective enterprise in the market system creates islands of command coordination in a sea of market mutual adjustment. . . . The very existence of a collective enterprise or corporation represents an entrepreneur's choice of command over market system for some range of activities. . . . The more the coordination by corporate management, the less by the market system" (*The Market System,* 78). Second, the "control of assets of the conventional corporation lies in the hands of a small number of executives chosen by members of a de facto self-perpetuating governing board or by an executive team." "It no longer so much matters who formally owns a corporation as how its executives operate: by what rules, for what objectives, subject to what incentives, with what rewards, and to whom responsible" (81–82). Third, as already mentioned in chapter 5, the Supreme Court decision in *Citizens United v. Federal Election Commission* is likely to increase dramatically the political power of corporations and those who run them.

118. This explanation is defended in Thomas Frank, *What's the Matter with Kansas? How Conservatives Won the Heart of America* (New York: Henry Holt, 2004). It has, however, received decisive refutation from Larry M. Bartels in "What's the Matter with *What's the Matter with Kansas,*" *Quarterly Journal of Political Science* 1 (2006): 201–26. See also Bartels, *Unequal De-*

mocracy: The Political Economy of the New Gilded Age (New York: Russell Sage Foundation, 2008), 83–97.

119. The massive significance of resident aliens, legal and undocumented, in the overall political picture of social stratification is demonstrated in Nolan McCarty, Keith T. Poole, and Howard Rosenthal, *Polarized America: The Dance of Ideology and Unequal Riches* (Cambridge: MIT Press, 2006), chapter 4: "How has the median voter's economic position been sustained, while that of the median family has declined? Part of the answer . . . is that lower-income people are increasingly likely to be noncitizens. The median income of noncitizens has shifted sharply downward, and the fraction of the population that is noncitizen has increased dramatically" (116). Exclusion of a sizable fraction of the country's actual residents from the political process has effectively tilted the electorate away from redistributivist economic policies. It is in the perceived self-interest of the corporate elite: (a) to have low-income workers; (b) for those workers and their dependents to lack the legal rights of citizens; and (c) for residents who have the legal status of citizens to regard resident aliens as unworthy of citizenship.

120. See Douglas S. Massey, *Categorically Unequal: The American Stratification System* (New York: Russell Sage Foundation, 2008), especially chapter 4, which analyzes how the new underclass was made. In correspondence, Molly Farneth pointed out to me that in "three states, ex-felony offenders are permanently barred from voting, and in dozens of other states, ex-felony offenders must wait several years after being released from prison and jump through a number of legal hoops to regain the right to vote. Such disenfranchisement laws disproportionately affect African American men; nationwide, 13 percent of all African American men are ineligible to vote due to these laws."

121. Alain Badiou, *Metapolitics,* translated by Jason Barker (London: Verso, 2005), especially chapters 2 and 5. It is hard to know what to make of Badiou's approving discussion of Lenin on the related issue of the need for "iron discipline" (*Metapolitics,* 74–77), a topic on which Badiou seems to swerve ambiguously between Cavarero's insistence on honoring singularity and a taste for the revolutionary sublime. The more closely Badiou approaches the important question of what modes of organization and restrictions on means are to be deemed acceptable when push comes to shove, the harder it is to figure out what he is saying. I am here simply applying the same standard to Badiou that I have already applied to Alinsky, who was much more forthcoming on the relationship between leaders and the rank

and file, but was suspect on the question of permissible means. It seems to me that there are good reasons to demand clarity on such matters, especially from writers who express suspicion of appeals to human rights and belittle people who rejoiced at the fall of Soviet domination as "statue-topplers"—two things that Alinsky would never have done. For the latter remark, see Badiou, *Theoretical Writings*, translated by Ray Brassier and Alberto Toscano (London: Continuum, 2004), 132.

Slavoj Žižek expresses the hope for a *"return to Lenin"* in: *On Belief* (London: Routledge, 2001), 2–4, italics in original; *The Ticklish Subject: The Absent Centre of Political Ontology* (London: Verso, 2000), 236; and *The Fragile Absolute—Or, Why Is the Christian Legacy Worth Fighting for?* (London: Verso, 2000), 2. The key expressions, which Žižek appears to be using with a positive valence, are: "cruel," "secret police," and "dirty work." He takes Leninist cruelty and liberal niceness to be our only options. His rite of passage for joining the neo-Leninist left is to imagine oneself inflicting cruelty on capitalist villains and perhaps on their liberal enablers. Why, one wants to know, must the force that proves necessary in the struggle against domination be cruel? Žižek's answer appears to be that the attempt to adhere to an ethically scrupulous way of acquiring and exercising power inevitably collapses into ineffectual niceness. In his view, only Leninists like himself and conservatives like Dick Cheney are serious about politics, and thus authentic.

122. The quoted phrase comes from the following passage in Robert Duncan, "A Poem Beginning with a Line from Pindar," in *Selected Poems*, revised and enlarged edition (New York: New Directions Press, 1997), 64–72: "It is across great scars of wrong / I reach toward the song of kindred men / and strike again the naked string / old Whitman sang from" (67).

123. The sort of identification I am recommending therefore differs significantly from the one recommended by Rorty in *Achieving Our Country*, 1–38. Rorty's preferred mode of political identification is pride in one's country, whereas mine is participation in a tradition of democratic struggle. As I see it, identification with some such tradition is required to make sense of the normative point of view being adopted when one criticizes this or that arrangement or relationship as a violation of liberty or justice.

Any tradition's contemporary inheritors are responsible for justifying their current normative commitments *retrospectively* (in relation to the strengths and weaknesses of previously held positions) and *comparatively* (in relation to the strengths and weaknesses of currently held positions and conceivable positions not yet held). Justifying the commitments constitutive of one's own point of view ultimately involves constructing a narrative that presents the emergence of the preferred point of view as a rationally acceptable outcome of a dialectical progression, rather than *merely* as an effect of nonrational factors (such as who was able to impose their will on whom at this or that time and place). This means that narratives intended to debunk some outlook or set of arrangements (in the mode of "ideology critique" or "critical genealogy") need to be supplemented by narratives intended to justify the commitments taken for granted by those engaged in the debunking. For a technically demanding, but illuminating, attempt to make sense of the latter kind of narrative, see Robert B. Brandom, *Reason in Philosophy: Animating Ideas* (Cambridge: Harvard University Press, 2009), chapter 3. See also Alasdair C. MacIntyre, "Epistemological Crises, Dramatic Narrative, and the Philosophy of Science," in *The Tasks of Philosophy: Selected Essays,* volume 1 (Cambridge: Cambridge University Press, 2006), 3–23. I discuss "the problem of point of view" in *Democracy and Tradition,* 55, 119–21.

124. Sheldon S. Wolin, *Politics and Vision*, expanded edition (Princeton: Princeton University Press, 2004), 598.

125. As Molly Farneth has reminded me, chapter 13 of Wolin's more recent book, *Democracy Incorporated: Managed Democracy and the Specter of Inverted Totalitarianism* (Princeton: Princeton University Press, 2008), appears to adopt a position somewhat closer to the one I am defending. On page 291, he refers to the need "to encourage and nurture a counterelite of democratic public servants" and argues that this counterelite can already be found to a large extent in "numerous nongovernmental organizations." In effect, I am extending this thought, but at the expense of the "fugitive" democrat's distaste for hierarchy as such.

Chapter Nineteen. The Organizer President

The epigraph is from Barack Obama, *Dreams from My Father: A Story of Race and Inheritance* (New York: Three Rivers Press, 2004), 133.

126. Hillary Clinton, '"There Is Only the Fight . . .' An Analysis of the Alinsky Model," honors thesis, Wellesley College. The thesis was not available to the public during the Clinton presidency, but was placed in an open archive at Wellesley in 2001.

127. For his own account of his experience as an organizer, see Obama, *Dreams from My Father*, part 2. The most important expression of Obama's

views on the role of religion in politics is a speech entitled "Call to Renewal," delivered in Washington, D.C., on June 26, 2008.

128. The quoted material comes from Obama's victory speech after the Iowa caucuses on January 3, 2008.

129. Patrick Healy and Jeff Zeleny, "Clinton and Obama Spar over Remark about Dr. King," *New York Times,* January 13, 2008, consulted online at: http://www.nytimes.com/2008/01/13/us/politics/13cnd-campaign.html.

130. Obama, *Dreams from My Father,* 276.

131. For one of many occasions on which Obama has said this, see his interview with *Q-Notes*, April 30, 2008: http://www.q-notes.com/113/obama-change-comes-from-the-bottom-up/.

132. I consulted the site on August 4, 2009. The home page is: http://www.barackobama.com/index.php.

133. Joanne Bland, remarks at a conference on religion in the civil rights movement, Princeton University, April 3, 2009.

134. In her syndicated column of January 21, 2009, Amy Goodman claimed that Obama had told this story at a fundraiser in Montclair, New Jersey.

135. See David Bromwich, "The Character of Barack Obama," *The Huffington Post,* August 4, 2009: http://www.huffingtonpost.com/david-bromwich/character-of-barack-obama_b_251186.html. Gerald Kellman, who trained Obama in community organizing, found his trainee reluctant to polarize a situation. "He didn't gravitate toward confrontation, and would use it as a last resort," Kellman told the *New York Times*, "and it seems to me he's still there." Sheryl Gay Stolberg, "Gentle White House Nudges Test the Power of Persuasion," *New York Times,* February 23, 2010, consulted online at: http://www.nytimes.com/2010/02/24/health/policy/24persuade.html?partner=rss&emc=rss. I am grateful to David Bromwich for calling this article to my attention.

136. See David Bromwich, "Obama's Run against McCain Begins Today," *The Huffington Post,* March 8, 2008: http://www.huffingtonpost.com/david bromwich/obamas-run-against-mccain_b_90538.html. "Hillary Clinton," wrote Bromwich, "is the social-democratic candidate of the war establishment. John McCain is the right-wing candidate of the war establishment. Both Clinton and McCain know this. They look on each other kindly, and share a disdain that borders on contempt for Barack Obama." I am saying that the price of party unification, three months after Bromwich wrote this perceptive

analysis, was a commitment on Obama's part to appointing center-left members of the war establishment to his key foreign policy posts.

137. For illustrations of his long-standing concerns about who gets to be at what bargaining tables, see Joseph Stiglitz, *Globalization and Its Discontents* (New York: W.W. Norton, 2003), 225; *Making Globalization Work* (New York: W.W. Norton, 2007), 19, 116, 131. For a more recent expression of a similar concern in the context of the 2008–9 bailout issue, see part two of his Talking Points Memo video interview of February 13, 2009: http://www.youtube.com/watch?v=-sjHzw4DCB4&feature=channel. At roughly 2 minutes and 30 seconds into this part of the interview, Stiglitz says: "You ask the question, 'Who is at the bargaining table?' It's the people who created the problem in the first place." In the remainder of the interview he lays out how the people who were at the bargaining table benefited at the expense of taxpayers.

138. I am not applying a utopian standard. A close study of Lincoln's speeches would show how carefully he used his campaign oratory, as well as his presidential pronouncements, to form the mind of the citizenry in accordance with democratic republican principles. If Obama wishes to be Lincoln's heir, he has a good model of political eloquence in mind. I doubt, however, that he grasps what Lincoln was doing and what causal role Lincoln's oratory played in his governance.

To judge Obama by contemporary standards, one could ask whether there is anything in his oratory that frames the issue of economic justice nearly as well as Senator Jim Webb's formal response to George W. Bush's state of union address on January 23, 2007. Here is one brief passage in which Webb made his most telling point with breathtaking simplicity a year and nine months before the financial crisis: "The stock market is at an all-time high, and so are corporate profits. But these benefits are not being fairly shared. When I graduated from college, the average corporate CEO made 20 times what the average worker did; today, it's nearly 400 times. In other words, it takes the average worker more than a year to make the money that his or her boss makes in one day." http://www.washingtonpost.com/wp-dyn/content/article/2007/01/23/AR2007012301369.html.

If I were asked to name a single model of sustained rhetorical excellence on the part of a public official during the period since Obama's election, my answer would be Elizabeth Warren's performance as chair of the Congressional Oversight Panel for the Troubled Assets Relief Program (TARP). Warren, a professor at Harvard Law School, consistently explains the nature of the financial crisis and the inadequacies of the federal response to it in accessible terms, without for a moment losing sight of the concerns of ordinary people. For a vivid example of Warren's clarity, see her video interview with *New Yorker* reporter James Surowiecki: http://www.newyorker.com/online/blogs/jamessurowiecki/2009/11/video-elizabeth-warren.html.

In my view the best treatment of the significance of rhetorical excellence for the project of building a democratic polity of trust is Danielle S. Allen, *Talking to Strangers: Anxieties of Citizenship since Brown v. Board of Education* (Chicago: University of Chicago Press, 2004), chapter 10.

139. They were pleasant spring days, in which the winter of man's discontent was thawing as well as the earth, and the life that had lain torpid began to stretch itself. One day . . . I saw a striped snake run into the water, and he lay on the bottom, apparently without inconvenience, as long as I staid there, or more than a quarter of an hour; perhaps because he had not yet fairly come out of the torpid state. It appeared to me that for a like reason men remain in the present low and primitive condition; but if they should feel the influence of the spring of springs arousing them, they would of necessity rise to a more ethereal life. . . . On April 1 it rained and melted the ice, and in the early part of the day, which was very foggy, I heard a stray goose groping about over the pond and cackling as if lost, or like the spirit of the fog.

Henry David Thoreau, *Walden,* in *A Week on the Concord and Merrimack Rivers, Walden, The Maine Woods, Cape Cod* (New York: Library of America, 1985), 355.

Chapter Twenty. Walking in Our Sleep

140. Henry David Thoreau, *Walden,* 365, 396.

141. On the legal infrastructure essential to emergence of the mill and the railroad as novel forms of corporate organization, see Charles Perrow, *Organizing America: Wealth, Power, and the Origins of Corporate Capitalism* (Princeton: Princeton University Press, 2002).

142. John Bowlin has rightly pointed out to me that the examples of Lin-

coln and King can also be sources of self-deception for people tempted to imagine themselves as the next great public figure.

143. The phrase "Inert Concern" appears in Jonathan Kozol, *The Night Is Dark and I Am Far from Home* (New York: Bantam Books, 1977), 185. I am grateful to Andrea Sun-Mee Jones for pressing me to draw attention to the danger Kozol had in mind.

144. Frederick Douglass, speech celebrating West India Emancipation Day, August 1857.

145. Robert Duncan, "A Poem Beginning with a Line from Pindar," in *Selected Poems*, 67.

⁕ *Index* ⁕